Arizona's War Town

ARIZONA'S WAR TOWN

Flagstaff, Navajo Ordnance Depot,
and World War II

John S. Westerlund

The University of Arizona Press / Tucson

First paperbound printing 2003
The University of Arizona Press
© 2003 The Arizona Board of Regents
All rights reserved
Manufactured in the United States of America

09 08 07 06 05 04   7 6 5 4 3 2

Library of Congress Cataloging-in-Publication Data
Westerlund, John S. (John Stephen), 1945–
Arizona's war town : Flagstaff, Navajo Ordnance Depot, and
World War II / John S. Westerlund.
p. cm.
Includes bibliographical references and index.
ISBN 0-8165-2262-6 (cloth: alk. paper)
ISBN 0-8165-2415-7 (pbk.: alk. paper)
1. Navajo Ordnance Depot (Ariz.)—History—20th century.
2. World War, 1939–1945—Arizona—Flagstaff. 3. Flagstaff
(Ariz.)—History—20th century. I. Title.
D769.85.A71F53 2003
940.53'79133—dc21
2003004424

British Library Cataloguing-in-Publication Data
A catalogue record for this book is available from the British Library.

For

Katie, Marty, and Gail Westerlund

and my parents,

who came West because of World War II,

and the

Navajo Ordnance Depot ammunition handlers

and other employees

CONTENTS

ILLUSTRATIONS

MAPS

PREFACE

In June 1990 my family and I left Paris, France, where I had been assigned as the U.S. Army's instructor at the Ecole Supérieure de Guerre, the French army war college. My new posting was professor of military science at the Northern Arizona University Army ROTC program in Flagstaff. Shortly after arriving in July, I was invited to an open house and barbeque at Navajo Army Depot, located about ten miles west of Flagstaff at a small hub called Bellemont.

Bellemont was a peculiar place, a hodgepodge of old and new. Two major arteries crossed the large clearing in the ponderosa pines, U.S. Interstate 40 and the Atchison, Topeka, and Santa Fe Railroad tracks (today the Burlington Northern Santa Fe). To the northeast rose the volcanic peaks, and Arizona's highest point at 12,633 feet, of the San Francisco Mountains, named by Spanish Franciscan friars at the Hopi village of Oraibi in 1629. The peaks had for centuries been sacred to many Native Americans in the region. For the Navajo people, the mountain is Doko'oosliid, the Sacred Mountain of the West. It is their strength, boundary, identity, and home. The mountain represents the origin of their journey and elders pray to the peaks that represent doorways to the Earth. For the Hopi people, it is Nuvateekiaovi, or the "Kachina Place," the "Place of Snow on the Very Top," and home to supernatural beings.[1]

Just south of I-40 a half-dozen businesses dotted the area, along with a rustic cinder block building—Junior Whipp's Inn—landscaped with years of trash and discarded newspapers, one reporting the 1969 moon landing. Crumbling shacks of the earlier town faced south along the bed of old U.S. Highway 66.

Motorcycle riders flocked to Bellemont, and it was not uncommon to see a dozen bikers exit I-40 and head to the Grand Canyon Harley-Davidson store. Further east along Route 66, the Pine Breeze Inn gas station stood empty, wanting to collapse, a decaying monument in local lore from the 1969 film Easy Rider—the place where Dennis Hopper and Peter Fonda stopped their panhead chopper motorcycles, asked for a room, and made an obscene gesture as they roared off down the road.

Further south beyond Route 66 at Navajo Army Depot stood a few World War II era warehouses, administrative buildings, and a water tower. All in all, the beautiful setting was home to an unimpressive military base. There were few soldiers to be seen. There were no tanks, howitzers, or armored fighting vehicles; nor was there much activity. Those driving along the interstate recognized nothing unusual or anything of military interest. In the distance and out of view from the interstate, however, a few earth-covered structures resembling mounds protruded ominously from the wood line of ponderosa pines.

These mounds were bunkers, commonly called igloos, built during World War II. They were scattered about, each several hundred feet from the other. Hidden beneath the dirt exteriors were walls, floors, and ceilings of thick, steel-reinforced concrete. The bunkers held bombs, shells, mines, and ammunition—in military terms called "ordnance." To my surprise, eight hundred of these igloos were tucked away in a vast tract stretching across rolling hills of two national forests. They were the depot's raison d'être, and each was roughly the size of a two-thousand-square-foot home.

A few years later, I decided to dig into the depot records and do an exploratory paper or two for my history doctoral studies at NAU. As I worked into the material, the extent of the collection at Cline Library's Special Collections and Archives became apparent. It also raised many interesting questions. What was the history of the land that eventually became home to Bellemont and the depot? Who built the arsenal and why there? Why did several thousand Navajos and Hopis migrate to Bellemont? Where did they live? Flagstaff must have been a boomtown during the construction period. What was it like? What about the depot's Hispanic workers? What about women? Why were two hundred fifty Austrian prisoners of war at Bellemont? How did they get there? Why were sailors in Flagstaff—miles from the ocean and Pacific fleet? What really happened in Flagstaff during the war? To my surprise, none of the answers were readily available. It was obvious that this unique Arizona story had to be researched, carefully pieced together, and told.

Gathering thousands of pages of historical documents required a considerable amount of travel. I did six weeks of research during two trips to the National Archives Building in Washington, D.C., Archives II at College Park, Maryland, and the Library of Congress. I also conducted research at the National Archives at Laguna Niguel, California, and at the U.S. Army's Center of Military History in Washington, D.C., and at the army's Military History Institute at Carlisle Barracks, Pennsylvania. I went to the army's Soldier and Biological Chemical Command at Aberdeen Proving Ground, Maryland, and also traveled to Vienna, Austria, in search of former prisoners of war.

Perhaps the most difficult problem, however, was locating World War II era depot employees and veterans, former prisoners of war, former female students and navy apprentice seamen and marines who attended Arizona State Teachers College (today Northern Arizona University), and Native American families who lived in Indian Village. I wanted to interview as many participants as possible, not only to give the book a personal touch but to ensure historical accuracy as well. For many of those interviewed, almost sixty years had passed since the events.

Today, World War II era depot employees are scattered across the United States. To find them, I ran ads in publications that have a national audience—the *Army Times* (the U.S. Army's unofficial weekly newspaper) and *The Retired Officer Magazine*. I also used the National Military Personnel Records Center in Saint Louis, Missouri. Those who responded were enthusiastic about the story of Arizona's forgotten war town.

I was lucky, however, in locating the first of several former Austrian prisoners of war. While working on an NAU doctoral paper about

Austrian POWs at Navajo Depot, the Austrian national television company in Vienna, "ORF," coincidentally decided to do an historical documentary about Austrian soldiers of the German army who were held in American POW camps. One of their sources, Vienna-area resident and retired dentist Dr. Josef Papp, had been a prisoner at Navajo Depot. Papp emphasized that only Austrians were held at the Bellemont camp. In the fall of 1997, shortly after ORF personnel received a copy of my doctoral paper, their television crew arrived in Flagstaff and began filming. They also brought along Papp's address and telephone number. To locate other former Austrian POWs from Navajo Depot, I ran ads in a Vienna newspaper and in the German army veterans' newspapers *Soldat im Volk* and *Der Heimkehrer*, along with an ad in the Rommel Society's German Afrika Korps newspaper *Die Oase*. The International Chapter of the Red Cross, the German Red Cross, the Deutsche Dienststelle, and the Austrian Heeresgeschichtliches Museum in Vienna were also very helpful.

Finding wartime ASTC students was less difficult. Anne Walden of the NAU Alumni Office searched the database, prepared a list of female students who attended the college, and forwarded my request for assistance under a university cover letter. On the navy side, Capt. Robert S. Jones, USN, Ret., a national coordinator for the navy's World War II V-12 student information, provided a current address of several navy apprentice seamen and marines who were in the ASTC program. In many cases, former female students and seamen provided additional names.

Many residents of Indian Village live today on the Navajo and Hopi Reservations and in the Flagstaff area. Carol Hansen, a friend who lives and teaches at Kayenta on the Navajo Reservation, became interested in the project and was helpful in locating and interviewing former village residents for her own graduate paper. I was fortunate to locate and visit with John Billy—who served on the depot's first Navajo Tribal Council—and his wife Mary in Tuba City, along with Flagstaff residents Rev. Scott and Amy Franklin.

For the Col. Arman Peterson story, Jon Hales graciously retrieved family records about his uncle. The Netherlands Red Cross, local Dutch officials, the German Bundesarchiv-Militärarchiv, and the Imperial War Museum at Duxford, England, were also very helpful in putting the missing pieces of this story together.

As my work progressed, many friends helped locate those who were in some way associated with this Flagstaff story. I extend my sincere gratitude to all who have provided assistance during this six-year project.

I am especially indebted to Professor Andrew Wallace, who provided direction and encouragement throughout the project. I am also indebted to other faculty at NAU: Larry McFarlane, Margaret Morley, Michael Amundson, Howard Salisbury, and David Kitterman. I also thank Jim Byrkit, Al Richmond and the Grand Canyon Pioneers Society, Richard Mangum, Francis McAllister, Arthur Gómez, and Arnold Krammer of Texas A&M University.

I wish to thank the Camp Navajo staff, especially Larry Triphahn, Tim Cowan, Don Hack, and Tom Shimonowsky, for their support in making much of the research possible. I also wish to thank the NAU Department of History for their assistance, which partially funded earlier portions of the research. I thank Bruce Dinges and Bill Broughton of the Arizona Historical Society for their assistance with articles published in the *Journal of Arizona History*.

I owe a special debt of gratitude to the staff of the NAU Cline Library Special Collections and Archives, to include Karen Underhill, Brad Cole, Laine Sutherland, and Richard Quartaroli. Cline Library's Lee Gregory helped in many areas, as did Bob Coody. I thank Randy Wilson, editor of the *Arizona Daily Sun,* for his ongoing interest in this project. I thank the University of Arizona Press and editor Rose Byrne for a marvelous job.

I have also been encouraged by my mother, Helen E. Westerlund, and my sister Janet. Most important of all, I have been sustained by the loving support of my wife, Gail Roberts Westerlund, and our children Katie and Marty.

INTRODUCTION
An Armed Camp

World War II turned Arizona into an armed camp. At Luke Air Field west of Phoenix, home of the world's largest fighter pilot school, more than 13,500 pilots trained, as did more than 10,000 combat air crews at Tucson's Davis-Monthan Field. Williams Field, east of Chandler, and Thunderbird II, north of Scottsdale, also trained pilots and cadets. The Army Air Corps established new bases at Kingman, Marana, Douglas, and Yuma. Camps Bouse, Horn, and Hyder helped prepare soldiers at Maj. Gen. George S. Patton's Desert Training Center. Prisoners of war were scattered at two dozen camps across the state, and Japanese Americans were interned at Poston, Sacaton, and Leupp. Other camps, fields, and war production plants were built. Del Webb expanded Fort Huachuca, and army engineers built an ordnance depot west of Flagstaff.[1]

The study of Flagstaff and Navajo Depot involves several themes. Federal influence in the San Francisco Peaks area began in the mid-nineteenth century and continued until the 1942 depot construction resulted in a significant federal presence. Since the first American settler came to the Bellemont area in 1876, the landscape has been altered in many ways. Some of the changes are reversible, some not. And finally, the depot became an extraordinary experiment in the convergence of peoples. African Americans, Anglos, Hispanics, and Native Americans from six tribes found good paying jobs and sometimes careers at Bellemont. Women of every group worked at the depot as ordnance versions of Rosie the Riveter.

Historian Frederick Jackson Turner proclaimed an end to the frontier West in 1893. The westering process, however, continued and accelerated during the Great Depression and World War II. Families from the Midwest, the South, and especially Arkansas and Oklahoma flocked to Flagstaff in 1942, looking for construction jobs at the depot site where eight thousand workers were urgently needed—far more than the number who had labored on Hoover Dam at maximum employment.

Flagstaff, with a population of about five thousand, was overwhelmed as fifteen thousand workers and family members tried to squeeze in somewhere. Many went to Bellemont, some lived in their cars, others camped in the woods. It was a merchant's dream come true but a city nightmare. The acute housing shortage forced the government to build emergency homes. Racial tensions simmered beneath the surface. A labor union moved in and city businesses temporarily closed their doors in protest. For years the primary focus of the chamber of commerce would be the depot, as it accelerated the urbanization process and crammed more than two decades of growth into just a few months. The depot became an economic force in Flagstaff and surrounding areas, defining the regional economy and relationships with the federal government.

Much has been written of the four hundred Navajo Code Talkers and Hollywood even launched a film. Nothing, however, has been said of the thirty-five hundred Navajos and Hopis at Navajo Ordnance Depot during World War II. Leaving nearby reservations, they were drawn into the white man's world by the unprecedented demand for labor. Steady employment and good-paying jobs were available at Bellemont. After years of stock reduction had pauperized the Navajos, steady wage labor proved attractive. Most Indian workers lived just west of Bellemont in something new—a community called Indian Village on the depot grounds.

Flagstaff was turned into an armed camp with the depot to the west, trainloads of soldiers and equipment passing through at all hours, a military police training camp for African American soldiers at the base of Mount Elden, prisoners of war at the depot, and a boatload of sailors at the college. The city was absorbed in war bond drives, rationing, and Victory Gardens. There were jobs at the depot, and more workers were needed than Flagstaff and the surrounding area could supply.

The navy's V–12 officer training program in Flagstaff began on the Arizona State Teachers College campus in the summer of 1943 and continued through the duration of the war. The program came just in time; enrollment had slumped below one hundred and officials anticipated closing the school. More than one thousand apprentice seamen and marines came to Flagstaff, bringing federal relief and a vibrant campus life to the beleaguered college.

Two hundred fifty Austrian prisoners of war were held in Bellemont between March 1945 and April 1946. Their experience illustrates problems on both sides of the barbed wire fence. Flagstaff citizens living under strict wartime rationing and price controls resented the prisoner sugar allotment, paid prisoner labor, and the appearance of an easy life.

Navajo Depot was not closed after the war's end. It remained operational and supported the wars in Korea, Vietnam, and the Persian Gulf. The Arizona Army National Guard assumed control of the installation and took advantage of the storage space by leasing igloos to the nation's armed forces. Today, Camp Navajo stores thousands of intercontinental ballistic missile motors, deactivated in accordance with treaties signed between the United States and Russia following the end of the Cold War. Camp Navajo—perhaps more than ever—is woven tightly into our regional fabric and national security strategy. Evidently the Russians think so. They frequently come to inspect.

ARIZONA'S WAR TOWN

1

SUMMER 1941

Flagstaff and Bellemont

The migration lasted about one week. The sight was fascinating—something witnessed only in the American West. The travelers came from across the Southwest, and each evening hundreds of campfires popped up along the lonely roads leading to town, flickering like tiny candles in the wide expanse of darkened mountain and desert country as families and small groups paused overnight on their slow journey to Flagstaff.

They timed their journey to arrive on Thursday evening or Friday morning of the Fourth of July weekend. Many traveled by creaking wagons pulled by a team of horses or mules. Others rode on horseback. Some came in squeaking cars. A few drove trucks loaded with relatives and gear. The scene was enchanting, almost hypnotizing, especially at night when Navajo wagons finally reached Flagstaff and passed beneath the streetlights. The horses' hooves clicked a rhythmic beat on the pavement along Route 66, adding to the din from wood and iron wheels and bleating livestock and riderless horses tethered alongside the wagons. Inside the wagons, yet visible through evening shadows, Navajo families wrapped themselves in colorful Pendleton blankets as they rode through the cool mountain air to their annual celebration and holiday.[1]

The Navajos were not alone. Native Americans from more than twenty Southwestern tribes began trickling into town for the twelfth annual Southwestern All-Indian Pow-Wow held at the city park. There were Hopis, Zias, Zunis, Piutes, Jemez, Santa Annas, Grosventres, Utes, Taos, San Juans, Acomas, Cheyenne-Arapahoes, Apaches, Lagunas, Havasupais, Maricopas, Mohaves, Hualapais, Tohono O'odham (formerly called Pima and Papago), and several other tribes. They came from Arizona, New Mexico, Oklahoma, Nevada, Utah, California, and even as far away as North Dakota. They headed for the woods beside Mars Hill adjacent to the rodeo grounds and when that filled they settled into hundreds of camps in the nearby forests. Their numbers soon swelled to ten thousand, doubling the size of Flagstaff for the holiday weekend.[2]

Flagstaff, a border town located next to the Navajo and Hopi Reservations, had a history of intercultural relations that began when early travelers, settlers, and Indians met at the springs below the San Francisco Peaks and traded on the nearby reservations. Organized Native participation in the town's Fourth of July celebration began in 1912 when a "long string" of mounted Indians added a true Western appearance to the parade and an Indian sports committee established games. By 1920 about six hundred Indians from five northern Arizona tribes came into town—the Supai, Hualapai, Navajo, Hopi, and Piute—and many participated in events. Officials, recognizing that many Natives had traveled hundreds of miles, gave the Indians a royal welcome. Local citizens were urged to go out of their way to ensure their neighbors felt at home. Cattlemen and merchants donated steers and food and a committee divided it among the tribes.

In 1930 organizers revised the weekend program and created an all-Indian event—the Southwest All-Indian Pow-Wow—and the Museum of Northern Arizona started the Hopi crafts exhibit. The two events coincided nicely. By 1933 many Native Americans felt comfortable in Flagstaff and thirty-five hundred came into town for the Fourth of July weekend. Universal Newsreels gave moviegoers across the nation a glimpse of the pow-wow and Associated Press began running feature articles.

In 1934 the pow-wow committee incorporated as a nonprofit organization, Pow-Wow Incorporated. Committee members served without pay and soon reflected the list of town dignitaries, so much so that those not chosen to serve felt snubbed. Although the show brought in business, Flagstaff officials had a more important reason to sponsor the pow-wow. They recognized that the treatment of Native Americans

Many Navajos traveled by wagon to Flagstaff for the annual Fourth of July celebration.

had been regrettable. Most city leaders and citizens supported the all-Indian Fourth of July program to honor and recognize their Indian neighbors.

The pow-wow committee used revenues from ticket sales to pay rodeo prize money and make contracts with tribal dance teams from across the Southwest. Pow-Wow Incorporated paid their transportation to and from Flagstaff and provided meals, tents, and wages for each performance. The contracts specified arrival times, when and where the dancers would appear in full ceremonial regalia, and the specific rituals to be performed. Bureau of Indian Affairs agents gave unofficial advice on the best and most dependable dance teams. Judges rated dancers on tradition, singing, and dancing, helping the committee keep only first-rate shows. The performers received half of their wages in advance and the remainder after their performance. Contracts were also made for Native rodeo livestock. Pow-Wow Incorporated also provided bales of hay for wagon teams in the parade and placed hay at various locations along the wagon routes across the reservations to Flagstaff. Tribal leaders assisted in making rules and deciding how events would be handled. Expenses mounted over the years, forcing Pow-Wow Incorporated to purchase rain insurance for each program.

Although cities like Prescott, Pendleton, and Cheyenne had their traditional rodeos or frontier holidays and Gallup had its intertribal council, it wasn't long until nothing in North America measured up to the Flagstaff show. In 1937 "one of the greatest Indian events on the nation's calendar" was broadcast live across the United States, Canada, and England, from Flagstaff's city park by the National Broadcasting Company, and the program was translated into French and German for an enthusiastic European audience.

The weekend, however, was not without its problems. It was illegal to sell any type of alcoholic beverage to Native Americans, on or off the reservations. Some shysters took advantage of the Native presence to sell them liquor. Others sold them "bonded" whiskey—the lowest grade homemade concoction dressed in a fancy bottle with a bogus label. There were stickups and robberies and it was not uncommon to come across an Indian who had passed out on city streets or in someone's backyard.

In the summer of 1941 spectators poured into Flagstaff from around the country. Hotels, boardinghouses, and tourist courts filled. Officials set up hundreds of regimental tents at Fort Tuthill south of town for the overflow. Many went to Williams or Winslow; others brought their camping equipment. Flagstaff homes filled with guests from neighboring states, some coming from the East. It was not uncommon to see a half-dozen buses from Georgia or another distant state parked along Aspen Avenue. Flagstaff mobilized its civic organizations and hundreds of volunteers to help with the weekend events.[3]

It was some show, indeed. Although new events were added each year, the three-day format remained relatively unchanged. The 1941

All-Indian Pow-Wow included a Native American parade down the streets of Flagstaff each day at noon, rodeos each afternoon, evening ceremonial dances, rituals, and chants, and an all-day open-air crafts market. Non-Indians who asked to participate in an event were turned down, thus preserving the exclusive Native atmosphere. Federal agencies set up exhibits around the park, gave lectures, and discussed projects on the reservations.

There were few in the Southwest who did not know about the Flagstaff Fourth of July weekend that summer. For months, Greyhound buses traveling between New Mexico and southern California carried large banners advertising the show. The governor came and asked for support from the entire state of Arizona, calling on everyone to retain the Native ceremonies, dances, and prayers. Travelers passing through town could not help but notice the spiffy store windows, flags, and brightly colored bunting. A city ordinance requested everyone dress in Indian or western attire for several weeks prior to the event. College professors to maintenance workers sported ten-gallon cowboy hats—twenty-four gallons in President Tormey's case—Levi's, scarves, and boots. Women wore satin and velvet along with turquoise jewelry. Young and old moved about in a "blaze of brilliant colors of every hue and shade." The out-of-uniform nonconformists were tossed into one of several downtown "Red Cross birdcages" for a few hours.

The chief of police led the miles-long parade in the company of two or three impressive looking Native chieftains and medicine men. The rodeo participants followed, wearing chaps, spurs, cowboy hats, and bright scarves. They twirled their ropes, sometimes lassoing a tourist. Next came hundreds of ceremonial dancers adorned in beautiful feathers and regalia. Apache spirit dancers wore black leather hoods with towering headdresses adorned with horns, eagle feathers, and seashells sewn into their costumes. At times they would swoop down, scoop up an excited child, and dance a few steps along the street to the amusement of the crowd. Thousands of Indians dressed in their tribal finery passed by on foot, horseback, in wagons, cars, trucks, and even buses. For some young spectators standing in front of the crowds along Route 66, the excitement made it almost impossible to breathe. The unforgettable proximity of the Indians, the ancient costumes, the beating of drums, the chants and dancing, created lifetime memories.[4]

Following the parade, the thirty-five-piece all-Indian Pima band from Sacaton (about twenty miles southeast of Phoenix) gave a half-hour concert at 1:30 P.M. to start the rodeo, where a professional Phoenix radio personality announced the events over a state-of-the-art public-address system.

The amateur Indian cowboys and cowgirls were mostly from local Arizona tribes. They competed in pony races, wild horse races, saddled and bareback bronco riding, steer riding, bulldogging, wild cow milking, calf tying, team roping, women's tug-of-war, footraces, and a Navajo chicken pull—an ancient sport where the rider astride a running pony attempts to pull a buried sack of sand (formerly a chicken) from the ground. The program also included a pow-wow princess and Indian baby contest, a women's horse race, a potato race, a bed race, and even a wagon race.

It was not the routine brand of Western rodeo. Instead, the shows generated a free-flowing spirit where humorous scenes were abundant and crowds often roared with laughter, especially during the chicken pull. It was the Native way of enjoying the sport of playing cowboy. Nevertheless, there was also fierce competition between tribes. The prize money was substantial, as were the specialty prizes donated from major companies such as Justin Boots, Levi Strauss, Stetson, Pendleton Blankets, and Hershey Chocolate. Natives gambled on almost every event, as did many spectators. The livestock were not trained rodeo animals. They came from Indian reservations and were "wilder than a scared cat and tougher than a lumberman's boot."[5]

Later each evening, thousands of tourists, local spectators, and Indians wrapped in blankets squeezed into the large stands surrounding the rodeo grounds to watch the night ceremonials. Tribal dancers appeared first, along with the slow, dull booming of the drums. Four huge bonfires sent out an "eerie blazing light." The atavistic and sometimes haunting rituals, hundreds of pitched tents, flickering campfires and drifting smoke, primitive rhythms, and dances that preceded the Spaniards took spectators back centuries, as if they were witness to their own native ceremonies.[6]

Native Americans began participating in Flagstaff's Fourth of July parade in 1912. In 1930 it became an all-Indian parade and part of the town's Southwest All-Indian Pow-Wow.

Floodlights burst upon the dancers, enhancing the brilliant colors of beautiful traditional costumes handed down from generation to generation for centuries with few changes. Cheyenne-Arapahoes started with their shield and hoop dances. Then came the Jemez crow and eagle dances, the Santa Anna mountain sheep dance, the San Juan war dance, the Navajo fire dance and war chant, the Apache devil dance, the Hopi hoop dance, the Kiowa feather dance, and so on until around midnight when the spectacle finally ended. Indians drifted back to their camps where more dancing continued in tribal and intertribal

The all-Indian rodeo took place at Flagstaff's city park. Contestants were mostly amateurs from northern Arizona tribes. Rivalry between tribes was intense and many gambled on the events.

groups. Navajo women would sometimes choose their male partners, often resulting in an amusing struggle when some young men preferred not to dance. At times spectators even joined in.[7]

On Saturday morning another regular feature of the pow-wow took place as one hundred chiefs and tribal leaders gathered for a grand council breakfast at Hotel Monte Vista. Some wore elegant traditional costumes, others came in jeans or informal attire. They ate and talked about tribal problems and pow-wow administration, in addition to any problems that might arise over the weekend. Chee Dodge was there, the last of the great Navajo war chiefs, and told of his first visit to Flagstaff in 1879. So was Chief Watahomogie of the Havasupais, whose mustache and goatee accentuated the flat-brimmed hat, plaid shirt buttoned at the collar, and sport coat.

One chief shared the tale of his trip to Flagstaff: "We have had bad luck all the way but we are glad we are here. We had blowouts, bang! Then another, bang! Then another, bang! Then we get just inside your town of Flagstaff and fourth tire goes bang! Me and my boys we get out, kick the tire, say to hell with it, let's go to the pow-wow and have a good time." Another chief said something should be done about the young Indians shouting and dancing and beating drums all night preventing him from sleeping. One chief added that he went to sleep at three o'clock in the afternoon so he could be ready for the excitement.[8]

The Indians were guests of Flagstaff. Pow-Wow Incorporated fed everyone from their arrival until the close of the last show and also provided water and firewood in the camps. The Natives did their own butchering and cooking, and the city provided truckloads of sheep and beef cattle on the hoof, tons of flour, white bread, potatoes, and onions, along with large quantities of coffee, sugar, baking powder, and other essentials. Huge portions were cooked up twice daily by the campfire chefs at 10:00 A.M. and 5:00 P.M.

The Indian camps were one of the picturesque features of the weekend where spectators walked at will among tents, strips of hanging jerky, and lots of watermelon and red soda pop. They smelled coffee, juniper and pine campfire smoke, and rich mutton stew. They bought jewelry and traditional crafts from Natives who displayed their entire year's work. Bargain hunters waited until after the last show when prices dropped dramatically. Camp visitors often came across the carcass of a horse destroyed following a rodeo injury, strung up in a tree and butchered. They might also pass by a butchered lamb, the sorting of organs into various piles, and the milking of excrement from intestines—all as hordes of flies hovered overhead.

The Natives came to town for fun as well as work. The children, mothers and fathers, grandparents and relatives packed up and came ready for the biggest event of the year. At the pow-wow they feasted, laughed, and a few even remembered wars between tribes. They met friends and recounted adventures of previous pow-wows. But perhaps their greatest source of entertainment was the whites—people who had such funny, sometimes crazy, but always strange customs and unusual side attractions.

Carnival operators were well aware of the Flagstaff celebration and set up their rides and games at the city park site.

One of the strange attractions was the carnival. Carnival operators were well aware of the pow-wow and always set up on the city park site. Most Indians had never seen anything like it. One distinguished elderly Navajo man, for example, enjoyed the children's small roller coaster ride so much that he remained seated in the car with his arms folded, handing the operator another ticket at the end of each ride, never smiling or saying a word, but thoroughly enjoying himself.

The Indians began to leave town Monday morning. That evening hundreds of campfires once again lit up the roadside across the Navajo Reservation. The tourists also moved on. More than 18,500 participants and spectators had taken part, at times straining public services. Thousands had been turned away from some shows for lack of seating. Thirty major newspapers from Los Angeles to Boston, as well as NBC, reported on the colorful all-Indian weekend.[9]

The pow-wow had brought considerable attention to Flagstaff. In the summer of 1941, however, it may also have represented the nation's most well-received, enjoyable, and generous offering at the local level to Native Americans. Many of the Indians certainly thought so.

The weeks of anticipation and excitement over the town's largest celebration ended abruptly. Flagstaff reluctantly returned to its usual routine after the pow-wow, not too different from that of ten years earlier, or even twenty. Few if any of the Indians remained in town. Once again, the reputation for the pow-wow had grown, as had the number of tourists passing through en route to the Grand Canyon located about seventy-five miles northwest. For those who lingered that summer, however, these two attractions could not overshadow Flagstaff's cultural and historical legacy from its roots of sixty-five years.

This legacy was reflected in the city's numerous nineteenth-century buildings; in the vibrant blue-collar population of black, Hispanic, and white cultures; in the college that dated from 1899; in the Museum of Northern Arizona established in 1927; and with the sheep and cattle ranchers, lumbermen, saloon keepers, railroaders, merchants, public officials, and tourist court and restaurant owners. They were all part of the city's landscape. The force of history rolled through daily in the form of huge Atchison, Topeka, and Santa Fe Railroad locomotives that pulled their cargo up and across the Arizona divide, or at the Hotel Monte Vista where many of Hollywood's stars lingered, or along the well-worn concrete sections of Route 66 where thousands had fled west from the Great Depression.

Flagstaff was not a haphazard settlement. Federal interest in the area south of the San Francisco Mountains began immediately after the Mexican War. The nation wanted pathways to the Pacific Ocean and the government dispatched military expeditions in the 1850s to search for routes. Although the Civil War interrupted the westering process, several Union expeditions passed by en route to the mining digs around the Hassayampa River in the vicinity of today's Prescott. Volunteer Springs, the watering hole ten miles west of today's Flagstaff at Bellemont, was named in honor of the California volunteer soldiers. Although Gen. William Jackson Palmer surveyed along the thirty-fifth parallel route for the Atlantic & Pacific Railroad between 1867 and 1869, construction was delayed during the nation's hard times of the 1870s.

The first settler in the San Francisco Mountains area, Thomas F. McMillan, drove a flock of sheep in from California in 1876 and was soon followed by a few other ranchers. To the west at Volunteer Springs, another hardy sheep man named Walter J. Hill settled on land that would years later become part of Navajo Ordnance Depot. About the same time, two parties from Boston passed through the area. On the nation's centennial they raised the flag on a pole made from a large ponderosa pine. The Bostonians stayed just long enough to appreciate the inhospitable climate. They left the pine pole standing, probably giving the name of "Flag Staff" to the tiny settlement that consisted of fewer than a dozen ranchers.[10]

Homesteading in northern Arizona Territory coincided with the rapid growth of the sheep industry to the south. Between 1870 and 1876, the number of sheep grazing in Arizona—outside Indian reservations—rose from 803 to 10,000. Flagstaff sheep men may have run more than one-third of Arizona's flocks in 1876. They gave the business their full attention and many of the local ranchers prospered as did sheep men across the territory.[11]

The approach of the Atlantic & Pacific Railroad east of Flagstaff in 1881 quickly changed the quiet ranching settlement. A stage and relay service, surveyors, lumberjacks, carpenters, engineers, mechanics, graders, and laborers moved ahead of the track-laying operations. Many were rough characters—laborers, frequently uncouth, unwashed, foul-smelling, and at times reinforced with cheap liquor.

Railroad construction fell into three general stages. First came the final surveys and engineers who laid out the exact line. Next came the graders, and finally the tracklayers or "gandy dancers," using tools made by the Gandy Tool Company of Chicago. They paced their labor with a melodic singsong chant and moved in a pattern of rapid, unforgiving, and precise steps not dissimilar to a dance, as they lifted, carried, and dropped the heavy iron rails and pounded in the spikes.[12]

The frenzy of activity leading A&P railroad construction, commonly called "the front," finally reached Flagstaff in August 1882 when the town became "Terminus, Atlantic & Pacific" with the corresponding flurry of excitement, activity, and disorder. Along with contractors, workmen, and payrolls came "gamblers, dance hall girls, and other riffraff, like hogs following a swill wagon." About the same time, Chicago industrialist Edward E. Ayer built a sawmill in town that quickly began churning out railroad ties, adding yet another industry to the ranching settlement.[13]

The A&P needed the copious water from Volunteer Springs, the most reliable source between Winslow and Williams. Westbound trains would be especially thirsty after the long climb up to Flagstaff and across the Arizona divide. Railroad engineers quickly set about digging wells and building two large water tanks along with a four-inch pipe to Walter Hill's spring where water was pumped to the railroad using a small steam engine. They named the water stop Bellemont in honor of Miss Bella Smith, daughter of F. W. Smith, General Superintendent of the A&P. Like Flagstaff, Bellemont soon boasted a Wells Fargo station, post office, and section gang boardinghouse, in addition to becoming a water stop for most local and many transcontinental trains.[14]

Once the Southern Pacific and the Atlantic & Pacific had laid tracks across Arizona, the territory's sheep population exploded to 698,404 by 1890. By opening northern Arizona to markets in the East and West, the railroad generated good fortune for many of Flagstaff's pioneer ranchers.[15]

The railroad stop at Flagstaff grew rapidly. Twenty-one saloons popped up around town, along with two stores. Drinks were two bits apiece and a bottle of beer one dollar. The town had a definite character. There were no peace officers and the occasional "lynching bee" was an orderly and subdued affair. Train robberies were not uncommon and stage robberies were all too frequent, especially between Flagstaff and Canyon Diablo before the railroad was completed. Shooting irons were carried openly, contributing to the "weekly pistol practice" in the town's numerous watering holes, or "deadfalls." It wasn't until

November 1883, fifteen months after the arrival of the railroad, that Flagstaff rejoiced because only eighteen shots had been fired in city saloons on a Sunday evening and only one man had been killed during the week. In the "skylight city," as it was also called, a generous volume of light flowed freely through many bullet holes in saloon ceilings.[16]

Although Flagstaff burned down a few times, including the lumber mill, it was rebuilt and the town continued to grow. Matt, Timothy, and Michael Riordan operated and then purchased the sawmill. Five Babbitt brothers moved in from Ohio and formed a partnership, the Babbitt Brothers Trading Company, along with a cattle company whose "C-O Bar" brand became renowned. The publishers of the *Arizona Champion* moved from Peach Springs to Flagstaff, believing the lumber, ranching, and railroad town had a brighter future.[17]

By 1890 Arizona Territory boasted 59,620 residents, and Flagstaff grew to almost 1,000. The town became the seat for the new Coconino[18] County, which was split off from Yavapai County in 1891. Flagstaff built a new courthouse using a fine red-brown sandstone mined from a quarry a mile east of town. The attractive stone was used locally and around the West as well.[19]

Good times for the sheep pioneers ended with the Panic of 1893, the worst depression in American history up to that time. Wool that had sold for twenty-seven cents per pound plummeted to seven cents. Northern Arizona ranchers were hit hard. The ranges were overstocked, two years of drought had stunted the grass, and cattle ranchers lost half their herds. Some Flagstaff ranchers survived. McMillan hung on and eventually became a prominent citizen.

In Bellemont, however, Walter Hill's story was the most strange and violent of Flagstaff's early pioneers. By the late 1880s Hill had become wealthy, due in no small part to hard work and the proximity of the A&P Railroad one mile north of his ranch. Hill owned between twenty and thirty thousand head of sheep and was the largest individual rancher in the territory. He employed about one hundred hands, built a two-story ranch house on his Volunteer Springs Ranch, and sold his wool and mutton on the West Coast and in the East. As

Walter J. Hill, the once wealthy and renowned sheep baron from Flagstaff, at the California State Prison at San Quentin in 1901.

Flagstaff's most prominent citizen, he founded the Masonic Lodge, the Odd Fellows chapter, the local militia company, and served as Territorial Fish Commissioner. He married and his wife gave birth to three sons. Hill traveled back East frequently and the *Arizona Champion* reported his comings and goings with pride.

Although on the surface he appeared to be a pillar of the community, there was a dark side to Walter J. Hill. In 1890 he began a series of affairs with several daughters of his Mexican sheepherders. His wife soon departed and his beautiful ranch house caught fire and burned down, resulting in considerable loss due to under-insurance. The Panic of 1893 sealed his fate. Hill was forced into bankruptcy. He sold out, went to work for the railroad, and had his wages garnished. When horse thieves stole his remaining stock, Hill and the sheriff tracked them down east of Flagstaff. As Hill crept up on the thieves, they shot him in the forehead. Amazingly, Hill survived the horrible wound, but the bullet—deeply lodged in his head—changed his personality. His mental decline was as precipitous as his story was bizarre. Hill could no longer hold a job and eventually became a drifter in California; he was sent to prison in San Quentin in 1901 for attempted rape, only to be released early for good behavior. Hill was sent back to San Quentin for parole violation and probably died destitute somewhere in California, quietly forgotten by the Flagstaff community.[20]

By the time Arizona became the forty-eighth state in 1912, Flagstaff's population had reached about two thousand, and the town was well on its way to becoming the economic and cultural center of northern Arizona. Percival Lowell's observatory, established on Mars Hill in 1894, continued to expand despite the declining health of its founder. Enrollment at Northern Arizona Normal School (later Arizona State Teachers College and Northern Arizona University) reached 136 students, with a faculty of 9 instructors.[21]

Although dozens of men from Flagstaff's National Guard Company I fought in World War I, the city's scourge of 1918 was not enemy soldiers but rather the deadly and deceptive worldwide plague of influenza that killed millions. The flu hit Flagstaff in early October 1918 when the number of cases in town jumped to several dozen. Doctors and public health officials could do nothing except ban all public meetings and close schools and churches. Three waves of influenza hit the town through the spring of 1919 and left a horrible trail of sixty dead, far outnumbering the nine soldiers who died in the war—and even some of those were from the flu.[22]

By the 1920s the American love for automobiles began to result in better roads. Flagstaff followed suit and paved 1.8 miles of Railroad Avenue as part of the National Old Trails Highway. By 1926 this section of pavement became part of the federal Highway 66, or Route 66, stretching across the West. Better roads increased access to northern Arizona's wonderland and the flow of tourist dollars jumped accordingly, resulting in Flagstaff's first motel—DuBeau's Motor Inn.

Although the local chapter of the Grand Army of the Republic held meetings in Flagstaff for years, the city had no military ties except for the militia company, originally called the Flagstaff Rifles, that had been organized by Walter J. Hill on March 25, 1890 and eventually became Company I, 158th Infantry. Local servicemen who fought overseas in two wars did most of their serious training elsewhere. Finally, in 1930 the state built a National Guard summer training camp a few miles south of town. They named it Fort Alexander M. Tuthill in honor of the Phoenix physician and army brigadier general who served during World War I.[23]

As the Great Depression gripped America, Flagstaff's growth slowed almost to a standstill. Its population registered 3,891 in 1930, an increase of only 700 during the entire decade of the Roaring Twenties. Federal money came to town in the summer of 1933, when the doors of Santa Fe Railroad cars swung open and several hundred slightly confused-looking young men stepped down and stared out into the thin air. Most of the first group were from Texas and Oklahoma but eventually they were replaced by men from Pennsylvania. They were skinny, half-educated, unmarried, poor, and in need of work that President Franklin D. Roosevelt's Civilian Conservation Corps provided. A few, however, were seasoned army sergeants along with some reserve officers who supervised the company. Flagstaff had two of the five CCC camps in the county—one at Schultz Pass and the other at the base of Mount Elden.[24]

Ranching and lumbering hung on during the Great Depression, and many new faces traveled through town. Okies, Arkies, and refugees from dust storms, dying lands, and awful times moved west on the long concrete path that twisted across the country from the Mississippi River to Bakersfield, California. Route 66, the mother road as John Steinbeck described it in *The Grapes of Wrath*, brought people in flight across the road of flight. They came over red lands, gray lands, deserts, and mountains, often with mattresses or washtubs on top of their cars and all kinds of things tied to the sides. After the climb up to Flagstaff many stopped for awhile. One woman, on the last of her possessions, traded a small diamond for blankets and bedding before moving on to the rich valleys of California. Some helped the town, although many hungry and destitute souls were housed and fed for free.

Some stayed for a few weeks or even months and migrant children flooded the Flagstaff schools.[25]

Flagstaff fared reasonably well, however. The pow-wow helped, and the CCC poured thousands of dollars into town each month. Several Public Works Administration projects renovated buildings at the college. The National Highway Recovery Program, one of FDR's relief measures designed to build roads as well as create jobs, built the railroad underpass in 1934, streamlining traffic through town.[26]

Bellemont, however, was not as fortunate. Heavy railroad logging around Volunteer Prairie gradually ended, and the population dropped from its peak of 692 residents in 1910 to 113 by 1930. Many were Hispanic AT&SF Railroad workers, along with a handful of Native Americans.[27]

By the summer of 1941 Bellemont was home to only fifty or sixty people who hung on any way possible. The settlement consisted of the Santa Fe section house, a couple of tourist courts, a gas station, a few railroad workers' homes and perhaps ten other family dwellings, several chuck wagons, some outlying ranches, four rail yard stock pens and scales, an old bar located next to the schoolhouse, and Thompson's store.[28]

Ranchers bought their supplies at Delbert and Maude Thompson's store, which also included a small butcher shop, two gas pumps, and some slot machines. Behind Thompson's store—where one woman had danced in the 1920s—five women sold themselves in what was commonly called the "old whore house." They were especially busy during spring and fall when many cowboys came in from the range to ship livestock. Some of the women were quite well known but usually referred to as just Sadie or Susie. The brothel was part of the small community and rumors, though unlikely, circulated in the summer of 1941 that the sheriff was getting a nice cut from its gambling and prostitution.[29]

Time seemed to stand still on the clearing southwest of the San Francisco Peaks. Most viewed Bellemont and Volunteer Prairie from the windows of their Santa Fe Railroad car or their automobile as they drove along Route 66. Bellemont, like many small settlements in the

American West, had enjoyed a few good years but was almost a ghost town by the summer of 1941. The people had moved on or to neighboring Flagstaff where some jobs were available at the tourist courts, the teachers college, and the lumber mills.

Thus, no one noticed when, on August 17, a stranger stepped out of his sedan parked alongside Route 66 and took a leisurely stroll around Volunteer Prairie and Bellemont. The stranger was Charles M. Steese, an army colonel assigned to the Field Services Division of the Office of the Chief of Ordnance in the War Department. Steese and his party of railroad officials didn't say much. They quietly began, however, to thoroughly inspect the area.

The group walked around Bellemont and the Volunteer Prairie range where Walter J. Hill had once been a rich man. They admired the lands that formed a large, picturesque, high-country bowl encircled by rolling hills pushing up several hundred feet and backed by larger pine-covered cinder cones. To the north, they saw low-lying green knolls that were disciples of a three-tier ancient volcanic range extending twenty-five miles into the distance. Steese noted the foothills braced by the much higher Wing and A-1 Mountains, each over 8,000 feet high. They in turn seemed dwarfed by Agassiz and Humphreys Peaks at 12,356 and 12,633 feet respectively.

For the quiet and mysterious strangers the panorama from Bellemont was one of distinct images: rolling rangeland and mountain park, ascending perimeter peaks of volcanic rock, meadow Arizona fescue, heaving swells along ancient faults and seeps flanked by prolific springs. All were surrounded by dark green ponderosa pines. It was beautiful Colorado Plateau high-country at its best—a welcome contrast from the cramped army headquarters in Washington, D.C.

The group wandered over to the cluster of springs where cool, clear water percolated profusely near the middle of the clearing about a mile south of Bellemont. The water gave life to the range. In Steese's search, the springs were critical.

The foundation for Volunteer Springs had been laid by volcanos spewing miles of molten lava, in combination with earth movements over 4.5 million years ago. The surface layers of basalt, a dark volcanic rock extending sixty to eighty feet deep, were frequently covered in the open range by layers of Kaibab limestone, a sandy sedimentary rock. Immediately below the surface basalt an impermeable layer of clay acted as a barrier to prevent moisture from escaping, thus creating an aquifer. Shifting of the earth's surface over time created several distinct fault lines. Deep-seated earth movements between 1.5 and .8 million years ago along Volunteer Fault forged an elevation offset of three hundred feet, and created a crack between the two earth surface sections that offered an upward escape for water trapped under pressure between the basalt and clay layers eighty feet below.

Colonel Steese watched the water bubble generously up to the surface, water that once cut a path across the landscape, eventually flowing southwest through Volunteer Canyon toward a junction with Sycamore Canyon—one of the most rugged and primitive areas of the United States—and eventually reaching the Verde River. Steese had seen enough. They returned to their sedans and drove away.[30]

Meanwhile, in Flagstaff, one man—Leo Weaver—had finally settled into a work routine as secretary of the chamber of commerce. Weaver would soon be flooded with questions about strangers, the army, and wild rumors.

2

WILD TIMES
Building Navajo Ordnance Depot

Leo Eugene Weaver was just what the Flagstaff chamber of commerce needed as the city inched out of the Great Depression in the summer of 1941—someone to savor the positive, wink at the negative, and promote just about anything as peaches-and-cream. The fifty-five-year-old Weaver was one of those Arizona characters that few forgot, and many returned to visit. Likeable, interesting, and colorful, he was also an excellent salesman, a natural after-dinner speaker, and someone who spread his boundless energy in thick layers. Especially fascinated by places and things that had a history, Weaver was also a romantic, an entertainer, and a showman.[1]

Weaver was tall, six feet one inch, with an upright posture that made him seem even larger. His piercing slate blue eyes were "always smiling" and they quickly evaluated whether or not he liked someone, labeling them as either ".45 or .22 caliber." He was rugged, thin— never weighing over 175 pounds—and believed in physical fitness. Despite chronic smoking, Weaver enjoyed exercise and often ran four or five miles.[2]

Weaver admired the popular cowboy film star Tom Mix, thought he resembled Mix, and began to dress like the Hollywood actor. He sported fine western clothes that included an oversize cowboy hat, striped gambler pants held up by a large belt and buckle, a black kerchief knotted and pinned at his neck, sharp Mexican spurs, and lizard skin boots. Weaver advertised himself as a horse trainer, but knew little about horses or stock. In reality, Weaver was, as the saying goes, all hat and no cattle. Yet his overall impression "made feminine hearts flutter." In short, Leo Weaver had style.[3]

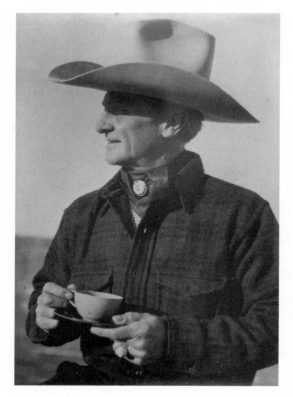

As secretary of Flagstaff's chamber of commerce, Leo Weaver assisted Navajos and Hopis in their relocation to Bellemont.

In 1919 Weaver bought a ranch in Wickenburg, named it the Circle Flying W, coined the term "guest" rather than dude ranch, and launched Arizona's modern guest ranch tourist industry. Unable to pay bills, he eventually sold out and accepted a loan offer from noted Flagstaff guest Dr. Harold S. Colton—founder of the Museum of Northern Arizona and formerly professor of zoology at the University of Pennsylvania—to buy the M. I. Powers ranch north of Flagstaff at Fort Valley. There Weaver started another guest ranch, again named the Circle Flying W.[4]

Never making a go of his Flagstaff ranch, Weaver postponed loan payments to Colton and found work as the secretary of the chamber of commerce and manager of the Monte Vista Hotel. He married Hazel Barbeau in 1931 and, despite increasing debts, bought the John D. Lee ranch at the mouth of Pahreah Canyon at Lee's Ferry on the Colorado River, naming it Paradise Canyon guest ranch.

Weaver provided a personal touch at his Lee's Ferry ranch with tours, wonderful stories, music on his small Steinway piano, and singing of popular songs. His published articles and watercolor paintings added even more. Weaver ensured that each customer had a pleasant experience in northern Arizona. As receipts ultimately proved, however, he did this for an unusually modest fee.

A few of Weaver's peculiarities went unnoticed, or at least overlooked. He was impractical and always in financial straits because he never charged customers enough to cover expenses. He was not interested in making money. Weaver lived on credit and never carried a wallet. He believed some bills were not meant to be paid, especially those received by mail, which he always tossed into "File 13," the wastebasket. Weaver had a bizarre relationship with the Babbitt store where he brought customers for outfitting, believing sales earned credits for himself because guests copied his handsome outfit. The store billed Weaver regularly and he tossed the bills out regularly.[5]

In the end, Weaver failed to make his Lee's Ferry ranch profitable, just like he failed at Flagstaff and Wickenburg. His ideas were impractical, he didn't charge enough, he lacked business skills, and he was unlucky. His customers, however, relished the guest ranch experience provided by the handsome and entertaining Arizona cowboy. He, in turn, remained an idealist who loved northern Arizona and Flagstaff with a passion. Weaver and his family returned to town in the late 1930s where he went back to work for the Flagstaff chamber of commerce.

In the summer of 1941, the city was fortunate to have Leo Weaver at the commerce helm, despite his obvious shortcomings. For the unimaginable events that were about to unfold, few could have filled his shoes. Weaver's style was complemented with a love for the Navajo and Hopi people and their country, where he had cultivated many friendships. They, in turn, liked and respected the colorful cowboy who had been studying their languages and by 1941 spoke Navajo and some Hopi. Weaver was always interested in the Indians' welfare and did what he could to prevent their exploitation. Neither he nor others realized at the time how important this relationship would soon become.

Weaver's duties with the chamber of commerce were far removed from America's growing problems with Imperial Japan. Flagstaff was getting back to work all across town. Construction at Arizona's air bases revived the city's major industry—lumber and finished timber products—to the highest level since World War I. Two large lumber companies were operating mills in Flagstaff. The Saginaw & Manistee Lumber Company left their Williams mill and took over Arizona Lumber & Timber Company on March 1, 1941, employing 350 men at the Flagstaff mill and in the forests. Southwest Lumber Mills and the two or three smaller mills in town probably employed about 200, bringing the total to around 550. Other industries in town included about 50 employed in food-related businesses, a half-dozen employed with saddles, leather products, and Indian jewelry, and 20 or 30 with the city's four hotels and seven tourist courts. Arizona State Teachers College employed 42 faculty for 535 students. Flagstaff was also a livestock town and depended heavily on the industry. Six stockyard pens supported about eighty thousand head of range cattle in the county, along with eight hundred thousand head of sheep during the summer months. All together, between 700 and 800 people found employment in 1941 in or around Flagstaff.[6]

The dog days of summer slipped by quietly amidst the beautiful mountain pines and school-age children relished their final days of freedom. Flagstaff citizens, focused on promoting their community as the site for a military airport, failed to notice the strangers who stopped at Bellemont on August 17. Colonel Steese and the railroad officials were searching for possible sites for a massive munitions storage and shipping depot. The quintet had just visited a site at Lake Mary and were driving west toward Williams when Steese noticed the large clearing south of the Bellemont railroad tracks. The colonel believed the site had merit and ordered a prospectus drawn up. The party then continued on to Chino Valley, completing their inspection the following day.[7]

Colonel Steese's tour of northern Arizona was part of a War Department plan to construct ordnance facilities in the West for receiving, storing, maintaining, and shipping ammunition, explosives, and bombs. At the end of World War I, the army's ordnance depots were concentrated along the East Coast, where they were more susceptible to sabotage and enemy attack. In 1920, the War Department moved to correct the problem by constructing new depots at Ogden, Utah, and Savanna, Illinois. The subsequent closure of nine reserve depots in the East drastically reduced the country's munitions storage facilities. Postwar budget reductions worsened the situation.

The outbreak of war in Europe, and in particular the fall of France in June of 1940, forced the War Department to scramble for new facilities. Congress responded with increased appropriations in early 1941 that enabled the army to construct additional depots at Fort Wingate, New Mexico; Umatilla, Oregon; Anniston, Alabama; and Ravenna, Ohio. Construction had hardly begun when the United States' escalating involvement in the European conflict called for the accelerated production of ammunition. Secretary of War Henry L. Stimson responded by approving the establishment of twelve more depots, bringing the total to sixteen. Half of the new facilities were designated "A" program depots, consisting of administrative buildings and warehouses designed for indefinite use; the other half, designated "B" program depots that eventually included the Flagstaff facility, would be shut down at the end of the war.[8]

Investigation of potential depot sites continued into the fall of 1941. Relations with Japan rapidly deteriorated during the several months that Maj. Carroll H. Deitrick spent touring western states, which held only 7 percent of the country's ammunition storage facilities at the outbreak of the war in Europe. With the surprise Japanese attack on Pearl Harbor on December 7, the War Department immediately ordered rapid construction of one-thousand-bunker ("igloo") ammunition storage depots at sites in California, Colorado, and South Dakota, as well as somewhere in the Flagstaff-Prescott area.[9]

On December 27 or 28, Colonel Steese returned to Flagstaff with Major Lyle Rosenberg of the Army Corps of Engineers to select the Arizona site. In surveying the Bellemont and Chino Valley locations, the pair were looking for reasonably flat, open terrain that could accommodate a thousand igloos at a safe distance from nearby cities; a cool climate; sufficient water to sustain two thousand military and civilian personnel; and proximity to a railroad. The Bellemont site met all four criteria.[10]

One additional item proved critical. The threat of a Japanese invasion of the West Coast and an inland battle loomed over planners for several months after the surprise attack on Pearl Harbor. The army's danger zone—where a depot would not be safe from a coastal invasion—extended from the California coast almost to Seligman, west of Flagstaff. The cities just outside of the zone yet closest to the port of Los Angeles—Seligman and Ash Fork—did not have a sufficient water supply to support a large depot.[11]

Other factors also weighed heavily in Bellemont's favor. First of all, only a few small ranches dotted the Volunteer Prairie. Most of the range and surrounding forest was owned by either the federal government, the State of Arizona, or the Atchison, Topeka & Santa Fe Railroad. Steese and Rosenberg estimated that it would cost the government no more than $2.50 per acre to buy up any land that was in private hands. A transmission line near Route 66, on the northern boundary of the site, furnished electrical power, while fuel oil and coal could be easily shipped by rail from Gallup, New Mexico, 180 miles to the east. The dry, high-country air would reduce maintenance costs. And, finally, nearby Flagstaff offered convenient housing and office facilities during the initial construction stages. On December 30, Steese and Rosenberg turned in their report recommending the immediate construction of a one-thousand-igloo munitions depot on twenty-eight thousand acres of land at Bellemont.[12]

Flagstaff residents, meanwhile, had gotten wind of the army's plans to construct a huge ammunition storage facility somewhere between Albuquerque, New Mexico, and the Colorado River. Pleased with a thirty-five-thousand-dollar appropriation to improve the National

Guard facility at Fort Tuthill, community leaders renewed their arguments for establishing a military airport in Flagstaff. Their pulses quickened when government surveyors, quietly going about their work, popped up at several different locations near town. With the support of local businessmen, Leo Weaver, as might be expected, far outspent the chamber's annual phone budget, deluging Senator Carl Hayden and Arizona's other representatives in Washington with requests for information and assistance. By late December, Maj. Gen. C. M. Wesson, the War Department's chief of ordnance, was fully apprised of the ample water supply at the Bellemont site. Although Flagstaff boosters may not have realized it at the time, their energetic self-promotion and the ties they were about to forge with the military during World War II would profoundly affect the future development of their community.[13]

Flagstaff was not the only city to experience vague and mysterious rumors. In other parts of the West, word often leaked out concerning the army's interest in their region. Cities and even states engaged in heated competition as they promoted and exaggerated their own peculiar advantages. Some cities like Edgemont, South Dakota, for example, went so far as to refrain from publishing any stories about the proposed depot in its area, afraid that additional publicity would cause neighboring cities and states to increase their lobbying efforts. After all, the stakes were enormous for small towns like Flagstaff—sometimes a matter of survival. Despite gradual economic improvement, many cities had not recovered from the Great Depression and still yearned for better times. They were thrilled by rumors of thousands of jobs and gigantic payrolls.[14]

Events moved quickly. Rumors raced through Flagstaff on Monday, January 19, 1942, after someone telephoned the *Coconino Sun* asking about the availability of well-lit office space for an engineering crew. The caller was also looking for a room large enough to do drafting work, a two-bedroom house for himself, and other facilities to accommodate a "large number of men." The following day, a caller from Gallup, New Mexico, asked what the *Sun* knew about the work that was about to begin "on a munitions dump project" near Flagstaff. He had heard that the facility would be larger than the 650-igloo Gallup depot and far exceed its two-hundred-thousand-dollar weekly payroll.[15]

Leo Weaver once again contacted Senator Hayden, who responded on January 21 that he had no definite information. He reminded Weaver that the War Department would be reluctant to reveal the location of the proposed depot for fear that the news would drive up land prices. That same day, Maj. Demmie H. Cox and eight men from the Army Corps of Engineers district office in Albuquerque arrived in Flagstaff "on government business." Suspense and curiosity surged through the community as the newcomers set up headquarters at the DuBeau Motel just south of the Santa Fe tracks. Although Cox admitted that he was looking for a one-year lease on a house for his family, he refused to divulge any other details of his business. Undeterred by the major's reticence, bold headlines on the January 23 edition of the *Coconino Sun* trumpeted "U.S. PROJECT MEN HERE." The paper went on to predict that a facility "immense in proportion" would be located at Bellemont.[16]

The reception Major Cox received at Bellemont, however, did not go well. Cox, a no-nonsense engineer who was very good at his profession, was noted for being strict, military, and efficient. He was also aloof and unapproachable. Many steered clear of Cox and one stenographer "almost froze up" in his presence. Perhaps, therefore, it was no surprise that when Cox, apparently in civilian attire, first drove out to inspect the site, someone telephoned the sheriff's department reporting "a suspicious character who got water at Del Thompson's store. He was very secretive, a stranger." Deputy sheriff Pete Michelbach, concerned because the Bellemont whorehouses were behind the store, raced out and "collared the guy." Much to his embarrassment, Michelbach learned that he had just apprehended Major Cox, the army engineer in charge of the project.[17]

The excitement generated a small boom in rental property, business, and housing. By the following week, every available home in Flagstaff was rented. Business improved and merchants were eager to expand their inventories. They hesitated, however, awaiting some type of confirmation that the rumored depot was a reality. Like most of their fellow townspeople, they were very happy with the situation but were "afraid to bust loose." Meanwhile, Weaver alerted Senator Hayden to be prepared to snare a federal housing project for the city.[18]

Local residents were stunned when the Office of Censorship in Washington finally unveiled the secret in a January 30 telegram to the *Coconino Sun*. The news release announced that the $17 million project (over $175 million in today's dollars) would begin immediately. The depot would cover forty-eight square miles and, at the peak of construction, would employ six thousand laborers in three round-the-clock shifts, constructing eight hundred "major units" (the terms igloo, bunker, ammunition, and depot did not appear in the news release), scores of buildings, a locomotive repair shop, 185 miles of paved roads, and 50 miles of railway. When completed, it would employ about two thousand workers for the duration of the war. It was an enterprise beyond the wildest dreams of Flagstaff residents whose town then supported eight hundred jobs at most. Construction of the Bellemont depot would be the second largest 1942 defense expenditure in Arizona—exceeded only by the $38 million open-pit copper mine at Morenci. Something momentous was taking place. Life in the small lumber and college town was about to change.[19]

Along with the good news, the press release also cautioned anyone who might contemplate taking advantage of the situation. Merchants were warned not to impose "boom-town" prices as thousands of workers descended upon the city. Although the government would be offering higher wages in order to give contractors the choice of available workers, citizens were reminded that this was not a "gravy train." Good pay demanded good work. To finish the project as fast as possible, the government would issue "cost plus 10 percent" contracts. The *Coconino Sun* alerted its readers that wage and price controls would be imposed should businesses and individuals "get too greedy."[20]

Despite the announcement, some Flagstaff residents still could not quite believe their luck. The federal government had already awarded a three-hundred-thousand-dollar contract for engineering plans to Prouty Brothers of Denver. Nonetheless, the arrival of carloads of engineers, surveyors, and chain men on Sunday, February 1, sparked wild rumors that the project had been canceled. Even reassuring telegrams from Senators Carl Hayden and Ernest McFarland failed to calm the jittery nerves of Flagstaff businessmen, merchants, and Leo Weaver at the chamber of commerce.[21]

Things changed, however, once the land appraisers appeared in town. The big question on everyone's mind was whether the property holders on Volunteer Prairie and adjacent land would sell without condemnation proceedings. Fortunately, the majority of the 28,978-acre reservation was already owned by the federal government—17,245 acres. Another 9,080 acres was in state hands, leaving only 2,624 acres to be acquired from private owners. Negotiations were long and complicated. With the horror of Pearl Harbor fresh in their minds, the largest land owners responded unselfishly and patriotically. C. J. Babbitt, president of the CO Bar Cattle Company; Dr. R. O. Raymond; and cattleman John D. Osborne immediately offered to turn over their land to the government at no cost. The Atchison, Topeka, & Santa Fe Railroad, the largest private landowner, gave up some of its Volunteer Prairie land in exchange for tracts elsewhere. One notorious cattleman, however, threatened to derail the entire process.[22]

Described by those who knew him as an ethical, dynamic, and complex individual, Cecil Miller Sr. never played for fun—he only played for keeps. At about age thirty-four, Miller and his partners bought the DK Ranch near Woody Mountain, southeast of Volunteer Prairie. He obtained grazing rights to 140 acres of Forest Service land valued at two dollars per acre that fell within the projected depot site. Miller not only refused to part with his grazing land, but he informed Senator Hayden and the War Department that the army engineers had selected the wrong site for the depot. He demanded that the government move to another location west of his leased property. If not, he would use his considerable influence to have the project stopped—regardless of what his Flagstaff neighbors might think.[23]

Community leaders were aghast that Miller would place himself above home and country, not to mention jeopardizing millions of dollars in local business. Andy Matson, chairman of the Coconino County

Board of Supervisors, described Miller's position as "selfish" and "un-reasonable." A flurry of correspondence between Senator Hayden, the Ordnance Department, engineers, Leo Weaver, and the Arizona state land commissioner continued for two weeks, while Flagstaff business-men fretted over the potential loss of the project due to one unsavory cattleman. In desperation, the chamber of commerce suggested mov-ing the depot boundaries two miles south and west of their present location. Considering the stakes involved and the anger in the com-munity, it is surprising that Miller was not found hanging from a tree.

Major Cox, thoroughly disgusted with the quibbling, finally re-ceived word from Albuquerque that the boundaries would not be moved a single foot. The matter was settled and work commenced. Still, it would be August 31 before the federal government finally issued an order for condemnation and immediate possession of land still remain-ing in private hands.[24]

The pace of business in Flagstaff immediately picked up. Frank Prouty established his company headquarters in the Morrow Garage on west Santa Fe Avenue, just north of the railroad underpass, in the vicinity of today's city hall. Local merchants banded together to pledge "just and fair treatment to all customers during any boom period." Placards outlining their policy appeared in store windows all over town. City officials canvassed rental property, including tourist courts and hotels, to determine what accommodations were available. The Wil-liams–Grand Canyon chamber of commerce extended a helping hand by forwarding lists of available housing in the neighboring communi-ties. Flagstaff chamber of commerce president C. R. Brown traveled with several local businessmen to glean what information they could from Gallup's boomtown experience with the Fort Wingate construc-tion.[25]

Labor was a major concern for contractors as well as army plan-ners. Flagstaff and surrounding cities simply did not have enough workers to build the Flagstaff Ordnance Depot—as it was first called—nor to staff it once it was completed and placed on a wartime footing. The army turned to the nearby Navajo reservation, which had played a valuable role in building the Fort Wingate depot. On February 5,

1942, the War Department issued General Orders No. 9, renaming the Flagstaff project the Navajo Ordnance Depot, in honor of the thousands of Native American workers it would call on to help build and operate the Bellemont facility.[26]

Major Cox set up an office in an old building on Volunteer Prairie and immediately encountered obstacles. Deep snow, temperatures of minus fifteen degrees Fahrenheit, and ground frozen to a depth of almost three feet hindered survey work in January and February. Extremely rough and often muddy terrain made it impossible for engineers to compile comprehensive data in the time allowed. As a result, the district engineer office in Albuquerque received penciled draft designs that they then reproduced for the various contractors. By February, the bad weather was compounded by acute shortages of both labor and housing. Only a few local laborers and a handful of Navajos had signed up.[27]

Before long, Flagstaff was churning with excitement as army and civilian engineers, company officials, and construction workers poured into town looking for office space, lodging, and food. Merchants, land owners, chamber of commerce representatives, elected officials, and army personnel met in an effort to anticipate problems and devise plans for dealing with the turmoil. Even so, during the second week of March, Major Cox noticed that several local landlords were demanding unreasonable rates. Some renters were moving out of the houses they were leasing for fifty dollars a month and subletting them for hundreds of dollars. Cox announced that "if Flagstaff does not change its ways," he would protest the price gouging to Washington, which would likely launch a formal investigation. Hoping to preclude profiteering, Leo Weaver and the chamber of commerce urged moderation. Greed not only harmed the project, they said, but gave aid and comfort to America's enemies.[28]

As if the community did not have enough problems, two announcements in March 1942 once again caught Flagstaff residents by surprise. First of all, Major Cox revealed that the project, already proceeding at a hectic pace, would be speeded up. The starting date for construction was being advanced to April 1. The second bit of news

In 1942 Capt. Demmie H. Cox, the army's engineer for the construction of Navajo Ordnance Depot, placed his headquarters in an old building on Bellemont's Volunteer Prairie, ranch lands that once belonged to sheep baron Walter J. Hill.

was even more staggering. Chamber president Brown and his colleagues returned from New Mexico with predictions that, based upon the Gallup—Fort Wingate experience, Flagstaff could expect an influx of ten thousand laborers at the peak of construction—two-thirds more than Cox had estimated. Moreover, Flagstaff would have to house, feed, and perhaps school three additional persons for every one worker. Brown warned that Flagstaff could end up taking in forty thousand new residents.[29]

Meanwhile, around the Grand Canyon region, many cities suffered from the sharp drop in tourism caused by the war. Grand Canyon visitors plunged by 55 percent compared to May of the previous year. In Flagstaff, however, things were different. The city shifted into a genuine boomtown mode as the weather improved in April. Officials and technicians continued to arrive, and were joined by hundreds of Navajo and Hopi workers and their families who had left the reservation for jobs with the army project. Hordes of transient workers poured in from around the West and the South, some of them seeking a way out of hard times while many others were pursuing a quick buck. The feverish activity overwhelmed the sleepy lumber village. A temporary town mushroomed overnight at Bellemont, directly on the construction site, where some early arrivals were already living and working. Thirty-three construction companies rushed to northern Arizona to fulfill their government contracts. The Atkinson-Kier Company, the depot's major contractor, had helped build the enormous Grand Coulee Dam on the Columbia River. Atkinson-Kier rented the Stroud tourist court at the junction of Route 66 and Oak Creek Road. Other companies found offices elsewhere in town.[30]

Although the accelerated schedule pushed contractors to their limits, work proceeded smoothly at first. Prouty Brothers completed much of the design work by mid-March. The E. W. Duhame Company of Phoenix began construction of aboveground magazines and buildings on schedule, April 1, with contracts for $1.6 million. On April 14, Atkinson-Kier began work on their $13.6 million contract for eight hundred earth-covered concrete igloos, along with shelters, loading platforms, and ramps. Many other contractors pitched in during May. Finally, on June 20, Arizona Contractors of Phoenix began their $3.3 million project for railroad tracks, roads, and highways. The Jerome A. Utley Company of Detroit commenced work on July 28 for the last major project, combat storage buildings costing $2.3 million.[31]

Flagstaff residents were enjoying pleasant summer weather and construction companies were churning at full steam when Carl Hayden dropped another bombshell. On July 20, he wired Leo Weaver that the War Department had just allocated an additional $2 million to expand Navajo Depot, bringing the total contract to almost $20 million. The work would begin immediately and had to be completed before December 15.[32]

For Atkinson-Kier, the depot project was far more complicated than Grand Coulee Dam because of the sprawling forty-four-square-mile construction site. The company had to first build access roads to each of the eight hundred igloo sites. Then they cleared trees, leveled the hilly volcanic ground, and prepared the igloo foundations. They

The largest depot construction contract was awarded to Atkinson-Kier for $13.6 million to build 800 steel-reinforced concrete igloos, along with loading platforms and docks, on 800 acres of land. Atkinson-Kier was a seasoned company that had helped build the foundation for the Grand Coulee Dam. The igloo frame shown is ready for concrete, which will be poured thickest at the base to direct the blast from an accidental explosion upward rather than outward.

poured concrete slabs of about two thousand feet square each. When the slabs were set, carpenters built the inner wooden forms for each bunker's curved roof, followed by the outer form. The walls were made thicker at the bottom so the blast from an accidental explosion would be projected upward rather than outward.

Once the rounded frame was complete, cement trucks lumbered over miles of crude roads to each igloo site to fill the spaces between the inner and outer forms. Workers stuck special hose-type vibrators down between the forms to settle the wet concrete. When the concrete was dry, operators covered the bunker with dirt, taking their twenty-ton bulldozers to the top of the igloo—often protesting against the obvious danger. Then they moved on a few hundred yards to the next igloo site.[33]

The new deadline turned up the heat even further, and the construction lurched into chaos by late summer of 1942. Eight thousand men swarmed like ants across Volunteer Prairie day and night, building igloos, magazines, warehouses, roads, utilities, railroad tracks, and loading docks. Noise never ceased from the rock crushers, cement plants, cars, trucks, heavy equipment, and blasting. Concrete was king. Atkinson-Kier, having learned much from the Grand Coulee work, made, transported, and poured thousands of tons of concrete, day and night, in shifts from 5:00 A.M. to 1:00 P.M., 1:00 to 9:00 P.M., and 9:00 P.M. to 5:00 A.M. Scores of trucks scurried concrete across makeshift trails of dust or cinders leading from batch plants to carved-out berths among distant pines where they belched the mud into wooden forms still fresh of smell and shaking from the carpenter's hammer and nail.[34]

Shelton Dowell, who worked in the timekeeping department, drove across the construction site to verify that those who had checked in were actually on the job. Although most men had been relieved of their knives, guns, and whiskey at the gate, Dowell knew he was risking his life with every trip. "Powder monkeys" were everywhere, loading their dynamite capsules and running wires across roads, often smoking a cigarette, perhaps smelling of whiskey, and oblivious to any danger to themselves or others from their frequent explosions. Swarms of workers raced across the site in hundreds of Ford Model As and Chevys, darting around cement trucks and Caterpillars that often moved erratically due to untrained drivers.[35]

Contractors were now hiring everyone and anyone, even those with little or no experience. In fact, they didn't care who they hired. Howard C. Wren, a sixteen-year-old in the summer of 1942, had just finished his sophomore year at Flagstaff high school and, like others his age, was glad to get on with Atkinson-Kier for 97.5 cents per hour as an oiler, even though he had to first pay a fee and join the union. Labor at Bellemont was a closed shop and the unions included carpenters, teamsters, and several others. Wren's crew of six, all of whom were from Oklahoma but for Wren and his brother, dashed across the construction site searching for graders, bulldozers, and rollers that needed an oil change or lubrication.

As with others from Flagstaff, building Navajo Depot was a family affair. In Howard Wren's home, three found jobs at Bellemont. His father, a grader operator with years of road construction experience, and his brother both worked on the site. They all earned good wages and the income brought into the Wren home was significant. Around town, many other parents and their high-school-age children found good jobs with Atkinson-Kier.[36]

Keeping the heavy machinery running was no easy task. With wartime construction in full swing across the state, new machinery was at a premium. Construction companies were often forced to use old equipment. Atkinson-Kier even brought one of their two old steam shovels to Bellemont, a huge Bucyrus 50-B. The unusual machine had character—it would perform one task and then vent steam with a loud "pphhhtt" sound, and then repeat the cycle. The contraption, dripping oil from almost every hose, kept Wren's crew busy. Construction companies did not care where the machines came from as long as they worked. Although Atkinson-Kier had a central repair shop, they also did repairs out in the field. Around the site, tensions mounted as veteran equipment operators became frustrated with substandard machinery and the many novice operators, especially when those who had faked their experience caused confusion, delays, and breakdowns.[37]

Colonel Steese understated the case when he predicted that Bellemont's volcanic soil would only slightly increase the cost of construction. Excavators frequently struck solid rock that damaged their heavy equipment. As a result, machines often sat idle for long periods while they waited for difficult-to-obtain replacement parts. To fill the void, the government rented equipment, as many as 150 pieces at one time just for Atkinson-Kier. Drilling and blasting slowed operations considerably.[38]

For most workers the days were long, hard, stressful, and often dangerous. Jack Connelley, a young shovel operator, was under constant pressure to produce more and faster. At the same time, the draft was coming and he worried about his wife, Elgymae. On the site, Atkinson-Kier knew what needed to be done, how to do it, and how to get the most out of their men. The company was tough and efficient.

The 1942 construction of 8 aboveground magazines represented only a fraction of the 1,060 structures that provided 3.5 million square feet of enclosed storage space at Navajo Depot.

"Things just happened," Elgymae recalled, "just like the movies." Atkinson-Kier "didn't mess around." Workers either produced or were fired on the spot. The Connelleys lived in a small trailer at one of Bellemont's several trailer parks where Elgymae enjoyed walks in the forests while Jack was at work. She watched troop trains pass by and would often throw bouquets of flowers to the young soldiers.[39]

Construction of Navajo Ordnance Depot reached its peak in September 1942 as contractors scrambled to meet deadlines. Automobile travelers heading west on Route 66, across the Arizona divide, observed mountains of freshly cut lumber and acres of gleaming stacks of construction materials stretched out across Volunteer Prairie as far as the eye could see. The speed with which the depot was built inevitably resulted in waste that shocked some Flagstaff residents. On slack days, some contractors paid unoccupied workers just to ensure that they wouldn't become dissatisfied and leave. Leo Weaver, who had "never seen such a needless waste of money," was convinced that Atkinson-Kier was profiting from their cost-plus contract.[40]

Like Volunteer Prairie, Flagstaff was virtually unrecognizable. Housing was unavailable while the sidewalks, bars, and restaurants teemed with transient workers and their families. Some slackers actually spent their work time in the local barrooms—signing in at the construction site, returning to Flagstaff to drink beer, and then slipping back to Bellemont to sign out at the end of their shift. These loafers added to the already congested and often dangerous traffic conditions—especially during shift changes—on Route 66 between Bellemont and Flagstaff. H. T. Wilson's Nava-Hopi buses transported between six and seven hundred laborers in round-the-clock shifts at forty cents per round trip. Wilson could have used more buses if any had been available. Prices soared and crime increased. Although Brown's estimate of forty thousand new arrivals proved greatly exaggerated, Leo Weaver calculated that eight thousand construction workers were accompanied by seven thousand family members. All told, fifteen thousand people flocked to Flagstaff and Bellemont in the summer of 1942, quadrupling the area's prewar population.[41]

Tiny Bellemont—where two restaurant owners were forced to shut their doors because they could not handle the rush of hungry workers and still maintain adequate sanitation—was particularly hard hit. Workers and their families were living everywhere. They were under trees, in the tent city that mushroomed outside town, and in cars, tin shacks, and trailers. About one thousand construction workers lived on the site, where Atkinson-Kier built and maintained bunkhouses and a mess hall, both continuously filled to capacity. As many as a thousand Native American workers and their families lived in temporary shelters erected in the wood line a half-mile north of Bellemont.

Bellemont itself was home to a colorful mix of Indian, Hispanic, African American, and Anglo workers, but these local employees were often overshadowed by thousands of unruly transient laborers. Deputy Sheriff Pete Michelbach grumbled that every "hijacker, drifter, draft-dodger, and slacker" in the West passed through the town. Many lived and worked at the site, where drinking, gambling, robbery, and fighting were the order of the day. Liquor was the primary lubricant that flowed freely in Bellemont's numerous watering holes. Although town officials ran background checks on many of the workers, it was impossible to keep track of everyone's comings and goings.[42]

Thousands of itinerant workers flocked to Flagstaff as well, where they strained community services and goodwill. Many of the newcomers couldn't care less about law and order, failed to comply with government rules and regulations, refused to cooperate with contractors, showed little respect for public property, and seemed unconcerned over how the war might end. Their sole interest was to make money, preferably with as much overtime and as little work as possible. Although forbidden, whiskey, gambling, and firearms contributed to nightly battles in the construction area that sent dozens of workers to the Atkinson-Kier infirmary. Other fights broke out when guards tried to confiscate whiskey from roughnecks as they passed through the entrance to the compound. The guards didn't always win.[43]

It is no surprise that prostitution flourished in this raucous environment. When the five hookers who worked behind Thompson's store in Bellemont multiplied to twenty, the FBI threatened to close down the business. Sheriff's representatives protested, however, arguing that it would increase rather than diminish their problems in controlling vice by forcing customers to leave Bellemont for the Wagon Wheel Inn at Pitman Valley between Parks and Williams or, worse yet, into Flagstaff's notorious brothels like the El Paso Del Norte on south San Francisco Street and Pearl Polk's place on south O'Leary Street.[44]

Policing the construction area was a daunting task. Major Cox hired James Noble as security chief, along with David Lowry, Ernie Yost, Percy Benson, Milton P. Richards (father of Sheriff Joe Richards) and others to deal with the situation. Cox took on additional guards at the peak of construction, although the total force never exceeded sixty men. Officially known as the Auxiliary Military Police, the guards dressed in an array of cowboy clothes, "high-heeled boots and all," and wore side arms of all makes and sizes that they employed frequently. Their salaries of $1,320 per year were a quarter of the wages paid some construction workers and turnover was high.

James Noble supervised cowboys who rode the perimeter of the construction site. Affectionately called the "Southwest Mounted

Mounted patrol members Ernie Yost, David Lowry, and James Noble (along with a dozen others, including Milton P. Richards, father of Sheriff Joe Richards, and Percy Benson) rode the 26-mile perimeter of the depot at all times and in all weather. When "Slim" Betts hired on as a "mountie" he was required to provide his own horse, saddle, Colt .45, and feed. He was paid 89 cents an hour and "glad to get it." The mounted guards continued until 1952, when the last horses were sold.

Police," they received $1,860 per year from which they were expected to furnish and feed their own horses. Unfortunately, they did not mesh well with the "Okie" and "Arkie" truck drivers and crew who delighted in yelling out "hi-ho Silver!" whenever the guards passed by. Finally, one of the cowboys reached the limit of his endurance. Taking down his rope, he lassoed one of the jokers and jerked him off his truck into the dusty road. Although military authorities hardly condoned such unusual police measures, the cry of "hi-ho Silver" never again echoed across the construction area.[45]

Theft was a major problem, and the guards spent much time inspecting laborers who might be smuggling stolen property off the work site. They even looked in lunch buckets and thermos bottles. Surprise searches conducted around 11:00 P.M. once or twice every ten days on the swing shift always produced the same results. Automobiles lined up one behind the other for over a mile as guards on horseback and on foot methodically inspected for guns, whiskey, picks, shovels, tools, and other contraband. The unmistakable clatter of thousands of tossed articles echoed across the prairie as word of the inspection passed down the long line of stopped cars. In the early morning light, the guards looked out on a ribbon of discarded tools and liquor bottles stretching along both sides of the road. They emptied hundreds of full and partially full liquor bottles onto the prairie, "leaving [behind] the aroma of a distillery running at full blast."[46]

Security guards were not the only ones who searched for stolen property. Atkinson-Kier even periodically inspected the carburetors of their workers' vehicles to see if they were burning company fuel. To discourage theft of their precious gasoline—a rationed wartime product—the company added coloring to its fuel to ensure it would make a noticeable stain on the carburetor when used in any engine.[47]

There were more serious crimes, including a shoot-out at the Bellemont cinder pits led by local redneck Edward "Doc" January. In town, bullets flew through the floor of Flagstaff's Weatherford Hotel. Stabbings, armed robbery, and bootlegging filled Hotel St. Francis, as the county jail was called in honor of sheriff J. Peery Francis, to an all-time high by December of 1942.

The flagrant sins of Bellemont moved the County Ministerial Association to offer religious services for workers and families alike. Groups erected large tents at Bellemont, the Whiting Brothers gas station, the Maine (Parks) school, and in the forest west of town where evangelist James Carter conducted nightly services. Presbyterians even recruited a special field representative from Tennessee—a former football coach at Rutgers University who had "boomtown experience." The Church of the Epiphany and the First Baptist Church (South Beaver Street) provided organs. As examples of iniquity mounted, most Flagstaff denominations chipped in with something.[48]

The accelerated pace of construction took its toll in human life. A number of deaths and serious injuries occurred when trucks and vehicles collided with westbound trains before an overpass was built. In

A World War I veteran and an engineer, Major Myrick was instrumental in establishing the Fort Wingate Ordnance Depot near Gallup, New Mexico. He arrived at Bellemont in July of 1942 with a small staff and faced a bevy of personnel, administrative, and organizational problems at the fledgling depot.

other cases, heavy trucks backed over workers. Nevertheless, Atkinson-Kier established a national safety record among its seventy-two hundred workers at Bellemont.[49]

On July 1, 1942, Major Exum B. Myrick arrived at Bellemont with his secretary Lucile Michael, two army officers, and twenty-three civilians—all specialists in munitions work—from Gallup, New Mexico, where he had been influential in launching the Fort Wingate Depot. An easygoing, likable officer, Myrick assumed command of Navajo Ordnance Depot on July 10, when the arsenal was activated for ammunition storage despite the ongoing construction. Major Cox continued to supervise contractors, while Myrick and his staff tackled the multitude of organizational, labor, housing, and personnel problems. Myrick soon hired the first depot employee and first facility engineer, Charles W. Dryden.[50]

Myrick and his tiny staff went to work in a small makeshift building not far from Cox's office, about two miles west of the eventual headquarters area. Unfortunately, their office was adjacent to the horse stables where there were certain disadvantages, as Lucile Michael noted, during the hot summer days.[51]

By far Myrick's greatest headache was the severe labor shortage in northern Arizona. Few of the construction workers were interested in staying on as permanent employees, preferring instead to move on to the next boomtown where wages were highest. Realizing that the local workforce was inadequate, Myrick explored alternatives with Navajo and Hopi tribal representatives. Eventually, he came up with a novel solution—creating a Navajo and Hopi village at the depot and encouraging Native American workers to move in with their families. Enticed by the prospect of steady employment and good jobs, tribal leaders agreed on a plan to locate the village in a heavily forested area several miles west of the depot's main administration building. Throughout September workers constructed a cluster of hogans and put up dozens of tents. By October 1, more than one thousand Indians had moved into the compound, Navajos in one camp, Hopis another. For the first time in their history, Navajos had voluntarily migrated from a rural to an urban setting and were assembled in a single permanent "Indian Village."[52]

Although work on the depot would continue into February, the feverish pace of construction began to ebb by November of 1942. Most of the igloos were completed, while much of the combat equipment storage area remained to be finished. Myrick's permanent labor force had grown to twelve military personnel, one contract surgeon, and 813 civilian workers, 560 of whom were Native American, mostly Navajo. After eight furious months of construction, the ordnance depot was nearly operational.[53]

The project was indeed enormous. The base consisted of an "inner" depot surrounded by a seventeen-thousand-acre buffer zone. The inner depot was interwoven with a complex network of roads and railroads which served every igloo, workshop, warehouse, loading ramp, utility service, and magazine. The administrative area was located in the north central portion with the headquarters building facing east across the parade ground. Behind the headquarters area were the large shops and garages for vehicles and equipment. The combat equipment storage complex was about a mile northwest of the administrative area.[54]

It took Atkinson-Kier workers half an hour to travel from their temporary barracks to remote construction sites on the reservation. More than two hundred miles of roads eventually crisscrossed the base. The thirty-four-mile railroad was divided into three lines: a loop circled igloos on the eastern side of the arsenal (a round trip took fifty minutes without stops), a direct line serviced igloos on the west, and yet another direct line serviced igloos on the southwest and farthest from the administrative area. Despite the extensive rail network, some bunkers on the west side of the depot were almost two miles from the closest track.[55]

The installation's enclosed storage space was equally remarkable. The 802 earth-covered concrete igloos provided 1,611,827 square feet to house large and small munitions. More than 150 other buildings, magazines, and shelters contributed well over 1,000,000 square feet of additional storage capacity, most of it in the combat equipment storage area. Five warehouses each encompassed 90,000 square feet, four others held 88,982 square feet, and several more could store more than 50,000 square feet of materials. Other structures housed the depot's sewer, water, and electrical systems, not to mention reservoirs, stables, loading docks, and open storage areas. When all phases of construction were completed, Navajo Ordnance Depot's 1,060 buildings and structures were capable of safely storing 3,482,254 square feet of munitions and other materiel. And, an Indian village had sprung up in the forest.[56]

This extraordinary achievement was cause for celebration. On November 1, 1942, employees, families, and guests boarded a "Navajo Limited" sightseeing train for a twenty-mile tour of the new arsenal. At a site named "Tokyo," they disembarked for a day of festivities that included a barbecue, horseshoe contests, jeep and horseback rides, softball games, speeches, and music by the Flagstaff High School band and drum and bugle corps. Master of ceremonies "Slim Kite"

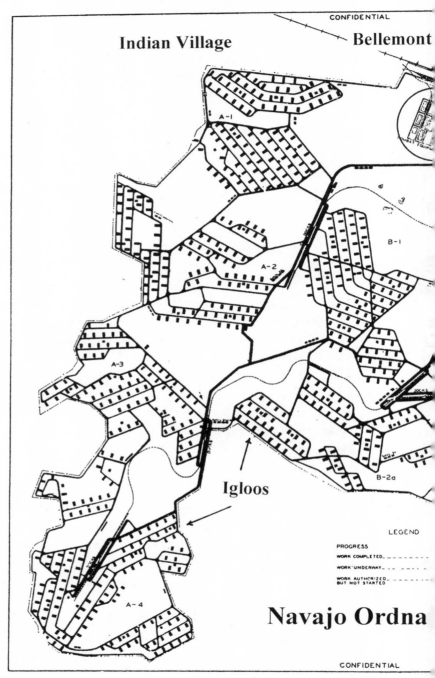

Indian Village

Bellemont

A-1

B-1

A-2

A-3

B-2a

Igloos

LEGEND

PROGRESS

WORK COMPLETED_____

WORK UNDERWAY__ __ ____

WORK AUTHORIZED_____
BUT NOT STARTED

A-4

Navajo Ordna

Navajo Ordnance Depot, 1942

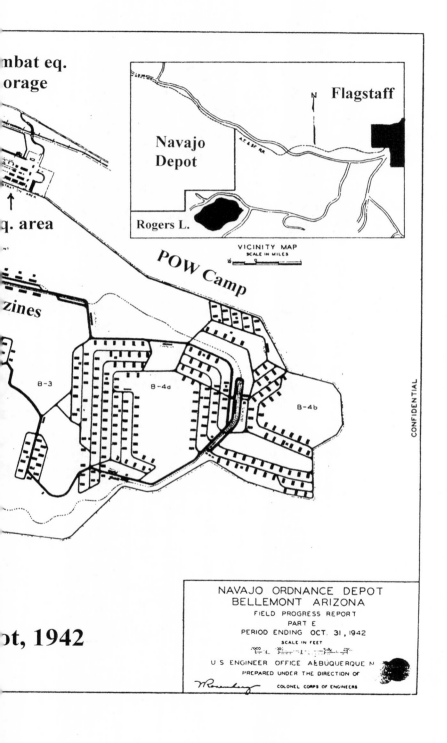

mbat eq.
orage

q. area

zines

B-3

B-4a

B-4b

POW Camp

VICINITY MAP
SCALE IN MILES

Navajo
Depot

Flagstaff

N

A.T. & S.F. RR

Rogers L.

ot, 1942

NAVAJO ORDNANCE DEPOT
BELLEMONT ARIZONA
FIELD PROGRESS REPORT
PART E
PERIOD ENDING OCT. 31, 1942
SCALE IN FEET

U S ENGINEER OFFICE ALBUQUERQUE N
PREPARED UNDER THE DIRECTION OF

COLONEL CORPS OF ENGINEERS

CONFIDENTIAL

When the concrete was dry, each igloo was covered with earth. The bunkers provided 1.6 million square feet of storage space, and although three railroad lines with 34 miles of track serviced them, some were still more than 2 miles from the nearest railroad loading ramp. Today, 152 igloos have been adapted to store intercontinental ballistic missile motors for the air force and navy.

entertained the eight hundred attendees with cowboy skits, after which vocalists Paul Tissaw, Marvin Bennett, and Patsy Hancock and the "Hill Billy" band provided musical entertainment. Other highlights of the day were cowboy trick roping and bronco busting.[57]

At 8:10 A.M. on November 5, the first carload of ammunition arrived at Navajo Ordnance Depot from the Denver Ordnance Plant. More cars rolled in, but it wasn't until six days later—Armistice Day—that Senator Carl Hayden placed a case of rifle ammunition on the first outgoing car. With a twinkle in his eye, Hayden announced the shipment of a "bundle of calling cards" for the Japanese Empire in the Pacific. Flagstaff postmaster George Babbitt Jr. loaded the second case of shells.[58]

At precisely 8:18 A.M. on December 7, 1942, exactly one year after the Japanese attack on Pearl Harbor, Major Myrick stood before hundreds of workers, public officials, and guests gathered in the quietly falling snow to officially dedicate the depot to the defeat of America's enemies. The solemn consecration, perhaps the most significant event in Myrick's brief military career, was a grim reminder of the past and a portent of the arduous road ahead. While acknowledging the contributions of thousands of workers to build this enormous "arsenal of democracy," the major expressed his belief that it would be presumptuous for him to thank them on the country's behalf. It was only right and natural that every citizen should sacrifice whatever was required in the fight for freedom.

On behalf of the Army Ordnance Department, Myrick accepted the depot from the chief engineer, Major Cox, as a symbol of a people aroused, armed for battle, and determined to fight to the death rather than relinquish their liberty. He pledged it to the relentless prosecution of the war. To Postmaster Babbitt the depot represented the sweat of hatred toward America's enemies, and the symbol of patriotism that would spell doom to mail-fisted warlords. As the crowd stood at attention, a bugle call pierced through the cold winter air and eighty-four-year-old Flagstaff lumber pioneer T. A. Riordan raised the American flag over the installation. Many eyes were blurred with tears of pride, loyalty, and determination.[59]

All in all, Flagstaff had accepted her unprecedented windfall in good stride. Despite the boomtown population explosion and all the inevitable problems that plague a rowdy labor camp, Flagstaff opened its doors to soldiers and civilians and forged ahead. While construction of the immense depot challenged the community's social fabric it was never overwhelmed. Because the Atkinson-Kier Company was skilled at public relations and handling men, many Flagstaff residents remained unaware of serious incidents that occurred at the work site.[60]

Flagstaff's boomtown experience was not unprecedented in the West. Similar stories took place in Utah, Colorado, California, Oregon, Texas, New Mexico, South Dakota, and Nebraska, where the War Department constructed other depots in 1941 and 1942. In northern Arizona, however, Navajo Ordnance Depot's impact extended hundreds of miles to remote corners of the Indian reservations where both

Navajos and Hopis were drawn to Bellemont in search of steady jobs. Above all, the depot brought a permanent federal presence to the high-country prairie that previously had been only a crossroads of exploration. Whatever the human cost, the project had been completed on time and on budget. For better or worse, defense plant work not only dwarfed Flagstaff's lumber industry but all local industries combined, and was a crucial part of the city's future.

Leo Weaver had been at the center of everything—working with Senators Hayden and McFarland, touting Bellemont to the War Department, finding housing for engineers and construction workers, sidetracking Cecil Miller's angry protests, urging caution to local merchants, and encouraging Navajo and Hopi workers to leave the reservations for steady jobs. Meanwhile, the change was readily apparent downtown as trains destined for Bellemont came more frequently, up the arduous climb past Holbrook and Winslow and across the Arizona divide. Mighty locomotives strained to pull their heavy boxcars that were now stuffed with tons of bombs, ammunition, and explosives destined for igloos hidden in the forests around Volunteer Prairie.

3

BOXCARS COMING
Trains, Bombs, Ammunition, and Igloos

Mid-January weather spread a warm blanket over the prairie, hills, and valleys of northern Arizona during the opening weeks of 1943. Workers at the newly opened Navajo Ordnance Depot took advantage of the unusual 65-degree daytime temperatures to empty railroad carloads of ammunition at a rapid clip. They were able to maintain the pace for several weeks, as most of the shipments were incoming and, as yet, only a few trains were departing with carloads of munitions on their way to American soldiers fighting in the Pacific. The situation at Bellemont quickly deteriorated, however, when the number of incoming and outgoing trains increased dramatically. Before long, the inexperienced workers and supervisory staff at the depot would be stretched to their limits. Then, just as it seemed that things could not possibly get any worse, the War Department drastically reduced the workforce. In the end, a crusty new commander, hard work, and community volunteers combined to save the troubled arsenal.[1]

The War Department assigned Navajo Ordnance Depot its first mission on December 4, 1942, just a few days prior to the facility's dedication ceremony. One of twenty-five Ordnance Department ammunition depots scattered around the country, the new Bellemont facility was designed to store combat vehicles, artillery pieces, small arms, fire-control equipment, and related supplies for eventual export overseas; stockpile all classes of ammunition, except chemical shells and chemical bombs; train civilian personnel; and perform preservative maintenance and minor repair of materiel—a French term for the equipment of warfare. It was also designated a reservoir depot for the Port of Los Angeles. Ammunition and war materiel was shipped to

Bellemont to be inspected and stockpiled until it was shipped out again by the boxcar load. Future War Department decisions would expand on this standard mission—with serious repercussions for the new depot.[2]

Major Exum B. Myrick, the initial depot commander, had helped launch Fort Wingate Ordnance Depot near Gallup, New Mexico, and knew what it took to get a new project off the ground. The Bellemont arsenal was larger than Fort Wingate, however, and posed complex problems for the World War I veteran and former civil engineer. He laid out the basic organizational structure that would oversee operations at the depot. Although titles and personnel changed several times during the course of the war, the general responsibilities of senior officers remained the same. The operations officer supervised the vast majority of the depot personnel. As such, he was responsible for rail and motor transport, stock control and accountability, and receiving, storage, and shipping of ammunition and materiel. The executive officer supervised most of the administrative work including oversight of the post engineers, the medical and signal staff, and the administrative, safety, security, depot property, salvage, civilian personnel, and surveillance branches. The surveillance branch grew into a major undertaking as its personnel inspected the ammunition prior to shipment and conducted repairs and renovations on munitions. Both the operations and the executive officers reported directly to Myrick, as did the depot-control branch, which was responsible for compiling data, studies, and reports.[3]

Also by late 1942, most contractors had completed their work and departed, often with all their employees in tow. Myrick, who needed approximately 2,000 workers to efficiently operate the installation, was immediately faced with a manpower problem. By the end of the year, he had managed to recruit only 915 laborers—less than half the required workforce. At the same time, his army command consisted of a medical corps physician, an engineer corps officer, and 14 ordnance corps officers. Except for soldiers temporarily assigned to the depot during surge periods, the number of military personnel assigned to the depot hovered around 35 officers and 30 enlisted men throughout the war. As was the case at Fort Wingate, where 13 officers supervised 1,550 civilians, military manpower at Navajo Depot was minuscule in comparison to the number of civilian employees.[4]

Despite the small and untrained workforce, the War Department dispatched 50 heavily loaded boxcars to Navajo Depot in November 1942 and 178 carloads the following month. Activity on the fifteen loading docks picked up, both day and night, as soldiers and laborers struggled to unload the incoming materiel. They even managed to ship out 43 carloads by the end of the year.[5]

As he had done a few months earlier, Myrick turned to the Navajo and Hopi reservations and looked outside the Flagstaff area for help. Realizing that almost all local laborers were either employed or in the service, in January of 1943 Myrick appealed to the Navajo and Hopi tribal leaders, the Indian Service, the U.S. Employment Service, and the War Manpower Commission for workers capable of handling heavy loads. He also advertised in Phoenix newspapers for skilled workers, such as semitrailer drivers. His efforts paid off. By the end of March, he had recruited a total of 1,769 civilian employees.[6]

Myrick depended heavily on Indian labor for depot field operations—moving ammunition from boxcars to trailers to igloos and the reverse. Trains usually arrived from the east and stopped just west of Bellemont, where boxcars were uncoupled and pushed back onto one of the half-dozen holding areas just south of the main tracks, where each crate of ammunition was counted and inspected for damage. Cars containing damaged crates remained in place until the contents could be shipped out to a repair facility. Meanwhile, one of the five depot locomotives hauled boxcars that had passed inspection to one of several spurs at the depot's ammunition holding area, about a mile and a half southwest of the administrative area. Here, inspectors from the transportation office checked serial numbers and quantities. Once this second inspection was completed, a locomotive moved the boxcars several miles to one of the loading docks scattered around the arsenal, where crews of mostly Navajo workers unloaded by hand tons of munitions from the boxcars onto semitrailers. Finally, the trailers hauled the ammunition crates, bombs, and shells another couple of miles to an igloo, where more Indian crews unloaded the munitions and carefully stacked them inside.[7]

Stockpiling of ammunition at Navajo Ordnance Depot began in earnest with the arrival of 115 railcars in January, 232 in February, and 310 in March. Similarly, outbound shipments climbed from 63 boxcars in January to 95 in March, most headed for the ports of Los Angeles and San Francisco. By March, the average weight of an incoming boxcar load of munitions was 65 tons, and the total weight of materiel processed tripled to 24,028 tons per month.[8]

Severe growing pains extended to almost all areas of Navajo Depot operations, wasting time, money, and effort. Personnel turnover climbed to more than 17 percent, with absenteeism often averaging 25 percent. Navajo absenteeism, a problem not yet addressed or understood, reached 63 percent. The accident rate jumped by almost 50 percent, mostly hand and foot injuries suffered by untrained workers moving heavy munitions. The continuing labor shortage, inexperience, language barriers, and the constantly changing work system caused other difficulties, at the same time that lack of standardization, inaccurate records, obsolete or unavailable forms, and equipment problems created confusion. Foremen, never sure of how large a crew would show up for work, wasted valuable time tracking down enough men to do the day's job. As experienced younger men were drafted into the service, depot recruiters turned to hiring untrained women, older men, and the disabled.[9]

Training these workers posed another set of problems. Depot operations included hundreds of specialties, many of which required technical knowledge, especially in performing dangerous tasks such as ammunition repair and renovation. Turnover and absenteeism made it difficult to instruct workers in detailed procedures that under the best of circumstances often took weeks to learn. Supervisors, themselves, were frequently absent at training sessions held at other depots. Because less than 20 percent of the Native Americans employed at the depot spoke English, translators had to be hired. It was a situation ripe for disaster. Work crews that rapidly moved tons of ammunition relied on training and teamwork that weren't always possible under the sometimes frenetic conditions at Navajo Depot. On one warm day, for example, crews opened both doors to create ventilation in the boxcar where they were working. At some point, they gave a five-hundred-pound bomb setting on the loading dock a good shove, and then stood back to watch it roll down the ramp, pass through both doors of the railcar, and crash to the ground—much to the horror of onlookers.[10]

Regardless of their levels of training, munitions handlers worked in round-the-clock shifts to deal with the mounting workload as the spring of 1943 faded into summer. Seven hundred twenty-nine heavily loaded railroad cars arrived at the depot in May—almost seven times the January figure; outbound shipments rose to 309 boxcar loads the following month. Total tonnage climbed to thirty-seven thousand tons in both May and June, with arriving shipments far outnumbering outgoing materiel. By the end of spring, 2,152 civilians were employed at the depot, many of them working twenty-four- and thirty-six-hour stretches to keep the ammunition moving. Even so, they were only partially successful. Unskilled workers, train derailments, and a disorganized effort to ship some munitions by truck slowed the process. Demurrage charges—fees assessed by the railroad for failing to load or unload within a specified time frame—soared to more than eleven thousand dollars as boxcars stacked up in Bellemont. Even with these serious problems, Myrick and his staff could take some satisfaction in knowing that at least deadline shipments were being made promptly, and that critical ammunition was arriving at the various designated ports on time.[11]

By the summer of 1943, the Navajo Depot railroad, with five locomotives and crews, was probably already the busiest in Arizona in terms of tonnage hauled. As with other heavy equipment, wartime scarcity left the depot to make do. The first locomotive was an old Texas Pacific steamer formerly used for passenger service in the plains country. The engine, already worn out and even less effective in the high altitude with inexperienced crews, was soon sold to Saginaw & Manistee Lumber Company and dismantled. About the same time, the depot received an old rotary snowplow from the Northern Pacific Railway Company. The plow, of 1880s vintage, was also past its best years. Following a two-foot snowfall, an engineer attached the plow to a locomotive and opened the throttle. A huge and unexpected blast blew cinders, lumber, rocks, sparks, and debris in all directions, seriously damaging the sides of a nearby warehouse. Crewman Harold Cameron had never seen anything like it in his life and was amazed no one was killed. As with the first locomotive, the plow was soon sold as salvage.[12]

Civilian employment at Navajo Ordnance Depot peaked at 2,172 workers in July of 1943. Recruiting in Phoenix and on the Navajo and Hopi reservations, along with improved retention of Native American workers, made the difference. At the same time, an increasing variety of munitions arrived at the depot, including trainloads of small arms and tracer ammunition, antitank mines, dynamite, and firing devices and blasting caps, along with every size of artillery round up to eight inches. Other boxcars contained rockets, hand grenades, pyrotechnics, smoke rounds, practice bombs, fuses, all types of propellant charges, and bombs weighing anywhere from one hundred to two thousand pounds. The sheer diversity of the materiel presented its own handling, storage, and shipping problems.[13]

Before long, Navajo Ordnance Depot constructed its own box factory to prevent damage of ammunition during shipment. The depot box factory consumed millions of board feet of lumber from its own sawmill and from local mills—which often could not keep up with the demand—to make dunnage (packing materials) and pallets.[14]

Just as the turbulent break-in period ended and Myrick's precious workforce—following months of hard recruiting—finally reached the required strength of around 2,200, the War Department dropped its own bomb and sent morale at Navajo Ordnance Depot plummeting. In order to release more men for the draft, the department established manpower ceilings in many agencies that employed civilians. In late July, 1943, it ordered a crippling 45 percent reduction of the depot's civilian workforce, from 2,172 workers to 1,200.

Coming just as operations at the depot reached full speed and with no letup in sight, Myrick and his staff were devastated. It had taken almost a year to bring the workforce up to full strength, and most civilian employees were still inadequately trained. Much of the hard work devoted to standardizing procedures and employee-motivated improvement would have to be scrapped. The timing could not have been worse, coming on the heels of a government-imposed 20 percent tax withholding from workers' paychecks. Myrick and his officers were particularly concerned for the Indian workers, who were now being charged five dollars per month for housing at the nearby Indian Village, where they previously had lived for free. Native Americans, usually the least paid and least skilled workers, were hit hard by the imposition of rent and the additional tax. By August, Navajo Ordnance Depot was both dangerously understaffed and in the throes of a serious morale crisis.[15]

A profoundly dispirited staff and civilian workforce greeted the arrival of Col. John Huling Jr., the permanent depot commander, on August 11, 1943. Originally from Towanda, Illinois, Huling graduated from the University of Chicago in 1917 and was commissioned a second lieutenant in the regular army, where he served in the Eighteenth Infantry Division. Transferred to the Ordnance Department in 1919, he performed numerous command and staff assignments throughout the United States and in the Philippines during the interwar period. Huling and his wife, the former Helen Moffet, raised two daughters and a son. Daughter Anna was married to an army officer, and Helen—nicknamed "Helen Jr." by depot employees—accompanied her parents to Bellemont. John W. was beginning his senior year at West Point.[16]

Unlike Major Myrick, Colonel Huling brought a career of Ordnance Corps experience to Navajo Ordnance Depot. Although Huling apparently made few friends either in Bellemont or in Flagstaff, no one failed to have an opinion about him. Newspaperman Platt Cline, who met the colonel several times, recalls that he was exactly what you would expect from an army officer of his rank. Around six feet two inches tall, thin, and ramrod-straight, he looked the role of a hardnosed base commander. Dressed in "the hard-boiled collar and the whole shiteree," according to Cline, he "half-way scared his own men." Cline said Huling "was military all right—a straight-edge, nose-in-the-air bastard."[17]

Smiling at the opening of the Victory Village store in July 1944, Colonel Huling was a World War I veteran and a career ordnance officer. He arrived at Navajo Ordnance Depot in the summer of 1943 and immediately tackled the numerous morale and organizational problems that had plagued the base from the beginning.

Huling impressed some local residents as a substantial, direct, and no-nonsense officer. Others thought he was a stern, exacting, businesslike, by-the-book sourpuss. He quickly acquired the nicknames "Honest John" (although not everyone saw the connection) and "No Fooling Huling." Beneath the spit-and-polish exterior, he was reported to be a kind person and good citizen who taught boys' Sunday school at the Episcopal Church and took a great interest in mentoring. Huling and his wife spent much of their free time horseback riding around Volunteer Prairie. But on one thing, at least, everyone seemed to agree—Huling appeared to be as hard as nails; perhaps just what the struggling arsenal needed during the bleak summer of 1943.[18]

With little regard for social formalities, Huling immediately tackled the deteriorating labor and morale situation at Navajo Ordnance Depot. At the same time, he quickly became aware that the War Department had gradually and unofficially modified the depot's original mission. What started as short-term preventive maintenance and incidental repair of materiel had become, by the fall of 1943, an undertaking of major proportions. Plants from around the country were shipping to Bellemont at an alarming rate thousands of tons of damaged bombs, defective shells and propellant charges, bombs with faulty wiring or inadequate packaging, unserviceable small arms ammunition, and munitions requiring replacement parts. To the casual observer, the depot appeared to be a dumping ground for unpainted grenades, unpainted or incorrectly stenciled artillery shells, corroded or badly soldered munitions, and bombs with incorrect shipping bands or leaking tail assemblies. The undermanned surveillance branch—responsible for renovation and repair—could hardly keep up with small projects, let alone immense quantities of defective munitions that often required extensive technical know-how to fix. Despite its huge storage capacity, Navajo Depot was rapidly filling up with munitions awaiting shipment, as well as material that required long-term storage until it was repaired.[19]

The War Department placed further strains on the depot's workforce and storage facilities when it authorized stockpiling at Navajo Ordnance Depot of mercury, a nonexplosive strategic item used in electrical apparatus, chlorine production, and industrial and control instruments. In late 1943, the Metals Reserve Company—a Reconstruction Finance Corporation subsidiary chartered on June 28, 1940 to procure and stockpile strategic and critical materials—shipped for the U.S. Treasury Department more than ten thousand flasks of mercury from Laredo, Texas, to Bellemont. Weight checks revealed that more than half the flasks were leaking and needed to be repaired. Mercury was the first of many unusual nonordnance items stored at Navajo Depot during and after the war as part of the nation's strategic reserve stockpile.[20]

Although Colonel Huling was hard-pressed to solve the repair problem, he quickly tightened up many other areas of operations in the opening days of 1944. Like Major Myrick before him, he first turned to the War Manpower Commission and the U.S. Employment Service in an effort to alleviate the depot's labor crisis and recuperate losses from the drastic July 1943 reduction in force. When that failed, he applied unsuccessfully to the U.S. Civil Service Commission. With still no relief in sight, he next asked for three hundred Italian prisoners of war to handle munitions. When Ninth Service Command denied his request, Huling doubled it to six hundred. In the meantime, Huling dispatched buses and recruiters to The Gap, Pinon, Rock Point, and Ganado to enlist any remaining able-bodied workers on the Navajo and Hopi reservations.

Finally, the spell was broken, or so it seemed. On May 20, 1944, Ninth Service Command approved transferring three hundred Germans from the new prisoner of war camp at Papago Park near Phoenix. The transfer would not take place, however, until housing was ready for them at Navajo Ordnance Depot. Delays in obtaining authorization for scarce building materials meant that day would not be soon in coming. Only later would Huling recognize the extraordinary good fortune of the delays.[21]

Huling next turned his attention to the unsettling morale crisis. He tried to mollify unhappy workers by transferring them into new jobs or assigning them to different supervisors. He provided a full hour for lunch and added morning and afternoon breaks, all without expanding the workday. At the same time, he cleaned up the post mess, improved the food, and added four field lunchrooms so that workers could enjoy a hot meal without having to trek several miles back to the main mess hall. To give workers a sense of participation in decision making, Huling formalized service awards, created an employee incentive and award program, and instituted grievance procedures. He also scoured the depot roster, looking for any worker with unique skills that were not being used, and standardized work shifts in order to reduce strain on the depot's limited transportation resources and eliminate bootleg taxi services. Finally, Huling opened a psychiatric clinic at the depot hospital, where employees referred by department heads and the outpatient physician could participate in one-hour weekly "job adjustment" sessions. A unique idea that was ahead of its time, the counseling service was designed to reduce turnover by keeping workers in a "more happy frame of mind."[22]

Huling also went to great lengths to improve depot efficiency and fiscal responsibility. As with any hastily created military or civilian organization turning at full speed, these problems existed at Navajo Ordnance Depot from the beginning. Major Myrick, focused on moving ammunition, had neither the time nor the experience to tackle larger organizational issues. Huling, with a career of ordnance-related problem solving behind him, was able to act immediately and effectively. Requisitioning supplies through military channels, rather than purchasing on the civilian market, reduced purchase-order expenses by 50 percent and saved the depot more than forty thousand dollars in a single quarter. Huling created other savings by eliminating unnecessary paper copies and by baling and selling the depot's wastepaper. Meanwhile, salvage teams combed the installation for excess steel and metal scrap, which Huling sold to the Allison Steel Company in Phoenix. Depot crews even retrieved the aluminum from bomber and other military aircraft crashes on the San Francisco Peaks for resale to Mallen Brothers of Phoenix.

By early 1944, yet another unexpected development was apparent—construction at Navajo Ordnance Depot had never stopped and no let-up was in sight. The first addition to the original plan, Indian Village, was only the beginning. In addition to the post mess and field kitchens, a commissary, a recreation center with a four-lane bowling alley, and a chapel were added to the central administrative area. A $1 million contract provided for construction of more roads on the depot grounds in 1943 and railroad tracks were extended. A fifty-four-bed hospital, dedicated on February 15, 1944, provided medical care for employees and their families. A delousing unit and a parking lot were eventually added to the building. Also in early 1944, work began on a smokestack for the heating plant, while new storage pads, cement floors, concrete platforms for loading docks, garages, shelters, and safety features were added in the combat equipment, standard magazine, and igloo areas. A new railroad overpass routed routine traffic and munitions trucks through the main gate and over the Santa Fe Railroad tracks to Route 66.

The ongoing construction doubled the depot's initial price tag to

more than thirty million dollars by mid-1945, making Navajo Ordnance Depot larger than any pre–World War II ordnance depot and
the second-largest depot of its kind in the country, exceeded only by
the 32,582-acre Sierra Ordnance Depot at Herlong, California.[23]

While most depot employees lived in Indian Village or Flagstaff, a
small civilian and military community settled into five senior officers'
quarters, seventy-two family apartments, and dormitories for 120 men
and women erected adjacent to the depot's administrative area.
Officially designated Victory Village by Colonel Huling on December
4, 1943, the rows of austere white dormitories and apartments seemed
strangely out of place on the broad volcanic plain where rocks had
been haphazardly shoved aside to make a path for automobiles and
pedestrians through the dirt and mud. Except for a few telephone lines,
some electric cables, and the occasional automobile, the long buildings with their wooden stoops and support posts could have easily
passed for nineteenth-century army barracks in the Old West. Inside,
incomplete partitions, unpainted walls, and exposed nails, joints, and
ceiling plumbing reminded occupants on a daily basis that the war
effort was their first priority. One job applicant—a good and much
coveted stenographer—took one look at the "sad" village, announced
"I won't live here," and quickly left.[24]

Although the buildings were new, bedbugs soon made their way
into the long strip of apartments. When officials sprayed one apartment, the bugs moved on to the next. Finally, the entire Victory Village
complex had to be sprayed.[25]

Despite the primitive surroundings, the close-knit community of
roughly 350 civilian and 150 military employees and family members—
about 30 percent of whom were Hispanic—took on a life of its own.
While mounted guards patrolled the depot perimeter, Victory Village
residents organized bingo tournaments, bridge and table games, community sings, dinner parties, and Thursday evening movies showing
the World Series, the Blitzkrieg, and the Battle of Britain. Other organized activities included sewing, crocheting, and knitting instruction;
musical programs; benefit balls; church services; Tuesday dances;
horseshoes; a model airplane club; pistol competitions; softball games;

The Victory Village dormitories were rapidly constructed in 1942 and provided decent living conditions under the circumstances.

United Services Organization (USO) shows; bowling leagues; a teen club; and an officers' wives club.

By 1945, many Flagstaff residents were driving out to participate in Victory Village events. At the same time, some locals grumbled that perhaps there was a little too much going on in the civilian apartments. Dubbed "whiskey row," the barracks-like colony soon earned a reputation as a place where liquor flowed freely.[26]

The effects of the war were felt everywhere at Navajo Depot. Civilian employees spent their days working with military ordnance, and many returned from their shifts to meager military quarters at Victory Village. For all, they lived in a world where gas, shoes, tires, cigarettes, cigars, sugar, and even Coca-Cola were carefully rationed. Many depot workers carried the additional burden of concern for relatives at the front. Even when the news was good, they knew their loved ones faced constant danger. Depot worker Lettie Peek, for example, learned in May of 1944 that her son, Capt. William E. Peek, a twenty-five-year-

Native American ammunition handlers and other workers gather for a war bond rally in 1944. Most adopted an informal uniform of a leather jacket, gloves, cowboy hat, jeans, and boots.

old Corsair pilot, shot down two Japanese Zeros in a five-minute dogfight over Rabaul, New Britain.[27]

It was also impossible to escape the daily routine that involved war bond quotas and rallies, where workers invested much of their paychecks. Fully 100 percent of the depot employees participated in the fourth bond drive, and one thousand depot workers attended the February 22 award ceremony. By June 5, 1944, the fifth drive was in full swing with lunchtime rallies generating average payroll deductions of more than 15 percent. Treasury Department films shown before the Victory Village Tuesday dance and at Indian Village sparked donations to the sixth and seventh bond drives. The high rate of employee giving consistently earned Navajo Ordnance Depot the right to fly the Treasury Department's honorary flag.

In January 1944, the depot handled 493 incoming and 334 outbound boxcars of munitions, averaging twenty-seven cars per day, its largest volume to date. Recognizing that ammunition shipments would soon overwhelm his reduced workforce, Huling appealed to Flagstaff civic groups for volunteers—called "Minute Men"—to help in Sunday emergencies. The Kiwanis, Rotary, and American Legion all submitted names of men from their organizations who were willing to lend a hand. On Sunday, April 2, 1944, forty-nine Minute Men answered the call to unload ten carloads of ordnance. Tonnage bound for Los Angeles continued to soar, keeping the depot's five locomotives and labor force working round-the-clock.

Then, in another unexpected turn of events, Navajo Ordnance Depot also began shipping munitions east to support the buildup for the Normandy invasion—121 carloads during the week of April 30 alone. On Sunday, May 7, Colonel Huling called out sixty Minute Men from Flagstaff and Williams, all depot officers, and Babbitt Brothers Trading Company volunteers to load more than ten railcars with 250- and 500-pound bombs, about 1 million pounds of high explosives, or enough bombs to conduct a medium-sized bomber raid. Between April 30 and May 27, 40 percent of Navajo Depot munitions were sent east.[28]

The depot strained to keep pace with the ammunition trains in early 1944 as the daily average soared to thirty-nine boxcars by April. With the Normandy invasion imminent, Maj. Gen. L. H. Campbell Jr., Chief of Ordnance at the War Department, reminded Bellemont workers in a stern message that their responsibility was inescapable, and that they must complete all shipments. Nothing should interfere, even if all administrative personnel had to be moved to igloos to load bombs and ammunition. By May, the declining workforce, which had again dropped to 1,516 from 1,662 in March, forced the War Manpower Commission to issue a directive for the northern Arizona counties of Coconino, Apache, Mohave, and Navajo. This, the commission's first severe action in the state of Arizona, required all unskilled laborers seeking employment to go through only the U.S. Employment Office in Flagstaff.[29]

The Minute Men played a critical role in keeping munitions moving when a second round of employee dissatisfaction threatened to disrupt work. This time it stemmed from poor living conditions. More than three hundred workers, mostly Native Americans, left the arsenal during the first nine months of 1944. By July, Navajo Ordnance Depot employed only 1,528 civilians, about 700 short of the depot's optimal work strength. On July 31, Colonel Huling, who managed to get away for a few days in June (perhaps to attend his son's West Point graduation), cancelled all leaves and furloughs and once again called out the Minute Men. On September 24, conditions deteriorated and Huling called out four hundred civilian employees and the depot's entire complement of officers to unload the largest Sunday shipment to date—twenty-six carloads.[30]

Still more trains rolled into Bellemont through early October, forcing Colonel Huling to send his new executive officer, Lt. Col. Lindley G. Schmidt, to plead for help in Flagstaff. On Sunday, October 8, the Flagstaff and Williams Minute Men once again responded to the SOS, assisting depot employees in loading three hundred tons more than their previous record. Some temporary relief finally arrived with the assignment of one hundred African American soldiers to the arsenal. As segregation still partitioned American society as well as the army, the black soldiers of the so-called NOD Detachment were assigned to barracks at the former CCC camp. They helped move munitions until March 1945, when they were transferred to other installations. Even with these reinforcements, carloads of munitions were arriving at Bellemont in such large numbers that Thanksgiving was declared a regular workday, albeit with a traditional turkey menu.

Some ammunition that arrived at Bellemont was beyond repair or dangerous to transport and had to be destroyed. After some trial-and-error experience gained from the explosion of small munitions in April 1943, depot personnel detonated a five-hundred-pound bomb on December 2, 1944. A memorandum invited spectators to witness the explosion in a remote area of the depot. It was the first of many blasts that could be heard and felt in nearby Flagstaff for years.[31]

The holiday season barely disrupted the frantic routine at Navajo Ordnance Depot. Military families continued to arrive, others de-

parted, and recruiters scurried across the Indian reservations searching for more workers. Depot trucks hauled an emergency shipment of
munitions to Albuquerque, while officers' wives organized bandage-
making parties for the post hospital and the bowling league provided
evening recreation. In the midst of this bustle, thirty-nine Flagstaff
residents traveled to Wilmington, California, to watch the December
22 launching of the California Shipbuilding Corporation's 10,500-ton
merchant vessel, S.S. *Flagstaff Victory.*

At the same moment back in Phoenix, U-boat Captain Jürgen
Wattenberg and twenty-four German prisoners of war made final plans
to escape from Papago Park. The next evening, these disciplined sailors and submariners, part of the group originally earmarked for transfer to Bellemont, carried out the largest prisoner escape of the war.
Many headed to the Gila River with a boat and were dumbfounded to
discover there was no water. All were captured within a few weeks.
Despite the humorous and colorful aspects of the breakout, Colonel
Huling was thankful the Germans had not been sent to his depot as
planned.[32]

Despite the perpetual labor shortage, at the end of 1944 the War
Department added yet another mission to the growing list of Navajo
Ordnance Depot tasks—storage of chemical shells and bombs. Unlike
World War I, chemical weapons were not widely used in World War
II. Still, the United States was prepared, particularly following
confirmation of reports that Germans were using gas against civilians
and of the widespread massacre of Jews in Poland and the Soviet
Union.[33]

The initial shipment of Chemical Warfare Service (CWS) ammunition rolled into Bellemont in January 1945 and consisted of phosgene (CG), cyanogen chloride (CK), and mustard-filled (H) bombs.
Their presence at Navajo Ordnance Depot caused considerable
apprehension among civilian workers and threatened to increase
absenteeism, especially among the Native American workforce. Films,
demonstrations, training sessions, and thorough inspections of the
hazardous munitions helped calm nerves. At the same time, the post
surgeon conducted first-aid training in chemical warfare for the depot

safety engineer, fire chief and captains, and other critical personnel. A disaster drill was carried out on the afternoon of February 7, but otherwise the depot guards continued their routine security operations. Work began immediately on plans for installing fifteen lavatories and remodeling a lunchroom into a decontamination area for ammunition handlers. The need for additional inspectors to maintain constant surveillance of chemical weapons placed an additional burden on already hard-pressed depot manpower.[34]

The initial shipment of chemical munitions was followed by seventy-six additional carloads in February, fifty-four in March, forty-eight in April, and thirty-six in May. The eighteen cars of chemical munitions that arrived in June included sixty-two one-hundred-pound chemical bombs. A few of the one-hundred-, five-hundred-, and one-thousand-pound chemical bombs were found to be defective. Inspectors disposed of one leaking phosgene bomb "in accordance with Ordnance Safety Manual, O.O. Form 7224"—probably by burning it in "chemical canyon," a remote area of the depot near the uppermost reaches of Volunteer Canyon. A one-thousand-pound chemical bomb with a leaking tail assembly, along with two one-thousand-pound phosgene bombs, were similarly disposed of, again probably in chemical canyon. Four one-hundred-pound mustard bombs and a five-hundred-pound chemical bomb also failed inspection.[35]

In the spring of 1945, depot inspectors began pressure-testing chemical weapons. By this time the inventory of chemical munitions at Navajo Ordnance Depot was probably around 13,000 bombs. Inspectors tested 4,363 five-hundred-pound bombs during June (after V-E Day) and estimated that it would take them three months to complete the backlog. Although there is no record of any chemical munitions leaving the depot, they were certainly available if needed for the invasion of Japan. Despite the high volatility of chemical weapons, there is no record of personnel experiencing either injury or illness.[36]

In the meantime, on March 24, 1945, Colonel Huling finally received some relief for his strained workforce as thirty Austrian prisoners of war arrived by truck from the large camp at Florence. They immediately set to work renovating the barracks that had formerly

Chemical bombs arrived late in the war and remained at Navajo Depot until 1966, when they were shipped to Rocky Mountain Arsenal. Although about 68,000 chemical bombs were stored at Navajo Depot in various configurations of phosgene, cyanogen chloride, and mustard gas, there were no accidents or injuries.

housed the black soldiers of the NOD Detachment. Although forbidden by the Geneva Convention from coming into direct contact with munitions and requiring close supervision, the prisoner of war contingent—which soon grew to 250—lifted the burden of many routine duties from the shoulders of depot employees.[37]

The war struck Navajo Depot in a very personal way in early April when Colonel Huling received word that his son, Lt. John W. Huling, had been killed while leading his men in an attack near Siegen, Germany.

Navajo Ordnance Depot personnel celebrated Victory in Europe (V-E Day) with two forty-five-minute rallies held at 1:00 P.M. on May 8, 1945. Flagstaff clergyman George E. Gooderham opened a rally in the Headquarters Area with a prayer of thanksgiving, followed by a speech in which Colonel Huling appealed to employees to stay on the job until the war against Japan was won. "We have not forgotten Pearl Harbor, or the Bataan death march," he announced, and reminded workers that squandering an hour or even a minute jeopardized the lives of their brothers, fathers, sons, and sweethearts who were slugging it out to the bitter end in the Pacific. Durfee Wren and Shine Smith added to Huling's comments. In the General Supply Area rally, Lieutenant Colonel Schmidt, the depot's executive officer, and Jim Boone, the general foreman for Indian workers, expressed similar sentiments. At the conclusion of the rallies, employees gathered beneath the garrison flag for the playing of the "Star Spangled Banner."[38]

Recognizing that the war was far from over, the seventh war bond drive started that afternoon set a one-day record for the depot of $11,225. Workers chipped in with their hard-earned cash as they celebrated victory in Europe. Meanwhile, the air war came to the depot that afternoon, just a mile or so from the administrative area, when Capt. Thomas A. White, on a routine training flight to Luke Field, crash-landed his P-38 airplane on Volunteer Prairie when he was forced down by bad weather at 4:20 P.M.[39]

As Colonel Huling anticipated, the end of the war in Europe meant that munitions would be redirected to the campaign in the Pacific and the planned invasion of Japan. Before long, each worker in the depot storage area was handling 7.3 tons per day, more than double the 3.3 tons per worker earlier in the war. An ominous order from the Chief of Ordnance doubled the Navajo Depot mission from forty-five to ninety boxcars of munitions per day. Mountains of bombs, shells, and ammunition were being stockpiled at the depot and at other arsenals in the West in preparation for the upcoming invasion.[40]

The sweat and toil from Navajo Depot workers stretched across the Pacific in mid-1945, when bombs from Bellemont were dropped on previously bypassed Japanese garrisons at Rabaul, Serang, Halmahera, and Timor, where enemy soldiers tended their crops and gardens. We just wanted to ensure "they aren't sitting this one out," quipped First Sergeant James D. Walkup of Flagstaff, who was in town on furlough recovering from a tropical disease acquired in the Pacific campaign where he had recognized ordnance coming from Bellemont.[41]

The surge in Pacific-bound munitions hit the depot on May 13, 1945. As heavily loaded trains rumbled into Bellemont day and night, Colonel Huling ordered the emergency mobilization of 598 civilian employees and the entire complement of depot officers to unload 2,012 tons of munitions from thirty-nine boxcars, again, a new Sunday record. The massive job began at 7:30 A.M., and when it was completed, Colonel Huling congratulated everyone who had participated. "People who are associated with us at Navajo know of the huge job ahead," he explained. "They see the increased numbers of carloads coming in, and going out to ports of embarkation. We are pleased with our accomplishment at the depot, and proud of our people's successful effort on Sunday. We're going to keep on the job. We're going to continue to meet demands that are made of us. When Japan is crushed, then—and only then—can we turn our thoughts to other things." Depot personnel handled a total of 1,618 carloads of munitions during May, a 61 percent increase over April and ultimately the busiest month of the war, averaging 52 boxcars per day. Expecting worse, Colonel Huling deferred calling out the Minute Men, preferring instead to save them for the crisis ahead.[42]

With operations turning at breakneck speed and still far short of the twenty-two hundred workers needed for maximum efficiency, Colonel Huling desperately searched for at least one hundred more employees. Fighting on the Pacific islands of Iwo Jima and Okinawa had consumed an enormous amount of munitions at the same time that the War Department was stockpiling ordnance for the invasion of Japan. Unlike the war in Europe, where America's allies had made significant contributions, the final campaign in the Pacific was strictly an American affair and Navajo Ordnance Depot proved the point. On Thursday, June 7, 1945, ammunition handlers and foremen were stunned when 502 boxcars arrived bringing more ammunition in a single day than had been shipped *and* received during the course of several months early in the war.

The next day at a 7:20 A.M. mass meeting, Colonel Huling praised

Most of the one thousand Navajo and Hopi employees at Navajo Ordnance Depot were ammunition handlers. Although some forklifts were available, about 60 percent of the 1.3 million tons of munitions were moved by hand.

the workers' fine record and noted in particular that, despite the heavy workload, turnover was only one-third of the 1943 rate. He announced that another sixty carloads of bombs would be arriving any day, and then asked every employee to put in a ten-hour shift on weekdays and eight hours on Saturday and Sunday. Huling asked all to work not only longer, but harder. He emphasized that careful planning was key to getting the job done quickly. Depot workers had six days—until June 13—to unload all 562 railcars so they could be dispatched to help move the country's grain crop. Employees did work longer and harder, and the depot met its deadline when the empty freight cars rolled out on time.[43]

As the pressure on Navajo Depot mounted, forty soldiers were dispatched from Stinson Field at San Antonio, Texas, to help out. At the same time, the Austrian prisoners of war took on many administrative and maintenance tasks, enabling civilian employees to move to the loading docks. And still ammunition continued to pour into Bellemont, forcing Colonel Huling to request 2,600 feet of additional railroad track to relieve congestion in the General Supply Area. In the meantime, Huling had no choice but to direct that workers store ammunition on pads out in the open areas between igloos—a dangerous location considering the approach of monsoon season lightning storms. Just as Huling began looking for an additional two hundred laborers, a strike by Arizona sawmill workers delayed delivery of 725,000 board feet of lumber for ammunition dunnage, leaving depot workers to scavenge for packing materials.[44]

At the end of June the improbable—many thought the impossible—finally happened. The massive Bellemont arsenal was full. Bombs, explosives, and ammunition were crammed into every igloo and magazine and onto every available outdoor storage pad. In addition, thousands of chemical bombs were carefully stored, and constantly inspected, at various locations around Volunteer Prairie. During April, May, and June 1945, Navajo Ordnance Depot received 2,893 boxcars of ammunition and shipped out 573 carloads for a total of 3,466 cars handled—the largest workload of any three-month period of the war. To quickly obtain more storage space, army engineers issued a $330,000 emergency contract to G. E. Kerns Company of Long Beach, California, for immediate construction of three hundred outdoor storage sites in the igloo area. Meanwhile, heavily loaded trains continued to pour into Navajo Depot through July in preparation for the invasion of Japan.[45]

Despite the daunting workload under very demanding circumstances in the summer of 1945, the arsenal finally hummed like a well-oiled engine thanks to excellent leadership and an extraordinary workforce. Local Flagstaff and Williams residents and organizations contributed much. But most of the burden of heavy labor, the day-in and day-out around-the-clock struggle with lifting, carrying, shoving, and stacking bombs and ammunition was borne by those coming from a different culture—the Navajo and Hopi ammunition handlers who made their home at Indian Village on the military grounds.

4

WARRIORS ALL
Navajo and Hopi Ordnance Workers

Boxes loaded with ammunition or grenades, crates of mines, heavy artillery shells, and bulky explosives had to be picked up by hand, moved, stacked, lifted again, moved again, and finally placed in storage, whether it was in an aboveground magazine, igloo, or on an outdoor pad. The ammunition handlers even moved heavy bombs by hand from railcars to semitrailers and then carefully eased the unwieldy cargo down ramps and into igloos for storage. Then, perhaps days, maybe weeks or even months later, this backbreaking process was repeated as they once again moved the munitions to semitrailers and then boxcars for shipment to the port of Los Angeles. Although the use of forklifts increased during the war, the majority of heavy labor was still done by hand even as late as August 1945.

Those struggling with these tasks were, for the most part, an extraordinarily hardy lot. The lifters and movers were primarily Native Americans. Although mostly Navajo, some Hopis were also ammunition handlers. Additionally, Indians from other tribes—Hualapais, Supais, Apaches, Lagunas, Maricopas, and Tohono O'odham—found jobs at the arsenal. Hispanics represented almost 50 percent of non-Indian laborers in late 1943. Fewer than thirty African American or Chinese workers were employed, a reflection of their small populations in the region.[1]

Navajos came to Bellemont because life on the reservation had been especially difficult during the Great Depression. Believing the erosion and plant cover problems stemmed from overgrazing and lack of range control, Commissioner of Indian Affairs John Collier, an active promoter of social change who valued Navajo culture, ordered severe cutbacks in the number of sheep and goats on the reservation. The Navajo Tribe complied, slaughtering several hundred thousand livestock, and in turn endangering not only a way of life but their self-sufficiency as well. Navajos had not seen such a grave disruption in their society since the days of Kit Carson and the Long Walk.[2]

Stock reduction influenced two other significant areas of Navajo life. The first was Collier's effort to reorganize tribes into constitutional tribal councils, establish tribal corporations for economic development, and adopt municipal ordinances. Congress passed the Indian Reorganization Act—the Wheeler-Howard Bill—in June 1934. One year later, however, Navajos voted by a narrow majority to reject the IRA. Much of their discontent sprang from goat reduction. In turn, Collier himself became the scapegoat for the entire stock reduction affair. Second, the devastation of stock reduction forced an economic diversification and families sought employment in construction and utilities projects, erosion control, and trading post jobs. Families which had previously relied upon livestock as their sole source of income were, by the late 1930s, dependent upon several sectors for their livelihood. Yet, even with forced diversification, Navajos were one of the most destitute and unemployed groups in the United States by 1940, suffering great hardships following the destruction of their animals.[3]

Although ravaged by the government's program and disenchanted with Washington, the Navajo stand toward America's enemies was firmly taken before Pearl Harbor. The Navajo tribal council sensed a German threat. Germany, befuddled by its World War I inability to break the Choctaw uncoded messages, not only sent anthropologists to learn Native American languages but mounted a Fascist propaganda campaign as well. The council, disdainful of Nazi concepts of racial superiority, submitted a resolution to the United States government in June 1940 from their annual tribal fair at Window Rock, Arizona: "We and the 50,000 people we represent, stand ready as in 1918, to aid and defend our government and its institutions against all subversive and armed conflict and pledge our loyalty to the system which recognizes minority rights and a way of life that has placed us among the greatest people of our race."[4]

In January 1942, as the first army engineers arrived in Flagstaff, the Navajo tribal council meeting at Window Rock once again affirmed the loyalty of the Navajo people to the United States, setting the stage for not only illustrious military participation in World War II but extensive civilian involvement as well—much of it at the new Bellemont arsenal. Meanwhile, Leo Weaver used his influence at the chamber of commerce to coordinate a systematic arrangement for Navajo and Hopi labor, stating, "We feel the Indians are our people and want to do anything we can for them." He worked to ensure the Native Americans were "given every opportunity to prove themselves and be protected at the same time from unscrupulous operators" who would no doubt try to take advantage of the circumstances. Weaver committed Flagstaff to help pay the salary of an official to assist the Indian workers in the many challenges ahead.[5]

The following month, selective service registration on the Navajo Reservation provided an indication of Navajo resolve and the changes that had come about since World War I, when fewer than a dozen had voluntarily entered the armed forces. No doubt the new requirements to register and serve imposed by the Indian Citizenship Act of 1924 were an influence. But perhaps more importantly, the ever increasing Navajo participation in and enjoyment of border town events like Flagstaff's historic All-Indian Pow-Wow familiarized them with newsreels, soldiers, airplanes, warships, and pictures of war, in addition to other aspects of acculturation. The Flagstaff Pow-Wow and similar border-town events during the 1930s inadvertently nurtured a concept among the Navajos of their place in the broader context of American society. This was best reflected on one single day, February 16, 1942, when 2,693 Navajos registered with the selective service, far exceeding numbers from any other tribe. If all Americans had registered with such enthusiasm and in such numbers, one observer noted, the draft would have been unnecessary.

This environment of Indian patriotism and support by Weaver and Flagstaff facilitated Major Myrick's mid-1942 recruitment of Navajo and Hopi workers from the reservations and their eventual settlement at Bellemont. Their familiarity with the area aided this passage considerably, and many Navajos and Hopis who had participated in the annual Flagstaff Fourth of July celebration continued to do so throughout the war.

In June 1942, even before taking command at Bellemont, Myrick reported that in addition to the hundreds of Native Americans working for contractors, he had hired twenty-five Indians as the first of over two thousand workers needed at his new depot. Military officials in Washington, however, were skeptical if not scornful despite the labor crunch and the arsenal's official name. Some Ordnance Department officers insisted it was a big mistake to rely on Indians for most of the heavy labor force. Myrick persisted, however, knowing full well from his experience at Fort Wingate Ordnance Depot that Indian loyalty was guaranteed and their work ethic commendable. By October 1942 Myrick had recruited a total of 560 Native Americans from several tribes.[6]

Although most of the Native Americans coming to Bellemont were Navajo, about 25 percent were Hopi. The Hopi, translated as "Peaceful People" and called Moqui Indians by the Spanish, are descendants of the prehistoric Anasazi culture. The westernmost of Pueblo peoples, they occupy the Black Mesa region of northeastern Arizona where their reservation, designated in 1882, is surrounded by the Navajo Reservation—a situation that resulted in a land dispute that continues to this day. Oraibi, undeniably the oldest continuously occupied settlement in the United States, dates to around 1350. The region of the Hopi towns has been occupied for at least ten thousand years. Although some have adopted modern conveniences, the Hopi have zealously guarded their cultural traditions.[7]

By 1940 the population of Black Mesa Hopi villages had grown to only 3,444 residents with perhaps 10 percent living off the reservation. A much smaller tribe than the Navajo, Hopis had, nevertheless, also been devastated by stock reduction. Although Hopi culture did not have a recent military history and opposed fighting in any form, several hundred would serve in World War II. Many would provide alternate service as conscientious objectors, and approximately 250 would find work at Navajo Depot where they furnished a coterie of skilled craftsmen and expert workers. Yet, with cultural misunderstanding on both sides, the Hopis would be the only American tribe persecuted for draft evasion.[8]

By midsummer of 1942, about one thousand Native American workers and family members had settled in tents and temporary shelters about one-half mile north of Bellemont in the Coconino National Forest wood line on the edge of Volunteer Prairie. Unsure how long jobs would last, they did not build hogans or permanent structures. Instead, they stacked volcanic malpais rocks several feet high to make circular foundations and then placed logs, wood, or any other available material on top. Shelters were close together, roads few, and sanitary facilities lacking. The village was called "Indian Town" by some, and the vibrant settlement was in constant motion as three shifts of workers came and went at all hours during the construction months.[9]

Conditions were disgraceful for many of these first Native American workers who came to Bellemont in the summer of 1942. In addition to the thousand who lived in temporary huts in the wood line north of town, many camped up and down Route 66 and slept in shelters made of cast-off crates. Dishonest traders put up shacks along the highway and charged exorbitant prices. Prostitutes flourished in the area, and venereal disease was believed to be rampant. Undiagnosed illnesses were commonplace. On paydays, some intoxicated Indians were robbed and left to die in Bellemont ditches. The deplorable situation was seen by officials as a broken link in the logistics chain that could eventually jeopardize the whole Pacific campaign because of the massive amount of munitions expected to flow through Navajo Ordnance Depot. Conditions at Bellemont and nearby Flagstaff, whether residents liked it or not, were cause for concern with the army's chief engineer Capt. Demmie Cox, along with some at the War Department.[10]

Every worker was precious for Major Myrick and his budding organization. Recognizing the size and quality of the Native American core of construction workers, Myrick proposed a novel solution to not only attract and keep Indian laborers and their families for the permanent force, but to also alleviate the serious problems in Bellemont.

Myrick, with the army's authorization and acting unimpeded by any similar precedent, decided to offer housing for the Indian laborers and their families in a communal setting somewhere on the military base. Tribal representatives quickly accepted the unusual but interesting idea and agreed to move to the more secure and permanent spot as soon as possible.

Myrick and his staff picked a beautiful and undeveloped area on the arsenal's northwest corner about three miles from the headquarters building. This second Indian settlement was probably located in a grassy lowland area with poor drainage. Regardless, the army quickly helped construct a village on government time at government expense. Although the army provided logs for hogans, most were too short and thick to be effective. Water, perhaps from late summer rains, seeped into the crude shelters and made the second Indian encampment more unsatisfactory than the original Indian Town in the Bellemont wood line.[11]

As soon as the lowland site was recognized as inadequate, the Native Americans, with army help, built a third and permanent camp on the high ground about five hundred yards to the north. This wooded area was south of the Bellemont cinder pits and the AT&SF Railroad tracks. It was far enough from Victory Village and the headquarters area to provide Navajos and Hopis the isolation they needed. At the same time, however, the camp was within walking distance of Bellemont. There was probably little if any Indian interest in placing the site closer to the mostly white community at Victory Village. Living a few yards from each other was no doubt sufficient challenge for those accustomed to moving with their flocks across the expanse of the reservation. At the third camp, what became known officially as "Indian Village," the pleasant surroundings soon attracted many family members. A few young single Navajo women, such as Amy Franklin, chose to live in the Victory Village apartments because they had no relatives or friends at Indian Village.[12]

Although a few Native American laborers may have lived in Flagstaff, most workers and families lived in Indian Village, where the new experience soon proved challenging. The majority came from isolated

Indian Village, a communal setting on the depot grounds, originally consisted of Navajo hogans built with army help in the fall of 1942.

homes or tiny communities scattered across the northeastern plateau of Arizona and northwestern New Mexico where contact with neighbors was infrequent if not rare. From this environment they moved into a settlement built by themselves and the army. Barbed wire surrounding the village did little to keep serious intruders out, but channeled workers, family members, and visitors to the gate on the north side of the camp where a soldier or village policeman verified passes and inspected for contraband, especially alcohol.[13]

The first Navajo and Hopi housing at the permanent Indian Village—the only army-built Navajo and Hopi town on record—consisted of fifty army tents erected in the late summer or fall of 1942. Stoves, installed for the coming winter, had no spark arresters and it was not long before the tents burned down or had so many holes that they provided little shelter.

Army tents were added to Indian Village, although hogans remained in use throughout the war.

The residents formed an Indian council and met with Major Myrick, asking permission to again build traditional hogans. Myrick agreed, and by October 1 they built a community of seventy-one traditional, well-constructed hogans, along with improved tents for Hopis several hundred yards east, as hogans were not part of Hopi culture. At this village, nestled among the tall ponderosa pines, the hogans and tents were not miles apart, but just a few feet, all neatly lined up with ten or twenty yards between rows. The hogans' hinged wooden doors—some displaying a war bond poster—faced east in accordance with Navajo custom. Animal skins lay drying in the sun on some of the rounded earthen roofs and an occasional stove pipe stuck up from the top. There were trappings of home, yet home for most still meant the open range of the Indian reservations.[14]

Despite continued recruiting of Navajo and Hopi workers, Myrick realized by Christmas of 1942 that he had a dangerous labor shortage on his hands. Although munition shipments were increasing rapidly, his Indian workforce was shrinking. More Navajos and Hopis were leaving than arriving. The number of Indian laborers dropped from 560 in October to 540 by December. This was an alarming trend considering that he needed about 2,200 workers and that Indians represented around 60 percent of his force and almost all of his heavy labor pool. Additionally, a high Indian absenteeism rate required 40 percent more Indian workers in order to meet deadlines.[15]

Myrick appointed one of his newly arrived lieutenants to investigate the worrisome Indian absentee and retention problem. Lt. Arch E. McGee reported for duty on January 22, 1943, and Myrick quickly made him the labor relations officer and also placed him in charge of all Indian affairs at Navajo Depot and Bellemont. McGee conducted an investigation and soon discovered that it was not the barbed wire fence, the guarded entrance, the military-controlled access, or the back-breaking work in around-the-clock shifts that were often extended that drove the first Navajos and Hopis back to their reservations. Nor was it the unfamiliar colonial setting of neatly arranged hogans and tents or homesickness. It was not the contact with Anglo culture and supervisors. Instead, it was a combination of several other problems that demoralized the new depot residents.[16]

The first problem McGee uncovered was transportation to Flagstaff. Although tractor-trailers picked up laborers at Indian Village and took them to and from the work sites, weekends and off-duty time were a different story. Then, most Navajos and Hopis had to walk two miles along Route 66 to the Bellemont bus stop, where—as Guy Multine, president of the Navajo Employees Club, pointed out—bootleg liquor dealers lurked in the shadows or along the road, waiting to sell Navajos whiskey and get them drunk. This walk, close to high-speed automobiles in the snows of winter and rains of summer, was unsafe and especially difficult when carrying groceries or other goods. Accidents happened and some Indians were injured.[17]

On Saturdays and paydays, once the workers and families finally arrived in Flagstaff, they ran into even more problems buying food, clothing, and other essentials. Many Navajos and Hopis had little if any previous contact with non-Indians and the majority spoke no English. They quickly became frustrated dealing with stores where few spoke their language. Only the Pay Less store cashed their checks, and then only if they purchased at least three dollars' worth of Pay Less goods—half a senior laborer's daily wage of six dollars—whether they needed the items or not. And then, after shopping and loaded with goods, the bus trip back to Bellemont and walk past the bootleggers was worse than the trip in. Even the most optimistic workers and families despaired. They became discouraged and finally just packed up and went back home to the reservations where life was harsh but more predictable and less difficult.[18]

As Lieutenant McGee continued his investigation he also noticed that many Indian workers, for reasons unknown, seemed to be slowing down in the afternoons and that some jobs were not completed. Wondering if this stemmed from fatigue due to an inadequate diet, he personally investigated many of the Indians' lunch sacks. The first sack he opened contained only a charred sheep's head with its black tongue flopping out grotesquely from the side of its mouth and singed eye balls glaring at the intruder. McGee continued the investigation and soon realized that the Indian ammunition handlers needed better food.[19]

Myrick sympathized with the Indian situation. Also, fearing the continuing decline in his heavy-labor pool would seriously threaten Navajo Depot as the war expanded, he searched for innovative solutions to the problems. He contacted Hubert Richardson, who built and ran the Indian trading post at Cameron, and William S. (Billy) Young, a Richardson in-law who had clerked the trading post at Leupp and worked for the Richardsons. Both Cameron and Leupp were on the Navajo reservation. Myrick asked Richardson if he would set up a trading post at Navajo Ordnance Depot somewhere close to Indian Village to accommodate Indian workers and families. Richardson and Young agreed to the plan and formed a partnership. In southern Arizona they found an old barracks building around one hundred feet long and large enough for a trading post and warehouse. They bought the building, hauled it up to Bellemont, and placed it between the Navajo and Hopi camps about three hundred yards from each.[20]

Richardson and Young quickly brought in goods and Richardson's Trading Post opened for business in the spring of 1943. The trading post was one hundred yards south of the Bellemont cinder pits and sandwiched between the depot's northern fence and the AT&SF Railroad tracks, where, to the amusement of some, the building shook considerably as trains passed a few feet away. A winding road directed traffic from Route 66 around the cinder pits to the trading post and guardhouse entrance at Indian Village.

Billy Young, who had been working on the reservation since 1920 and spoke fluent Navajo, knew immediately what to stock. He brought in a small flock of sheep from Williams, and was soon selling forty or fifty head per week, as mutton was the favorite meat. He kept a larger flock of about fifteen hundred sheep in the vicinity of today's Wal-Mart store in southwest Flagstaff. He stocked velveteen and satin for women's skirts, along with Pendleton shawls and "sing cloth" for ceremonies. He also stocked a variety of clothing, canned goods, cereals, dry goods, meats, and dairy products, and soon sold about eighteen hundred loaves of bread per week. Young added soda pop, cowboy hats, magazines, hardware, cigarettes, candy, and a large assortment of comic books. Shopping carts were available for customers, and Billy Young's son John often used the family truck to deliver groceries direct to the customer's door. Young brought in looms, and hired Navajo and Hopi interpreters. Finally, Navajos and Hopis could trade for or buy almost all they needed only a few hundred yards from their homes.[21]

The trading post provided a number of other services. As many as twenty Navajo and Hopi helpers were employed in the office, butcher shop, warehouse, and grocery. Young ordered meat from the Armour Company and had it delivered by train to Flagstaff or Bellemont. Young also provided an unofficial mail service with boxes so Indian Village residents need not wait for a trip to town or the reservation to get their mail. Many had never voted and Young helped them register. Young also gave his clients both groceries and gas on credit. For those who felt uncomfortable on the military base, Young went to the pay office and picked up their checks, deducted what he had given on credit, and returned the remainder. He cashed workers' paychecks at a trading post window, where long lines formed every payday. Young hired vil-

Elizabeth Johnson checks her mail at Richardson's Trading Post. The trading post provided everything needed, including mail service, for the 3,500 Navajos and Hopis of Indian Village.

lage children, or gave them candy, to fetch golf balls he hit from his parking lot tee into the clearing south of the trading post.[22]

Richardson's Trading Post gave a much-needed boost to Indian morale in the spring of 1943. Navajos had been doing business on the reservation with Richardson since 1918, and they were good friends. Navajos saw the trading post owners as honest and fair. Richardson and Young both understood and trusted the Indians. Their trading post prices were seen as "right" by village residents. The Navajo Employees Club council thanked Myrick for his efforts in recruiting the traders. As they expressed in their letter, "We thank you for our fine trading post. We are all very happy."[23]

Young, who managed the trading post, provided one more very important service for both Indian Village and Navajo Ordnance Depot. Almost every Monday morning he received a call from the Flagstaff chief of police who would say something like, "I've got fourteen Indians who were arrested over the weekend for drunk and disorderly conduct, and they say if they don't get back to work today, they'll lose their jobs. They've all got fines of ten dollars each, and if you'll pay it and make some arrangements with them, I'll let them go."[24] Young never hesitated. He drove into Flagstaff and paid the fines immediately, knowing full well there was a war going on and that Indian labor was critical. Young also believed that his customers were his good friends and in time of need he wanted to help. The Indians never failed to make restitution in one or two payments.[25]

Billy Young was described by some Flagstaff residents as the "nicest person you ever met." He and his wife Freeda, along with their daughter, Mary Jane, and their two sons, Bill Jr. and John, made Richardson's Trading Post a comfortable country store. If village residents needed an item, Young found it. He was known to be very caring of the Navajos and Hopis. One youngster, O. Tacheeni Scott, who grew up in Indian Village, remembers Young more than earning his pay as he loaded up bags of groceries for families traveling back to the reservation on payday weekends. Young also provided food to destitute Indian families who had used all of their cash and resources for train fare to Bellemont. He staked these newcomers until their first wages came in. Young donated all the candy, fruit, and nuts to fill five hundred Christmas stockings for the village children. He donated cash prizes for the Indian field day races and events, along with sweaters for the baby contest winners. In addition to selling much-needed items to his Indian customers, Young also purchased their traditional handmade rugs and jewelry. Families from Flagstaff and the surrounding area came to the trading post to shop for Native arts and crafts.[26]

If traders and Indians got along, they were friends for life. This was the case with Young. The Navajos and Hopis loved him and he in turn loved them. Indians from all over the area came to see, visit, and deal with Indian trader Billy Young.[27]

Although Richardson's Trading Post was important in keeping Navajo and Hopi labor, other depot improvements also helped. Myrick made arrangements through the Indian Service whereby Indians employed at the arsenal would not lose their farms for lack of tilling the soil at some time during the year. Likewise, with the new flock of trading post sheep nearby and fresh mutton readily available, fewer Navajos returned to the reservation for meat. One problem, however, persisted. Those who still owned sheep on the reservation returned to their flocks during the spring lambing season—much to the chagrin of War Department wise men in Washington who ordered depot officials to postpone lambing season in an effort to stamp out Indian absenteeism.[28]

As Lieutenant McGee continued his investigation, he no doubt observed that while Anglo and Hispanic women were employed at the depot, Indian women were not. At the same time, however, the male Indian workers' absenteeism continued to soar, once reaching 63 percent. The turnover rate, which was also high, reflected many discouraged Indian families who left Navajo Depot permanently. In February 1943, perhaps following a recommendation by McGee, Myrick hired twenty-four Indian women for light work.

The hiring of Native American women soon brought encouraging news. At first, although their absenteeism was less than the men's, the overall turnover rate remained high, and no significant change in the labor force was noted. The continued hiring of Indian women, however, along with other improvements, finally delivered results, eventually cutting the turnover rate to 20 percent and the absentee rate to 16 percent. The hiring of Indian women peaked at 290 in June 1943, about 14 percent of the entire workforce, at the same time when male Indian workers numbered 700. Indian women remained about 11 percent of the workforce through 1943 and about 8 percent in late 1944.[29]

All told, a combination of factors, some unexpected, finally kept Native Americans at Bellemont. The excellent trading post, arrangements with the Indian Service, improved housing, recreation, and food, and the hiring of Navajo and Hopi women finally stabilized the workforce in the summer of 1943.

Women worked in nearly all areas at Navajo Depot, including drop testing M51 fuses, shown here. Although Native American women were first hired for "light duty," the reduction in absenteeism and turnover rates quickly boosted their employment to almost 300.

Native American women, like other women workers, labored in a variety of jobs in almost every department (about a third of the depot's workforce was female). In early 1943, they crated explosives and ammunition, where the goal of two thousand crates per day was exceeded by five hundred on one summer day. A few were "checkers," responsible for ammunition accountability in boxcars, semitrailers, and igloos. Some worked along conveyor ramps which moved ammunition or other explosives. Others worked in the surveillance branch with tricky and technical repairs of ammunition, such as installing fin–lock-nut protectors on five-hundred-pound bombs. They made intricate repairs that required specialized training, such as the dangerous task of rewiring one-thousand-pound bombs. In other jobs, the possibility of accidental explosion was also high. Some Indian women salvaged old gunpowder from shells and replaced it with new, while others, with their small, delicate hands, carefully worked on grenades. Some handled lightweight ammunition, practice bombs, fins, fuses, and small boxes of other components. Others drop-tested grenade fuses. Indian women were especially adept at precise tasks, such as painting and stenciling ammunition, bombs, and containers. These talents were valued by supervisors because of the stringent requirements imposed by the War Department.[30]

Women were also needed in many areas not involving munitions. Alice Baloo, for example, was a twenty-year-old Navajo from Fort Defiance who had begun her driving career at Fort Wingate with semi-trailers. Navajo Depot officials did not believe the petite young Indian woman could climb up and into a large tractor-trailer, let alone handle one. They gave her a driving test and hired her immediately. She drove semitrailers, then the school bus, and also worked part-time in the transportation office. No one could park a semitrailer like Baloo. She always backed up only once.[31]

Some Native American women worked as nurse's aides in the hospital. Those Indian women not working at the arsenal made and sold crafts to trader Billy Young and took care of the children. Others formed a Navajo Women's Club to help with the many needs of their new community. The club elected Mrs. Roger Davis, Mrs. Leo Milford, and Mrs. William Dixon officers. They sponsored Indian Village projects such as the Thanksgiving and Christmas dinners where hundreds of people were served. Hopi women also formed a club that sponsored dinner fund-raisers for the Red Cross and other organizations or needs. Regardless of where they worked, the women of Indian Village had an important role at the depot. Much needed to be done and there were never enough workers to do it.[32]

One young Navajo woman, Amy Franklin, was in Shiprock, New Mexico, in September 1943, when she heard army recruiters tell about good jobs somewhere in Arizona at a place called Bellemont. She climbed aboard an army truck, having no idea where it was headed or when she would get there. She just went. Shortly after arriving at

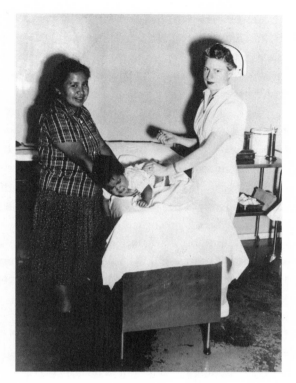

At Navajo Depot hospital, nurse Mora Huskey gives an inoculation to Melinda Harrison as her mother Hope looks on. For some Native Americans it was the first routine health care they had received. Many current Flagstaff residents were born in the depot hospital.

Navajo Depot she was put to work cleaning, packing, stamping, and shipping ammunition, alongside other Navajo women. She wore overalls and frequently worked all day and night "to keep the ammunition rolling." For Franklin, the steady paycheck was not as important as winning the war. The work was serious and there was little humor or horseplay. Franklin was young, wanted the boys overseas to return, and wanted to get married and have children.[33]

Another Navajo woman, Agnes R. Begay of Many Farms, Arizona, graduated from the Albuquerque Indian School in 1934. She and her husband Seth left their Bureau of Indian Affairs jobs in October 1943, to work at Bellemont, where they were assigned a "nice" two-bed-room apartment at Indian Village. She worked in the personnel office and as an interpreter before qualifying for the Indian Village police force, where she was equipped with a uniform, cap, and pistol. In this capacity Begay worked the night shift at the main entrance where she verified visitor passes and searched buses coming from Flagstaff for contraband. By the end of 1943, alcohol had become a problem in the camp, and tensions simmered among some families. Begay's major responsibility was to ensure liquor was not smuggled into the village during her graveyard shift. The Begays worked at Navajo Depot until the end of the war, when they returned to Many Farms.[34]

Navajo Depot's ammunition handlers were mostly Navajo men. They loaded by hand 60 percent of the 1,323,744 tons of ammunition that passed through the arsenal during the war. Discounting muni-tions moved by forklift (about 40 percent) and the emergency call-up of local Flagstaff and Williams Minutemen, every Navajo heavy la-borer lifted, moved, and stacked two tons of munitions by hand on an average day early in the war. By the end of the war, he lifted, moved, and stacked over four tons per day. The physical strength of Navajo men ensured the arsenal's success in moving munitions and meeting shipment deadlines. Without Navajo men, the depot would have been ineffective, if not shut down.[35]

Although most Navajo men were laborers, and made up almost all of the ammunition handling details at the loading docks, igloos, maga-zines, and storage pads, a few worked alongside Hopi men in semi-skilled and skilled trades and administration. Beginning in the winter of 1942–43, when many reported for work wearing jeans and a shirt with only a traditional blanket for warmth, the Navajo men quickly adopted more efficient work clothes. Soon, most wore an unofficial uniform consisting of a leather jacket, gloves, scarf, and a large flat-brimmed cowboy hat. Some worked as carpenters, forklift operators, mechanics, mechanic helpers, and firemen. Others found jobs in utili-ties maintenance, worked on the depot railroad, in the employees' mess, or as electricians or stonemasons. Some, like Kee B. Neversleep, worked

The munitions were moved by rail to the loading docks where they were then placed in semitrailers for movement to the igloos. In addition to boxes of ammunition and explosives, ammunition handlers moved bombs weighing up to 500 pounds by hand.

on salvage crews; others, like bespectacled Kee Manygoats, worked as truck drivers.[36]

For those who had schooling, many other jobs were possible. Scott Franklin worked as a clerk in the personnel office, where he did fingerprinting, wrote applications, interpreted when needed, and conducted safety demonstrations. Others with schooling worked as ammunition checkers. Ned Benally had vocational training, and was employed as an assistant director of recreation in Indian Village. By the summer of 1943, Indian men were serving in supervisory positions such as gang bosses, foremen, and assistant superintendents. One Hopi worker, Johnny Poseyesva, eventually rose to foreman of the roads and grounds section. Some were sent as far away as Ohio to study munitions.[37]

Navajos and Hopis overlooked their differences and worked side by side, many forming friendships despite the continuing land dispute back on the reservations. The first Indian leaders, Julius Begay and Maxwell Yazzie, came to the depot in 1942 highly recommended. Yazzie, who had worked in a coal mine for three years and also had painting, labor, and truck driving experience, spoke English. Begay was described as a very good man who had schooling and was foreman material. Leo Weaver, ever involved in expanding the Indian workforce, stated "there is no more honorable, dependable, or conscientious man, either red or white, that you could have in your employ than Julius Begay."[38]

Begay and Yazzie clearly understood the size of the task they faced each day. They began the routine of calling a camp meeting each evening in which they outlined the next day's work. Hundreds of men were divided into work gangs of twenty men each. Then, Begay and Yazzie drilled each group foreman about his responsibilities and their next day's labor. This system was unprecedented in the army's ordnance depots across the nation. At Navajo Depot, where workers were spread out over thousands of acres of rugged terrain, the nightly meetings saved time, money, and lives. Begay and Yazzie's leadership reduced confusion, instilled a sense of urgency, and inspired teamwork on a large scale.[39]

By 1943 the arsenal began to reap the rewards from excellent Indian leadership and centralization of the workforce. Most heavy laborers lived on depot grounds at Indian Village and were readily accessible for evening planning sessions. Likewise, the three hundred Indian women who hired on were also readily available to assist as needed. Other arsenals around the nation lacked a similar Native American presence or centralized labor pool and could not duplicate the Navajo Depot system that matured within months following the construction of Indian Village.

The wages were good for the Indian men who made up most of the depot's heavy laborers in the storage branch of the operations division—a force which fluctuated between five hundred and one thousand men. As the least skilled and least paid among depot workers, their 1943 pay started at $4.64 per day for a junior laborer and increased to a maximum of $6.00 per day for a senior laborer. The lowest income of Indian employees, however, compared favorably with the general income of Flagstaff. Depot wages varied according to skill and experience in eighty-two categories, including armorers, carpenters, foremen, gang bosses, laborers, and drivers. In general, most of the depot jobs paid very well for the area and provided residents of both Indian Village and many in Flagstaff with a secure income. The pay was usually better than the local lumber mills' and also included a retirement program.[40]

As the war progressed, Lieutenant McGee supervised the addition of more facilities in Indian Village, including a lunchroom, bakery, laundry, day school, and a completely equipped dispensary staffed with a physician and nurse for round-the-clock health care. Housing construction continued and afforded an interesting combination of old and new. Following the first experiment with traditional hogans and tents, the army added thirty-six winterized tents with modern chimneys. Large and able to hold more than one family, some were square, others oblong with high ceilings. Then, the army built some unusual wooden structures that simulated hogans. They were square with a pointed roof and chimney protruding from the apex. Called hogan huts or hutments, they were neatly lined up and only yards apart.

Engineers soon added forty-eight wooden apartments. They were covered with tar paper, and each housed two extended families. At the same time, Navajo Depot assumed responsibility for several old CCC camps around Flagstaff and began salvage of usable materials. In September 1943, Colonel Huling announced the letting of a contract to E. W. Duhame Company of Phoenix for twenty additional two-family units, to be split equally between the Navajo and Hopi camps. The houses were of frame construction and built from materials recovered from the two old CCC camps north and east of Flagstaff. McGee hired Hopi carpenters to help remodel the buildings, turning them into modest homes. Officials turned a larger CCC building into a community recreation center where sewing and weaving were possible with looms brought in by trader Billy Young.[41]

Some of the hogans and tents of Indian Village were replaced by CCC structures like these removed from camps in the Flagstaff area. Navajos and Hopis
moved to a new Indian Village of modular homes in 1958, located about 700
yards east. It was closed in 1964 although some tenants remained until 1970.

Myrick's long-range Indian Village plan included a total of 125
modern family units capable of holding more than one thousand people.
Construction was finally authorized in November 1944 and began in
February 1945. The $185,000 project was completed on August 30,
and included 104 family living units in thirteen apartments, each housing eight families. These "row houses" were 20 feet wide and 170 feet
long, and provided every family one room and a kitchen. The apartments were equipped with running water, lights, and a combination
cooking and heating stove. Overall, the new buildings compared favorably with those at Victory Village. Additional construction provided
two combination wash and bathhouses, thirteen double latrines, utilities and streets. Although original plans directed materials be salvaged
from Camp Williston at Boulder City, Nevada, the use of new materials was approved whenever necessary. The new units replaced sixty
hogans and were seen as critical in the effort to relieve the acute labor

shortage. All of the hogans, tents, hutments, apartments, and row houses were serviced by several roads running parallel through the village.[42]

All told, the high tide of Indian employment reached 999 workers in July 1943, about 45 percent of the 2,173 civilians and 64 military who worked at Navajo Depot. Indian Village probably held over 3,500 men, women, and children. Several sources, however, report at least 4,500. Hopis made up about 25 percent of the Indian labor force—about 250 workers. The Hopi population in Indian Village of about 750 represented about 22 percent of the entire Hopi population residing on Black Mesa in 1940. Later in the war when the Indian workforce dropped to around 500 laborers, 2,150 lived in Indian Village—about 1,700 Navajos and 450 Hopis in two separate camps about seven hundred yards apart.[43]

The drastic August 1943 reductions ordered by the War Department hit those with the fewest skills hardest, and the majority of departures were among Native Americans, with only 423 remaining at the end of the month—a 58 percent cut in Indian workers. Colonel Huling circumvented the reductions and soon hired more Indian laborers to handle the ever increasing boxcars of munitions that also headed east for the Normandy invasion. The number of Indian workers climbed back to 815 by March 1944, 49 percent of the civilian force, and averaged 47 percent during the remainder of the war.[44]

Despite the trading post and improved living conditions, all was not rosy at Indian Village. Public laws prohibited the sale of alcohol to Native Americans, resulting in some residents driving all the way to Two Guns, about thirty miles east of Flagstaff, to buy whiskey from a rancher who sold it out of the back door of his ranch house. They smuggled the alcohol into the village, contributing to friction among families. Leslie Cody, who lived in the village as a child, remembers the alcohol-related fights and the military police who dealt with them.[45]

Alcohol was not the only problem. Gambling, also forbidden, took many workers' paychecks. Some wives left their husbands, and some older men found younger women. Residents formed a disciplinary court of elected officers that spent many evenings hearing cases, which often led to the expulsion of repeat offenders. Scott Franklin, who served as court secretary, believed problems began when people who formerly minded their own business on the open range of the reservation moved next door to each other or, worse yet, lived in the same building. Although most residents were good citizens, the new environment contributed to an increase in teenage drinking and attitude problems. Indian Village was a "big change," and, according to Franklin, "young people ran over their parents and did as they pleased."[46]

For children of both the war and postwar years, life in the village revolved around the school, recreation hall, lunchroom, and local forests. The weekly movies were popular and often attended by residents of Victory Village. The children played baseball, basketball, and horseshoes, and hunted birds with their slingshots. Some hiked and played in the woods and adjacent hills. Daily life involved walking as only a few families owned trucks. John Young, son of trader Billy Young, made rafts of old dried-out railroad ties and floated around the cinder pit pond. Others fished in the depot's ponds. Years later, many relish memories of the beautiful water, forests, and Bellemont surroundings where they played "cowboys and Indians." Roland Dixon remembers fighting on the playground because some kids said that Indians always lost against the cowboys.

Some Indian Village children remember other things. For Al Henderson there were many wonderful distractions around the camp. He ditched school frequently and was often in trouble with his parents. Teddy Blake spent summers at Indian Village as a child and enjoyed barbecues and socializing with camp neighbors. For Leslie Cody, learning about the Hopi people helped him understand some of the differences between their two cultures. O. Tacheeni Scott fondly remembers the smell of tortillas and fried potatoes and watching the butcher slice bulk baloney at Richardson's Trading Post. For younger children, clothes were a burden and at times they ran naked through the camp. During the war, many loved watching the constant stream of freight trains loaded with war supplies and troop trains packed with staring soldiers pass just north of the village. Others remember the missionaries who came to the camp and conducted meetings on Wednesday and Sunday evenings.[47]

Navajo artist R. C. Gorman, also one of the village children, found the Austrian prisoners of war fascinating. The soldiers roamed freely about the Indian camp doing various jobs. The situation was friendly and the Indians treated them "quite nicely." Village residents did their own chores alongside the Austrians. Gorman showed the prisoners the latest news in *Life* magazine, and some of the soldiers gave him photographs. Some Navajos gave the prisoners copies of their official identification photographs. Many of the prisoners had families back in Austria and especially enjoyed time spent with the Navajo and Hopi children. Yet, for Gorman, they all seemed like prisoners inside the barbed wire fence. The Indians, however, were allowed to leave with a pass.[48]

The army established a two-classroom school in a temporary building at Indian Village because the city of Flagstaff did not accept non-English speaking Navajo children in its public schools. Called the Bellemont Day School, officials placed it under jurisdiction of the principal at Tuba City Boarding School. The Bellemont school, the second wartime school added to the Navajo Agency, was preceded by the Church Rock school located near Fort Wingate Ordnance Depot. Miss Anna J. Ring, formerly a teacher at the Moenave Day School in the Tuba School District, arrived at Indian Village and concentrated on teaching English to Navajo children so they would be accepted into Flagstaff public schools.[49]

Navajo children ages six to twelve attended day school classes that included instruction in English as well as in their native language. Hopis, however, preferred to send their children to schools in Flagstaff. Navajo parents were asked to pay the school fund fifty cents per week to help buy supplies. Years later, the day school facilities were seen as "tragically inadequate" by the Indian Village dispensary nurse, Sarah Brown, who also doubled as a teacher and librarian. The primary school teachers could handle only sixty children, and were unable to educate all who wanted to go to school. Most of the younger children did not speak English, and it was impossible to provide the language training necessary to adequately prepare them for public school.[50]

Sixty Indian children attended the Bellemont day school at Indian Village. Teacher Anna J. Ring made English instruction a priority so students could eventually be accepted into Flagstaff public schools. Those turned away from the Bellemont school due to inadequate facilities and staff became Flagstaff's forgotten children of the war.

After the war, and the departure of teachers Anna J. Ring and Ina Kingsley, the Indian Bureau employed two Navajo women, Teresa Salabye and Adele Mitchell, to assist Sarah Brown in the dispensary and with teaching. Another Navajo woman, Ramona Plummer, was hired to teach adult literacy. Still, no help came from the Flagstaff public school system. As Colonel Huling had done earlier, depot officials provided buildings, maintenance, utilities, and heat, and did everything possible within the army's capabilities. Although the Indian children were free to enter public schools at any time, the woeful lack of resources left the majority unprepared. In many respects, the first classes of Indian Village youngsters were Flagstaff's forgotten children of the war.[51]

The Native American children who did go to public school in Flagstaff encountered several problems. Most of their parents did not speak English and had difficulty finding support through parent-teacher organizations. Many parents were shy about appearing at crowded schools among white parents. Most did not have transportation into town at the proper time for their children or themselves to take part in school activities. For these children, just staying in school was difficult enough. Despite these difficulties and meager resources, depot officials promoted education as "the thing of today" and strongly encouraged school for all children up to twelve years of age.[52]

In the postwar years, nurse Sarah Brown proved to be a bright spot in Indian Village. She knew each child by their first name, along with their medical history. Brown also taught health courses to Indian mothers and children. Although she and her husband lived in Williams, Mrs. Brown remained at Indian Village Monday through Friday out of love for the village residents and concern for their welfare. She was assisted by a soft-spoken Navajo woman, Sybil Dick, a Red Cross certified nurse's aide. Together, with Sybil to interpret, they attended to many of the medical needs. As village nurse, teacher, and librarian, Sarah Brown's plate was full. There was no money for library or book mending supplies, so Brown purchased many items herself, including paper for the school children and a multivolume encyclopedia. A generous, understanding, and unselfish person, Brown was quick to give credit to anyone but herself.[53]

As with any military garrison, there were rules and regulations, which also applied to Navajos and Hopis at Indian Village. The soldier or Indian policeman who guarded the entrance kept out unauthorized persons, including local bootleggers, and also helped workers board the tractor-trailers in the morning and dismount in the evening. The Indian police force, in addition to searching vehicles and possessions, was responsible for maintaining order at meetings. The recreation center and theater remained open until 10:00 P.M., with the exception of Saturdays, when it closed at midnight. To prevent overcrowding at movies, women and children attended the first show and men the second. Health standards were enforced, and public toilets and buildings were cleaned two or three times per day. Spitting on the floor of any

Navajo Tribal Chairman Chee Dodge, a popular leader who remembered the
Indian wars, nevertheless encouraged Indian workers at the Bellemont arsenal to put forth their best effort to help win the war.

building was forbidden. Alcohol and gambling, along with stealing,
prostitution, and fighting, were also forbidden. At the soda pop stand—
an important place in the camp—unauthorized persons were not per-
mitted behind the counter. In addition to village regulations, regular
meetings provided a forum for many topics.[54]

Navajo Ordnance Depot, although the second largest ammunition
arsenal in the nation, was certainly the most interesting, colorful, and
rich in culture. In March 1943, Chee Dodge, the eighty-three-year-
old chairman of the Navajo Tribe and a very popular leader, visited
the arsenal and met with his people. In a thirty-five minute patriotic
speech he urged full cooperation in the war effort, total elimina-
tion of absenteeism, and the purchase of war bonds to the greatest

extent possible. Despite cold weather, he "held the undivided attention" of his audience. The significance of this event was not overlooked. Dodge, who as a child in the 1860s had run from his enemy—American soldiers on horseback—had now witnessed young Navajo men and women enlisting in the American armed forces. The horses had been replaced by tanks and airplanes. Somehow, Chee Dodge managed to feel at home in both worlds.[55]

Shortly after Dodge's visit, the depot commemorated the first anniversary of Indian labor in July with a celebration and games organized by the Indian camp council. Over one hundred participants competed. Many were veterans of the rodeo and Flagstaff pow-wow that continued throughout the war. They displayed their skills in calf roping, team tying, pony races, steer riding, cow milking, and men's and women's footraces. Festivities also included performance of the Hopi Buffalo Dance and the Navajo Yeibichai Dance. Around three thousand people attended the celebration and barbecue. In November another Navajo Yeibichai Dance climaxed a nine-day celebration with two thousand in attendance. A medicine man from the reservation did sand-painting, and dancers in full costume visited Flagstaff in a gesture of friendship to the city.[56]

The depot sponsored other events, such as the Indian field day held on Sunday, May 21, 1944. More than four hundred Native Americans from across the reservations, including visitors from Shiprock, New Mexico, participated in Indian Village festivities, which included softball, boxing, tug-of-war, footraces for children and adults, a baby contest, and a barbecue beef dinner. Cash prizes, probably donated by trader Billy Young, were awarded to winners in each contest. The depot's Hopi softball team played against teams from Tuba City and Shiprock.[57]

In 1942, the cultural gap frustrated both army officers and Native Americans. As the war progressed, however, the arrangement proved to be a unique experiment in Navajo and Hopi history. Working in the white man's world and living on a military base presented enormous challenges for those accustomed to distant neighbors and open range. Yet, once the first problems were solved in early 1943, the Navajos and

Indian Field Days were held each year. The festivities included softball, boxing, tug-of-war, foot races for children and adults, a baby contest, and a barbecue beef dinner. Trader Billy Young often donated cash and other prizes
for the winners.

Hopis adapted quickly to the new environment. Handling dangerous
explosives, using heavy equipment and power tools, organizing workers on a large scale, and maintaining strict accountability were skills
foreign to many. Official records note, however, that they "learned easily," and were at times ahead of supervisors in requesting safety schools
at night at Indian Village so they could master munitions handling
more quickly. Workers also requested training for Navajo and Hopi
gang bosses and foremen so that the Indians with schooling could do
their job more efficiently.[58]

The white culture presented many other challenges. The first Indian employees were reluctant to wear safety shoes when handling
ammunition. When in need of medical care, many preferred their own
medicine man and native herbs, using the base hospital only as a last
resort. Workers who received a plaster cast for broken bones frequently

removed the cast even before it was dry. Vaccinations, however, were not objectionable, and village residents took advantage of those available. Indian Village and the bathhouses were often the scene of ten or fifteen accidental and potentially dangerous fires per day, until residents were trained and placed in charge of fire prevention.[59]

Navajos and Hopis, jerked from one culture to another, made many significant adaptations. For most, their bank account had been the number of sheep they owned on the reservation. The army would not allow them to keep sheep on the military base, and they had to find ways to become less tied to their flocks. Billy Young's trading post sheep were supplemented by Navajo vendors who brought mutton from Leupp and set up shop in the back end of a pickup truck at Indian Village. Yet the meat supply in the village fluctuated, unlike on the reservation where mutton was readily available. At Bellemont they had to budget their meat, and some children remember eating "a lot of beans and fried potatoes" toward the end of the month.[60]

As Native Americans absorbed Anglo ideas, army officers and civilian supervisors were no less influenced by Indian culture. The Indian Village generosity in the purchase of war bonds was well known. Many often spent almost their entire paycheck on bonds, setting an invaluable example of patriotism and stimulating others to greater contributions. Word got around that one elderly Navajo man on the reservation, forced by the Indian Service to sell his cattle, put the entire three thousand dollars in war bonds. Likewise, Navajos and Hopis at Indian Village contributed generously to the Red Cross and other campaigns. For the Veterans of Foreign Wars "Buddy Poppy Day" for disabled veterans, some bought numerous poppies and wore them continuously for a week. Many Indian Village families had sons in the armed forces—some had as many as three. Others had brothers or sisters in the service. Agnes Begay's brother Keats, for example, who was first reported missing in action in 1942, was a prisoner of war in a Japanese camp for three years.[61]

As the war progressed toward the hearts of Germany and Japan and the number of incoming and outgoing trains increased dramatically, the Indian ammunition handlers worked long, grueling shifts, often putting in a fourteen-hour day to meet deadlines, all without a word of complaint. In the throes of lifting and moving tons of munitions by hand, long after others began to fade, the strong Indian laborers frequently eased into an atavistic rhythm—a slow cadence—moving in unison as a team controlled by a melodic chant which rose and fell in a succession of ancient tones until the last load was finished. Such rhythmic labor had not been seen on Volunteer Prairie since the gandy dancers laid rails in 1882. Supervisor Shine Smith was humbled by the spectacle of zest, enthusiasm, and dedication, wondering how he could perform his own job as efficiently and with the same light heart and courageous spirit.[62]

Time off was precious for all workers. For Native Americans, the runoff to elect a chairman of the Navajo tribal council provided an excellent opportunity for a free day or two, and they were encouraged to vote. Unfortunately, tribal laws specified that voters had to vote at the polling place on the reservation. Changing the law on short notice was impossible. After long and eloquent arguments were presented, Navajos at Bellemont insisted that their people would not leave the job no matter how bad they wished to vote. That "would be just like helping Hitler and those Japanese," one spokesman stated, "and this our people will not do."[63]

In addition to sings, ceremonial dances, sweat lodges, field day competitions, medicine men, and native herbs, the Navajos and Hopis brought other aspects of their cultures to Bellemont. One Christian missionary quipped that a few seemed to worship everything that crept or crawled. Others carried amulets around in their pockets and some held red ants in a position of esteem for their healing powers. Some had colorful names that fascinated Isabel Simmons in the personnel office, names like Many Mules, Many Goats, Many Whiskers, Boldest Brown Eyes, Hosteen Porthole, Cattle Chaser, Slim Whiskers, Sonny Many Children, Smiley White Sheep, Hosteen Sauerkraut, Mike Soda Pop, Braided Hair Son, and Yellow Man's Grandson.[64]

Coconino County Sheriff Joe Richards, a Bellemont youngster during the war, fondly recalls the sweat lodges scattered around the wood line of Indian Town north of Bellemont and Route 66. In the warm summer evenings of 1942, Richards heard the drums, songs, and chants from the ceremonies drifting melodically across Volunteer Prairie. He listened with a boyhood interest and fascination. At her trailer park, Elgymae Connelley heard the same sounds, which were especially clear when the air was still. Ultimately, Richards credits these evenings for giving him an awareness of a people with another culture. He appreciated those differences, believing it made him more sensitive to others. For Richards, the excellent wartime relations with Indian Village residents resulted in lifelong friendships.[65]

As Anglo, Hispanic, African American, and Native Americans worked more closely together as the war progressed, humor often bridged the cultural divide. Jim Boone, for example, was a large, powerful, and highly respected Navajo general foreman whose sense of humor and strength were legendary. Boone could carry a 155 mm shell weighing almost one hundred pounds by the index finger of each hand. Although he spoke almost no English, Boone was known by all depot employees—especially for his good-natured dubbing of officers as "easy money" because they worked behind a desk. Boone was, however, a natural leader and the depot's most valuable foreman.[66]

Over the years Boone earned a reputation as a very reliable weather forecaster. Despite limited English, he would accurately predict the weather in just a few words, such as "tomorrow snow" or "tonight rain." Even if sunny, he had an uncanny if not mystical sense for recognizing storms in the near future. His extraordinary gift became well known and respected. Workers constantly asked him how he knew. What was his secret? Where did his mysterious powers come from? After much speculation, and several years after the war, they finally pinned him down. Boone burst out laughing and finally let his secret out: "KCLS," he said, the local Flagstaff radio station.[67]

Boone enjoyed practical jokes. One day he killed a prairie dog, skinned and cooked it, stuffed it into his lunch basket, and took it to work. Offering to share his lunch with an Anglo coworker, Boone told him to help himself. The worker opened the sack and was startled to find the strange-looking creature. He asked Boone what it was. "A puppy dog," Boone replied.[68]

Jim Boone passes along the line in one of several field lunchrooms. Boone became a general foreman and highly respected leader. He could carry by the index finger of each hand a shell weighing almost one hundred pounds.

Boone also knew how to get things done. When one of his workers was not performing, Boone picked him up and threw him into a snow bank. In another incident, Boone was accidentally left stranded one evening at an igloo miles from Indian Village when tractor-trailers departed without him. Boone eventually made his way to a loading dock, and, unfamiliar with telephones, began dialing numbers at random until finally someone answered. Boone grumbled, "Jim Boone . . . no bus . . . goddamn!" and hung up. The listener wasted no time getting the important foreman back to camp.[69]

Meetings of Anglo and Indian supervisors at the headquarters were often interesting. At one conference it happened that only two whites were seated among many Native Americans. One Indian finally broke the ice, quipping, "Ah, Red power at last." At other postwar meetings, almost all except the base commander and Ward Olson (the senior civilian advisor to the commander) were Native American—Navajos on one side of the table, Hopis the other. The meetings progressed slowly and consumed hours because Ray Seumptewa had to translate for the Hopis, who apparently spoke limited English, and someone else translated for the Navajos. However, after getting around the arsenal a little, it dawned on Olson that most of the supervisors in attendance spoke excellent English. At the next meeting Olson got straight to the point, saying, "I know you all can speak English. Let's cut out this translating." An immediate silence fell over the group. Suddenly, all the Indians burst out laughing and someone ruefully said, "Well, I guess it's over."[70]

Depot leaders soon realized that Native American humor could be very intriguing. Isabel Simmons, at a meeting with about thirty Navajos and Hopis in the headquarters basement, called one to come to the front. As he walked through the aisles he was deliberately tripped and fell flat at Simmons' feet. As he got up, he never said a word and all of the faces in the audience were deadpan, solemn as could be—but dying of laughter on the inside. According to Simmons, "You didn't have a ghost of a chance of finding who did it."[71]

At the same time, depot leaders came to appreciate Native American self-restraint. One Navajo veteran had just returned from service in the Marines as a sergeant. His English was excellent and he "got along beautifully" with those interviewing him for a depot job. However, one administrator who apparently offended the young sergeant soon called asking why they had recommended a Navajo who spoke no English. As Isabel Simmons noted, some had passive resistance down to a science.[72]

Native Americans were not the only transplanted culture working at Bellemont. On the east side of the military base, soldiers held a group of young men under guard in the old CCC barracks. These men labored at all tasks around much of the base except those directly involved with munitions. They were lean, strong, and healthy, seasoned from service in North Africa, southern France, and months of picking cotton in southern Arizona's scorching fields. They were some of Hitler's former soldiers, now prisoners of war sent north from the overflowing camp at Florence.

5

"DON'T DO ANYTHING STUPID!"
Austrian Prisoners of War

The severe labor shortage at Navajo Ordnance Depot that attracted several thousand Navajos and Hopis to Bellemont also brought 250 prisoners of war. Part of the 425,000 captive enemy soldiers in the United States, they arrived at Bellemont late in the war and remained months beyond the war's end on V-J Day. They finally departed almost a year after the Allied victory in Europe. Their story, from capture to internment in the Bellemont stockade, provides not only valuable information about depot operations during World War II, but also sheds light on Flagstaff attitudes and concerns as well.

The transfer of prisoners of war to Navajo Ordnance Depot was part of a rapidly expanding program for which there was no World War I precedent. Fewer than six thousand POWs had been interned in the United States from 1917 to 1919, and most of those were enemy aliens. Postwar planning for future internments was incomplete. Even as involvement in World War II seemed inevitable by September 1941, the army's request for the construction of one permanent POW camp was disapproved for lack of funds. Hence, the United States entered World War II with no permanent camps in use or under construction.[1]

As late as May of 1942 only 32 prisoners of war—a single Japanese soldier and 31 Germans—were held in the United States. For the moment, the interwar reluctance to build camps appeared justified. In August, however, the U.S. State Department begrudgingly offered to accept POWs from Britain and share the burden by bringing some of the captured enemy soldiers back to the United States on otherwise empty supply or troop ships that had discharged their cargo in Britain or elsewhere. A few months later, in April of 1943, only 5,007 POWs were interned domestically. Following the May surrender in Tunisia of 275,000 soldiers of Rommel's Afrika Korps, prisoners began arriving in the United States at the alarming rate of 30,000 per month. By September, an astonishing 163,706 prisoners were housed somewhere in the United States and thousands more stepped off ships each month.[2]

The extraordinary 1943 influx forced the government to intern enemy soldiers at military and civilian installations throughout the country. Security was the most pressing concern. The War Department directed that camps be located away from coasts and international borders that might facilitate escape. Additionally, camps located in mild climates would hold internment costs to a minimum. Consequently, two-thirds of the base camps housing about three-fourths of the prisoners of war were located in the south and southwest regions of the United States.[3]

The military reservation two miles north of Florence, Arizona, fit the program nicely. As early as January 1942 the War Department directed that a permanent enemy alien camp, not a POW camp, be constructed on the desert site. Engineers designed the camp for three thousand internees, capable of expansion to six thousand. Completed in mid-1942, Camp Florence served first as a staging area for North Africa–bound soldiers in Operation Torch. Following their departure, the site was then expanded into a POW camp capable of holding six thousand prisoners with the December 1942 construction of barbed wire fences, guard towers, and additional barracks. The first prisoners of war were Italian soldiers who began arriving in May 1943. The Italians remained at Florence until August 1944, spending much of their time in political arguments, insulting each other, throwing stones, playing soccer, fighting, and rioting—which sometimes forced guards to go in with billy clubs and teargas. They were moved to camps on the West Coast to make room for German and Austrian soldiers captured in North Africa, Italy, and France.[4]

Josef Papp was an Austrian prisoner of war destined for camps at Florence and Bellemont. Drafted into the German army from his Austrian hometown of Hinterbrühl, Papp arrived in southern France on May 1, 1944, as part of the German Nineteenth Army of Army Group G. When General Alexander Patch's Seventh Army swept toward Papp's fighting position somewhere around Montélimar, France, in August 1944, Papp asked a Frenchman to find an American soldier so he could surrender. Papp had no intention of giving his life for Hitler.[5]

After a few weeks at interim camps at Oran or Naples, Papp, Otto Grünberger, Walter Gastgeb, and Friedrich Gröbner set out on Liberty Ships once again, this time for the naval base at Norfolk, Virginia. Friedrich Gröbner put his artistic skills to good use during the Atlantic crossing, trading his drawings with American servicemen for more than six thousand cigarettes. Walter Gastgeb was part of a July 1944 convoy of about one hundred Liberty Ships, many of which had just unloaded food and coal in Europe. After leaving their Italian ports, fifty warships joined the parade to ward off German submarines. After a tedious four weeks at sea, the large convoy arrived at Norfolk where the POWs were stripped, showered, shaved, and given a haircut and a new uniform with a large "P W" printed on back and front.[6]

The Arizona-bound prisoners spent three or four days on the train crossing the United States in what was undoubtedly an enlightening experience for some. The America they viewed from the train windows as they traveled west contrasted sharply from the images of a bomb–damaged nation and wartime economy crippled by strikes and dissension portrayed in Nazi propaganda. Pittsburgh's great industrial and manufacturing plants "caused their eyes to bulge," as did the number of automobiles cruising along streets and highways, or parked in the lots of war plants in full production. Astounded by the sheer size of the country they had been fighting, some of the captured soldiers sought answers from their fellow prisoners who had lived in the United States before the war.[7]

The railcars "continued to roll westward day and night and on and on." Some of the prisoners began to suspect that their trains were running in circles to further demoralize their passengers. "Is there no end to it?" they asked their comrades. The longer they rode the lower their spirits fell. As Friedrich Gröbner's train pulled into Chicago, people stood by the tracks and taunted the soldiers with photographs of prisoners being hanged. Others made grotesque gestures of someone hanging with a noose around their neck. Walter Gastgeb, on a southern train, was struck by segregation in the South where waiting rooms were marked for white and colored, not dissimilar to his own nation's separation of Jews and "Aryans."[8]

The influx of Austrian prisoners in 1944 presented problems at Florence and across the nation. Should they be confined with Germans? Some of the American public viewed Austrians as "redeemable" from the "hopelessly unsalvageable" Germans. Secretary of State Cordell Hull stated that the U.S. government had taken the position that Austria was not legally absorbed into the German Reich. Austria, after all, was not included in the official list of states against which the United States waged war and nine treaties or agreements remained in effect in April 1945. Adolf Berle, assistant secretary of state, noted that as early as October 1941, Austria's Archduke Otto Habsburg, although exiled in the United States, urged forming committees of national aspiration.[9]

As early as January 1942, the month after Germany declared war on the United States, Austria tried to separate itself from the Reich. In August the anti-Nazi monthly newspaper *Freiheit für Oesterreich*, published in New York by the Assembly for a Democratic Austrian Republic, called for the creation of an Austrian fighting force and recognition of Austria as the twenty-ninth state among the United Nations. Soon, some Austrian POWs requested permission to form an Austrian Legion to battle Nazi Germany. Meanwhile, the *Austro-American Tribune* also called for segregation of prisoners.

Despite these numerous arguments, it was difficult to overlook the fact that Austria had joined the Reich voluntarily. Many were happy to be part of Nazi Germany. Hitler was Austrian, as were several others in the Nazi inner circle. Yet, in mid-1944 at Camp Meade, Maryland, for example, only eight of the fifty-one Austrian POWs were considered hard-core Nazis. By April 29, 1944, Secretary of War Henry L. Stimson had agreed in principle to the segregation of Austrian prisoners and implementation eventually followed.[10]

When the train finally arrived at Camp Florence the prisoners were surprised by the size of the main camp, which held almost four thousand men, and the satellite camps holding an additional five thousand. They were greeted by the senior German officer who said something about "signing." As they marched into camp, veteran POWs yelled out "Don't sign it, or you'll be a traitor to the Fatherland!" The group, having no idea what they were talking about, was brought to a large hall where a table full of papers stood conspicuously in the middle of the room. Following an explanation of the special document in German, each prisoner gave his name and POW number. Then, each was given the opportunity to sign the document or decline. Additionally, they were given the right to withdraw the document at any time by submitting a written notice. Papp, Gastgeb, Grünberger, and Gröbner signed, as did at least eight hundred other Austrian POWs. By signing, they pledged on their honor as a German army soldier to work as required and accomplish all tasks to the best of their ability, to not attempt escape or encourage or aid others' escape, to return promptly to camp after work, and to do nothing injurious to the United States.[11]

Some, no doubt, believed signing the document was an early ticket home. The statement was carefully crafted by camp commander Col. Verne Snell and his staff to encourage discipline and reduce the guard requirement. Signers received more freedom and less guard supervision, but not necessarily better treatment. Snell ensured that there were no politically charged overtones. It was not an anti-Nazi document. It was merely a pledge to be a model prisoner of war—something Snell especially needed, considering the numerous discipline problems with hunger strikes, refusals to work, and agitation.[12]

The separation of Austrians into pro- and anti-Nazi camps at Florence was done carefully by an American army intelligence officer originally from Vienna. As Papp remembers, he was quite bright and used precise terms that had significant political and cultural implications. The officer offered separate camps for the "Ostmarkers" and "Oesterreichers" and let them separate themselves. *Ostmark* was a term for Austria that had pro-Nazi connotations, whereas *Oesterreiche* was the traditional German word for Austria. With the war raging and Allied victory still uncertain, many were afraid of eventual reprisals if they claimed national identity as Austrian or Oesterreichers. Those signing the document and identifying themselves as Oesterreichers were placed in a separate compound no later than early October 1944, in the Twenty-eighth Austrian Company.

The Austrians who signed were called traitors by some of the Germans. They called themselves the "Free Austrian" camp and were given a white armband labeled "Austria." They were also segregated by rank, with officers housed in a separate area. The senior German prisoner declared that the "Free Austrians" had nothing in common with Germans and therefore would no longer share the Red Cross packages coming from Berlin–Babelsberg.[13]

When the base camps like Florence and Papago Park filled to capacity in 1944, the army's provost marshal general directed decentralization of prisoners into temporary branch camps, provided the transfers did not require additional construction. To meet the need for more space, he instructed local commanders to use old CCC buildings and even tents to house POWs. By the spring of 1945 the army operated 155 base camps around the country, each holding several thousand prisoners, and over 500 branch camps, each holding between 250 and 750 men. Eventually, the POW camps in the continental United States held the largest concentration ever of enemy soldiers on American soil—an army of over 425,000 prisoners.[14]

In Arizona, the base camps at Florence and Papago Park sent POWs to twenty-two branch camps where most prisoners did agricultural work, many picking cotton. With the exception of Navajo Ordnance Depot, all of Arizona's camps were in the southern half of the state. They included Camps Parker, Yuma, Blythe, Roll, Buckeye I and II, Litchfield Park, Mesa, Queen Creek, Safford, Duncan, Stanfield, Casa Grande, Eloy I and II, Eleven Mile Corner, Marana, Cortaro I and II, Continental, and Davis–Monthan Army Air Corps Base.[15]

The Florence camp divided the Austrian "signers" into two companies, one destined for Bellemont, the other for Logan, Utah, where more than five hundred were eventually housed in the all-Austrian camp at the Cache County Fair Grounds and were visible to those

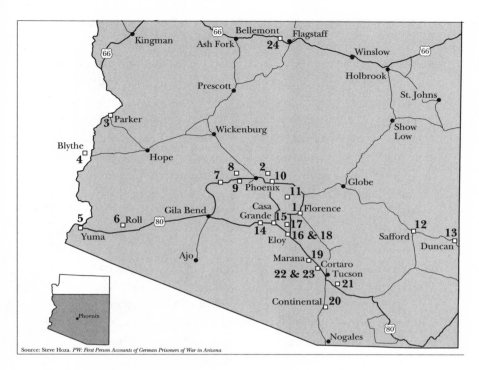

Prisoner of war camps in Arizona

Base Camps
1. Camp Florence
2. Camp Papago Park

Branch Camps
3. Camp Parker
4. Blythe Sidecamp (California)
5. Yuma Sidecamp
6. Camp Roll
7. Camp Buckeye II
8. Camp Litchfield Park
9. Camp Buckeye I (also known as the
   Avondale Camp)
10. Mesa Sidecamp
11. Queen Creek Sidecamp
12. Safford Sidecamp
13. Duncan Sidecamp
14. Stanfield Sidecamp
15. Case Grande Sidecamp
16. Camp Eloy I

17. Camp Eleven Mile Corner
18. Camp Eloy II
19. Marana Sidecamp
20. Camp Continental
21. Davis-Monthan Army Air Corps
    Base
22. Camp Cortaro I
23. Camp Cortaro II
24. Navajo Ordnance Depot
    (Bellemont)

passing by en route to the rodeo arena. The Logan camp was particularly detested because of the commander's lack of understanding and unnecessary strictness. Ultimately, tensions in Logan were so bad that the prisoners came "within a hair's breadth of being machine-gunned" when they protested against longer work hours. Utah was already the scene of tragedy when an American guard opened fire on sleeping prisoners at the Salina camp—killing nine, wounding nineteen.[16]

Ever haunted by the labor shortage, Colonel Huling had requested prisoners of war as early as 1943. Knowing full well that V-E Day would dramatically increase Pacific-bound shipments for the invasion of Japan, he was pleased when, on Saturday, March 24, 1945, a military police detail of one officer and fifteen enlisted men escorted thirty Austrian prisoners of war from Florence to Navajo Ordnance Depot. Huling ordered the men interned in the old CCC camp on the northeast corner of the base, just a few hundred yards south of the Santa Fe Railroad tracks and Route 66, a site that had formerly been occupied by the detachment of black soldiers before they were transferred elsewhere. The thirty-man Austrian advance party began turning the barracks into a stockade with barbed wire fences and guard towers.[17]

When the *Coconino Sun*'s bold headline of March 30, 1945 mistakenly announced the arrival of thirty "German" prisoners with 220 more enlisted men and noncommissioned officers to follow, many Flagstaff residents were justifiably concerned. Although V-E Day was just ten weeks away, the war continued to rage in Europe and everyone in town was aware of the great escape from Papago Park.

A January incident revealed the anxiety of a local Flagstaff policeman when he stopped two Winslow High School boys, George Spears and Ed Singer, who were walking to the train station after a basketball game. Ed Singer, in a smart aleck fashion, snorted "Was ist los?" [What's the matter?]. The remark triggered a knee-jerk reaction from the policeman who was fully aware of the Papago Park escape just a few weeks earlier. He drew his revolver and, with his arm shaking and the barrel pointing in the faces of the youngsters, demanded they get in the patrol car and shut up. Spears remembers the large cannon flailing wildly around the car as the nervous officer yelled "Don't say any-

About 250 Austrian soldiers of the German army were held at the prisoner of war camp, formerly the Civilian Conservation Corps barracks built in 1933. The camp was on the east side of the depot adjacent to the railroad tracks. The Austrians arrived in March 1945 and were not repatriated until April 1946.

thing, just stay where you are." At the Flagstaff police station the boys' true identity was finally determined. The chief, obviously embarrassed, offered the boys a ride home if they would not tell their parents. Spears' father, the editor of the *Winslow Mail*, only later learned of the incident.[18]

Colonel Huling quickly reassured the neighboring Flagstaff community that the Austrian prisoners were needed and posed no threat. He emphasized that POW labor would be restricted to maintenance at the depot and that the prisoners would not handle or transport munitions of any kind, nor material intended for combat units, nor would they be allowed in Flagstaff. Huling cited and the *Coconino Sun* printed fifteen pertinent provisions of the 1932 Geneva Convention dealing with prisoner of war treatment.

This, however, did not sit well with *Coconino Sun* editor Columbus Giragi who, in a front-page editorial, mocked the intent of Article 1 which dealt with protecting prisoners from violence, insults, and public curiosity. Giragi gloated that the Austrians were "more humble NOW than . . . when they were goose-stepping with the Nazi hordes, and prepared to kill every American possible." He went on, facetiously imploring citizens to be "DOUBLY cautious" about insulting our guests or injuring their "tender sentimentalities" by public nosiness— despite the Papago Park escapees who were recently "captured with whole slabs of bacon in their possession." Closing with the famous Battle of the Bulge comment "NUTS!" Giragi's column helped set an ominous tone in Flagstaff.[19]

But labor rather than purloined bacon presented the depot commander with his first real problems, according to the *Coconino Sun*. Within days of the POWs' arrival, Wade Church, president of the Arizona State Federation of Labor and formerly with the Atkinson-Kier Company during depot construction, protested to Arizona Senator Carl Hayden. Church claimed the prisoners were taking jobs away from Flagstaff workers and that POW labor posed a "great danger of sabotage." According to Flagstaff Labor Temple vice president W. H. Browne, plenty of civilian workers were available locally, but the army was unwilling to pay rates established at depots in southern California, Utah, and Nevada.[20]

In telegrams to Senator Hayden, Colonel Huling stated that, claims to the contrary notwithstanding, there was in fact a civilian labor shortage in the Flagstaff area and that the depot was two hundred workers below its personnel ceiling. Huling hoped that prisoner labor would release from depot maintenance civilian workers who could then be used to handle the expected 100 percent surge in workload after V-E Day. In response to Browne's allegations of unfair wage scales, Huling reminded Hayden that rates at Navajo Depot were based on a War Department survey and were comparable to those paid by other industries in the vicinity. He went on to point out that during the previous six months POWs throughout the nation had performed almost twenty-four million man-days of labor, much of it in areas of the country that were suffering from manpower shortages.[21]

The War Department's policy as authorized by the Geneva Convention was to work enemy prisoners. Creation of the decentralized branch camp system not only took pressure off base camps but, perhaps more importantly, ensured that precious prisoner labor would be used efficiently across the nation. Post commanders were responsible for ensuring that every prisoner of war performed a full day's work every day—regardless of where they labored. Prisoners at Navajo Depot were paid ten cents per hour, or eighty cents for a full day's work. This rate had been established in 1942 and was based on the monthly pay of an army private in 1941—twenty-one dollars per month. To prevent prisoners from stowing away hard currency for an eventual escape, the army paid them with canteen coupons from Florence or Papago Park or credited their pay to a trust fund. In addition, each POW was given ten cents per day in coupons to purchase personal items at the canteen.[22]

POW installations around the nation were generally divided into agricultural camps, where prisoners labored on nearby farms, and military camps, where they lived and labored on base. When helping farmers, their reception was much warmer, often forming lasting friendships that continued after the war. At Navajo Ordnance Depot, however, prisoners did not go into town, although they had contact with Flagstaff residents who worked at the depot.[23]

The POW company commander Lt. Adam Paskiewicz and his wife arrived at Navajo Depot during the first week of April 1945. He was the officer directly responsible for the enemy soldiers. Paskiewicz was a military police officer with extensive training and experience with POW camps, especially branch camps where prisoners numbered between seven and nine hundred. Paskiewicz knew his job, having also worked at Florence prior to Bellemont.[24]

The use of POW labor at Navajo Depot remained a contentious issue with Flagstaff union leaders. Many local residents also expressed their concern that the prisoners were being treated too fairly, if not leniently. Resentment boiled to the surface and Colonel Huling was forced to send officers into town to discuss the situation.

On Thursday, April 5, 1945, Lt. Donald H. Jones, the depot's public relations officer, spoke at the Flagstaff Lions Club meeting at

Hotel Monte Vista. He reiterated Colonel Huling's position on the use of POWs to alleviate the labor shortage at the arsenal. He also explained how the prisoners would help free up civilian workers to meet the anticipated surge in munitions. Jones also reacted to rumors and innuendos floating around the luncheon and the community by assuring his audience that the prisoners were not being coddled and were doing a full day's work. He emphasized that they were Austrians, and that none of them were members of the Nazi party or sympathizers. Jones' sweeping conclusion of no sympathizers, however, was probably questionable despite the prisoners' "signing."[25]

The following week, on Friday, April 13, Capt. Louis W. Regester, the depot's personnel officer, spoke at a courthouse meeting of the American Legion, Veterans of Foreign Wars, discharged World War II veterans, and other citizens. Public unrest about the local prisoner situation continued to fester, and many of those present again voiced their objections to the perceived coddling of POWs. Pointing to newspaper accounts of atrocities committed against American prisoners of war in Japan and Germany, a number of attendees characterized treatment of the Austrian prisoners as "too fair" and recommended harsher discipline.

In response, Captain Regester reminded the audience that the army had no choice but to handle prisoners according to the provisions of the Geneva Convention. He also pointed out that the depot employed 91 discharged World War II veterans and 123 World War I veterans, and was still 200 workers short. Tommy Burns, a North Africa veteran, called for cooperation to enable the depot to do its job. Another depot officer, Capt. Paul Bowsher, asked for "cool-headed understanding" to help shorten the war and save American lives.[26]

On Tuesday, April 17, just four days later, depot officers were called upon once again to clear up "rumors and misunderstandings" that POWs had access to scarce items when others in the community couldn't get them. Lieutenants Jones and Paskiewicz spoke at the weekly Rotary Club meeting to clarify the army's policy concerning rationed commodities and treatment of prisoners. Jones emphasized, for example, that prisoners had access to only cigarettes sent from their homeland through the International Red Cross. Despite Jones's assertion, however, the POWs probably already had American cigarettes or soon got them.[27]

Construction of the stockade proceeded despite Browne's continued criticism of prisoner labor and wages paid to depot workers. On April 12, as Navajo Depot and the world learned of President Roosevelt's death, the POW camp was officially established. By the end of April, after one month of prisoner labor on the stockade, Colonel Huling reported that "Civilian foremen, supervising the labor crews of prisoners of war, have spoken favorably of the work turned out, the eagerness and willingness of the prisoners to do a good job on any assigned labor. No favoritism is shown and there is no fraternizing or coddling, either in treatment or food. We are interested only in being enabled to do our job. Prisoners of war are giving us valuable mandays of necessary labor, at a time when labor is badly needed."[28]

The camp was finally activated on May 5 with a staff of three officers and twenty-seven enlisted men assigned by Headquarters, Ninth Service Command at Fort Douglas in Salt Lake City. The camp commander, Capt. Weldon M. Miller, was in charge of camp administration and security. He was assisted by an adjutant and Lieutenant Paskiewicz, the POW company commander. Six enlisted men handled administration and twenty-six guarded the stockade. All had received training in administration and handling of prisoners of war. The stockade was ready to accept the rest of the Austrian company.[29]

The remaining 220 Austrian prisoners of war from Florence arrived at Navajo Ordnance Depot the following week, bringing the total complement to a full 250-man company. About 40 percent of the men may have been veterans of Rommel's Afrika Korps and probably were not anti-Nazi or Austrian separatists. Regardless, they immediately set to work. Twenty-one prisoners worked inside the POW compound, where most were cooks. Others were responsible for barracks maintenance, or worked in company administration, latrine maintenance, or as barbers or carpenters.[30]

The remaining 229 prisoners were scattered across the depot, working in almost all activities except those involving direct contact with ammunition. Forty-three worked in supply, salvage, and dunnage; 30 on the railroad; 18 on sidewalk and asphalt repair; 18 on woodcutting details; 14 at the gas station and motor pool; and the remainder as forklift operators, janitors, plumbers, carpenters, in the hospital, on various engineering projects, and on POW camp repairs. Five worked at the most coveted job of all, as pinspotters in the bowling alley, where they competed against each other for the fastest spot and were soon recognized for their speed and efficiency.[31]

One of the prisoners' first tasks was to build a stone and cement marker for religious services on the north side of the compound. They set to work on May 11, with Josef Papp among those mixing concrete. The leader of the project, Isfried F. Schmid, was a noncommissioned officer and a Catholic priest who had been captured in southern France. Schmid placed a small glass jar inside the monument as a time capsule. The jar contained a photo of himself, an Austrian coin, pictures of Christ and Holy Father Pius XII, and a prayer: "We are thankful for the end of the tremendous terror and pray for our future. May all governing people negotiate rather than send their people into war." Schmid also enclosed a second prayer: "May the Lord not punish us any more with the swastika. Our past belongs to the grace of God. Our future belongs to the plans of God. Our present belongs to the love of God. Nothing is worse than sin alone, which separates us from the highest grace of God. Oh Lord, pour your Grace here upon us."[32]

After Schmid placed the time capsule inside the marker, the prisoners added more cement and rocks and finished the impressive monument that stood over six feet tall, a testament to the faith of the captives. An opening at the top contained a crucifix. In front of the monument, prisoners used rocks to outline an area to hold Mass.

The compound provided minimum necessities required by the Geneva Convention. The POWs lived in four barracks, two for sixty men, two for sixty-five. Although each building was about 160 feet long and 25 feet wide, with twenty-five windows and three coal-burning stoves, the prisoners were cramped. When the full 250-man company was present, the post surgeon noted that prisoners suffered from a large number of respiratory infections due to the congested quar-

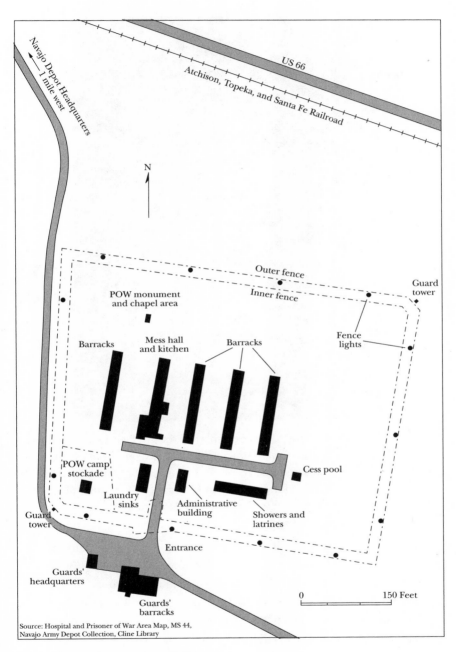

US 66

Atchison, Topeka, and Santa Fe Railroad

Navajo Depot Headquarters
1 mile west

N

Outer fence

Inner fence

Guard tower

POW monument
and chapel area

Barracks

Mess hall
and kitchen

Barracks

Fence
lights

POW camp
stockade

Cess pool

Laundry
sinks

Administrative
building

Showers and
latrines

Guard
tower

Entrance

Guards'
headquarters

0   150 Feet

Guards'
barracks

Source: Hospital and Prisoner of War Area Map, MS 44,
Navajo Army Depot Collection, Cline Library

The prisoner of war camp at Bellemont

Austrian Josef Papp, captured as an engineer in the German army, returned to the site of the prisoner of war camp in 1998. He has fond memories of his POW days at Bellemont, and stands over the monument he help build in May 1945. During restoration of the monument by Stan Cornforth and the Flagstaff Route 66 Car Club in 2001, the time capsule was discovered inside.

ters. An adjacent building had fifteen showers, twenty-one hand sinks, and ten laundry sinks supplied with large quantities of soap. The prisoners slept on white metal bunk beds with bedding similar to that of an army private. The kitchen had two stoves, an oven, a large refrigerator, and tables for the cooks. All kitchen workers received monthly medical inspections and certificates were posted on the wall. Although a liberal use of DDT ensured that the two large field latrines remained

free of most insects and rodents, flies were a constant problem throughout the stockade because the latrines, showers, mess hall, kitchen, and
barracks were all without screens.[33]

Papp, Gastgeb, Grünberger, Gröbner, and the other prisoners
voiced no complaints about the nature or quantity of their rations.
Two meals per day were served in the mess hall and prisoners usually
took a sack lunch to work. Meals on a typical day consisted of a breakfast of coffee, rolled oats, bread, and apple cake; a lunch of two cold
beef-heart sandwiches, one peanut butter sandwich, bread and water;
and a dinner of potato soup, macaroni with sugar, dried apples, bread,
and coffee. The hearty menu may have had something to do with the
high morale when they first arrived at Bellemont. Papp described the
food as "Very good. Nothing like this in the German army."[34]

Despite the depot's chronic labor shortage, Colonel Huling was
often forced to release prisoners for temporary labor at other branch
camps, usually working for farmers or picking cotton. Consequently,
prisoners were often coming and going, depending upon agricultural
needs around the state.

At first, life in the POW compound was satisfactory, if not comfortable. The men had two sets of clothes, good medical care at the
base hospital, a small library of 130 books (80 in German), magazines,
their own orchestra, games from the YMCA, and stenography and
Russian classes taught by fellow prisoners. A German Catholic priest
from Flagstaff, along with a Lutheran pastor and prisoner Schmid,
provided religious services each Sunday. The canteen was well stocked
to include good-quality smoking pipes and, contrary to the first reports, the men eventually received two ounces of tobacco per week.
Canteen profits went back to the prisoners.[35]

The magazine rack contained several magazines along with one
publication of special interest, *Der Ruf* (The Call). As Americans sensed
victory in 1944, many called for the education of liberal-minded prisoners in democratic principles to enable them to participate in the
postwar political makeup of Germany and Austria. Unbeknownst to
the American public, a secret War Department program had been in
place since early 1943. The concept provided historical and ethical

fundamentals of Western civilization to prisoners through motion pictures, music, art, educational courses, and news. The prisoner's own newspaper, *Der Ruf,* was a sophisticated German-language publication created by select German POWs at the indoctrination headquarters, secretly referred to as the "Factory," at Fort Philip Kearney, Rhode Island, and distributed to all camps. Secrecy was required to ensure that Nazi Germany did not reciprocate and try to indoctrinate our ninety thousand servicemen in German camps.[36]

Most of the base camps published their own newspaper written by POWs. The Navajo Depot camp, too small for its own paper, probably had access to the Florence *Arizona Sonne,* as did POWs rotating through Florence. Although not associated with the political indoctrination carefully woven into *Der Ruf,* the January 27, 1946, issue of the *Arizona Sonne* criticized Hitler's war. The twenty-four-page paper provided brief outlines of American and Arizona history, news from Germany, discussions of the Nazi regime, English lessons, an Austrian page devoted to music, news from Washington and Vienna, and columns on sports, the International Red Cross, and camp-related news.[37]

The climate and mountains of northern Arizona resembled parts of Austria and the prisoners of war found the location very appealing, especially after working in the sizzling cotton fields of southern Arizona. Artist Friedrich Gröbner found the Wild West lure of Arizona intoxicating. While in Florence he made pencil sketches of a bowlegged cowboy holding a rifle and a sheriff with revolver drawn, along with desert landscapes. At Bellemont Gröbner drew the scene from his barracks window—a barbed wire fence and Santa Fe train in the foreground overshadowed by rolling pine-covered hills and the San Francisco Peaks. He sketched the face of his Navajo foreman, and wooden knives with Indian-head handles. Another prisoner painted a watercolor of the peaks and gave it to depot employee Glenn Tinnin. Most were happy with their work, and one prisoner even declared, "If we could have our families here, we'd like to stay forever."[38]

The prisoners especially enjoyed working at Indian Village where they cut wood and dug irrigation ditches. They found the experience

Former POW Friedrich Gröbner was an accomplished artist who, during the Atlantic crossing, traded his drawings for thousands of cigarettes. He sketched this view from the window of his barracks inside the camp. Austrian POWs took comfort in the Flagstaff area mountains that reminded them of home.

rewarding because the local children were very friendly and, since many men had younger brothers and sisters, the Indian camp reminded them of home. Gastgeb found the experience fascinating and learned to appreciate the Navajo and Hopi cultures, especially when an Indian woman gave birth in the field, cut the umbilical cord, and returned to work with the crying child. Scott Franklin, who lived in Indian Village with his wife Amy, became friends with one of the prisoners while working in a warehouse. Artist R. C. Gorman, as noted earlier, remembers the prisoners roaming freely about the camp doing various jobs under friendly circumstances. Gorman could not visualize a similar situation with Anglos working alongside prisoners of war.[39]

The relationship between the Austrian prisoners of war and the Navajos and Hopis was unique to Navajo Depot. There is no evidence of any interaction of significance elsewhere in the army's POW camp system between prisoners and other Native American tribes. At Navajo Depot the prisoners sometimes worked under the supervision of Indians and sometimes worked alongside. Some prisoners and Indians became friends.[40]

Many prisoners of war were intrigued by the Indian cultures that were so foreign to Europe. The Austrians' fascination with the Navajos and Hopis stemmed, perhaps in part, from stories by the popular German author Karl May (1842–1912), whose adventures set in the American Southwest were very sympathetic to the plight of Native Americans. May's novels advocated Indian rights, bemoaned Indian extinction, and viewed marriage between races as normal. His Western novels sold almost one hundred million copies in German and dozens of millions in thirty-three other languages, easily making May the most successful German author of all time in the number of works sold. May captured the imagination of several generations of Europeans despite the fact that he had never visited the American West. Austrian and German fans, one of whom—despite May's advocacy of miscegenation—was Hitler, read about the noble Apache chief Winnetou and the moral cowboy Old Shatterhand.[41]

Josef Papp made several Indian friends. He enjoyed his hospital work alongside Navajos Grace Dean, Tall Whiskers, John Bluehouse, Rodger Begody, and Natney Bitney. At Indian Village, prisoners not only had contact with children and adults, but also assisted with daily village routines. Prisoners policed the area around Richardson's Trading Post and along the road where they might have seen a Navajo or Hopi ceremony. Walter Gastgeb remembers observing the differences between the two native cultures, and being especially intrigued by the Navajos, some of whom still lived in hogans at Indian Village.[42]

The Navajos, Hopis, and Austrian prisoners had several things in common. In some respects they were all refugees. The Indians had left the reservations and settled among foreigners. The Austrians, likewise, were even further from home. Living conditions were foreign—a residential setting for the Indians, a stockade for the Austrians. Most of the POWs and Indians could not speak English fluently with depot supervisors and employees. Yet, they managed to exchange ideas and form friendships. Both groups were living in a foreign culture with routines and tasks that were often unfamiliar. Although the barbed wire surrounding Indian Village was easily breached, Gorman recognized that the wire spoke of more than just security, it spoke about life.[43]

In addition to work at Indian Village, the Austrians also did repairs and maintenance at Victory Village where children like Sally O'Connell (Veazey) knew they were the "enemy." She remembers the prisoners had a wonderful time with the children and brought them piñon nuts, oranges, and other treats.[44]

When the anticipated surge in munitions heading for the Pacific hit the depot after V-E Day, prisoners did their share by freeing others to work on munitions. A few days later POWs were dispatched to fight a forest fire on Schultz Pass. Responding to a call from U.S. Forest Service supervisor R. W. Hussey, Colonel Huling sent Gastgeb, Papp and eighty other prisoners to assist 120 local firefighters who had been unable to contain the fire by themselves due to strong winds and steep terrain. Assigned to the highest and steepest sector of the fire where it threatened to break over into the Inner Basin, the POWs freed up local firefighters to concentrate on other sectors of the blaze. Once the fire was under control, Gastgeb couldn't resist a two-hour hike to the summit where he enjoyed the view. Another prisoner pinched a large case of firefighter rations, thereby supplementing his stockade food for weeks. Hussey praised the POWs as "willing, aggressive firefighters ... [who] did a first-class job of strengthening their part of the line and working the fire back from the edges of the burn."[45]

Although the POWs had proved their worth during the fire, some local residents continued to grumble about easy treatment. In fact, contrary to Colonel Huling's assertions, there was some merit to the rumors of leniency. Papp, for example, found conditions at Bellemont to his liking. It was much easier than picking cotton at the Continental camp just south of Tucson, his most difficult time. At Bellemont he labored on various depot projects and in the hospital ward where soldiers, depot workers, and prisoners were treated. Papp even assisted in two serious operations.[46]

Despite command efforts, the proximity of prisoners and civilian workers resulted in some fraternization in the camp and on the job. Walter Gastgeb, for example, had a brief liaison with a female employee. Josef Papp remembers smooching with a nurse. Johann Mitsch had an Indian girlfriend. One guard brought a guitar into the prisoner barracks and played songs, leaving his rifle in the corner of the building where it remained untouched by anyone. One day in the headquarters building, Lois Ferguson (Price), Mary Pitts, and other women were ogling a handsome young prisoner who was working high on a ladder and presumably did not understand their conversation. They talked admiringly about the rugged Austrian soldier—that is, until he turned around, grinned, and said in perfect English, "May I have a hammer?" Many prisoners and female employees were about the same age. With perhaps a third of depot employees being women, some, like Peggy Davern, found that working alongside prisoners of war was "exciting, dangerous, and fun!"[47]

Papp has pleasant memories of Bellemont: "It was a nice time for us . . . a much better life than I had as a soldier. We had food; we were safe. We frequently worked without guards. The war was over for us. I remember the beautiful sunrises and sunsets of Flagstaff."[48] The prisoners often moved about as they pleased and seemed quite content. Papp bought chocolate bars, cigarettes, soda pop, and pineapple juice at the canteen. There were no challenges and passwords at the security gate. Platt Cline visited the camp and said, "If you tore down the fences they wouldn't have left. They were usually grinning all over."[49]

Civilian foremen who supervised the prisoner labor crews spoke favorably of the work performed and commended the men for their eagerness and willingness to do a good job on any assigned task. Pete Michelbach supervised POWs in washing vehicles, chopping weeds, cleanup, and motor maintenance. He stated they were "damn good, damn good men . . . if I could have had that crew . . . I let them sneak back to help [with maintenance]. They knew their mechanics."[50] Ford McElroy, a depot employee, said that they were excellent workers, in fact, "that's all they knew was work." Overall, only 6 percent of the prisoners were unavailable for work on a daily basis due to illness or injuries.[51]

The good life, however, did not last long. Things changed drastically at Bellemont when the war in Europe ended on V-E Day, May 8, 1945. Until that time German army POWs in the United States and American POWs in Germany had been protected by the Geneva Convention, which guaranteed humane treatment during wartime. The American government wanted to ensure that the International Red Cross inspection reports of camps in the United States—all of which were relayed immediately to the German government—reported fair treatment, which they did.

Across the Atlantic, Nazi Germany held over ninety thousand American servicemen in German camps, and any mistreatment of German POWs in the United States would certainly have been reciprocated overseas. The conditions in German camps were atrocious, and even worse in Japan, but the German treatment was probably the best that could have been expected from a country that was under constant bombardment and losing the war. Although the treatment in Germany was much worse than in the United States, the Committee on Military Affairs of the House of Representatives reported in November 1944 that Berlin was keeping its end of the bargain.[52]

Following the Allied victory in Europe, the Geneva Convention protection no longer applied to the Austrian prisoners at Navajo Depot. And, most important, the ninety thousand American soldiers and airmen in German camps were liberated and soon repatriated. As the War Department debated the postwar status of prisoners in the United States, one thing was certain—the fear of reprisal against American servicemen held in German camps was gone. Gastgeb, at Florence on V-E Day, said the treatment turned "terrible." Rations were cut, milk and potatoes were out, as was beer and soccer. There was "nothing to eat." Trucks hauled away books, sports equipment, and other items.

Americans were angry with news of the concentration camps and some guards posted pictures of Nazi atrocities for all to see. Others were unhappy about the increased shipments to the Pacific in preparation for the invasion of Japan. The Florence prisoners of war went on strike for three days.[53]

At Bellemont things were black and white for many Flagstaff citizens whose loved ones had fought at Normandy, the Battle of the Bulge, Corregidor, or Bataan. According to Paul Sweitzer, the POWs were "the enemy—show no consideration. We were told not to go out to the depot and stare. But, if we wanted to go out and stare—WE WOULD!"[54] And stare they did. Walter Gastgeb remembers some workers and a few Flagstaff people glaring alongside the POW camp fences and even asking the prisoners "Where are the horns on your forehead?" Papp also recalls that about a half-dozen cars were parked every day off Route 66 just north of the camp. Some approached the barbed wire fence, asking if Hitler's people had horns.

Some Flagstaff citizens, many of whom worked at the depot and followed prisoner treatment, were delighted when the prisoner rations were cut drastically. The meager diet remained in effect at least through June when the Red Cross inspectors discovered that Bellemont rations were not sufficient for working men. Not only was the food inadequate, but the prisoners had not been paid. The mail system either broke or was shut down. Ten men had never heard from home, and most prisoners had not received any mail since late 1944.[55]

For those who received mail, the news was often not good. Otto Grünberger received letters written ten to twelve months earlier telling that his father was seriously ill. Walter Gastgeb, although writing often, learned that his family had not received his letters in over a year. Gastgeb's mother, finally hearing of his satisfactory condition, sent him "a thousand loving kisses." At the same time she affectionately cautioned her young son, "Don't do anything stupid." Grünberger found Bellemont "like a part of home." He worked a half-year on the railroad, saying he was "almost eligible for retirement." For Grünberger, the "sky was recently dark, but the sun will certainly come out soon." Writing to his parents he said it would take more than POW camp life "to finish me off."[56]

As the depot shifted into high gear with massive ammunition shipments for Operation OLYMPIC—the invasion of Japan—the prisoners continued to prove their worth, often working ten-hour days. The harsh treatment gradually ended, and Captain Miller, whom the POWs grew quite fond of despite the crackdown, departed by the end of June. The prisoners said Miller understood military life and had gained their respect. They were sorry to see him leave. Lieutenant Paskiewicz was promoted to captain and moved from POW company commander to POW camp commander.

Meanwhile, conditions continued to improve. Mail began to arrive and life for the Austrians began to return to normal by July. The rations improved, up from 3,400 to 3,700 calories per working prisoner per day, as required by regulations. Papp gained weight, eventually going from 165 to 220 pounds. Life was a far cry from the tree bark, pig fat and dried bread he survived on before capture.

Trains bulging with munitions headed for the Pacific continued rolling in and out of the depot, and a few prisoners even volunteered to help load bombs and munitions. Some resurrected the 1944 Austrian Legion idea and volunteered to fight National Socialism—a comfortable offer at the war's end. More books were added to the POW library. Medical care improved; post surgeon Captain Max Marks repaired Friedrich Gröbner's hernia, doing "excellent work" that has lasted almost sixty years. The men, however, stopped making improvements to the POW camp because the war in Europe was over and they expected to be on their way home soon.[57]

Although Flagstaff had been rather quiet about the prisoners of war following V-E Day, it didn't last long. A storm of protest erupted on July 27 after Platt Cline's *Coconino Sun* account of his recent visit to the POW camp. Rumors had already been circulating that the Austrians' lavish supply of sugar allowed them to mix it with water and use the solution as hair tonic. Cline inadvertently added fuel to the fire when he reported in a small human-interest column that the prisoners went so far as to sprinkle sugar on their macaroni! That did it. Tempers flared and many citizens were outraged. They couldn't believe prisoners had access to so much sugar. Sugar was rationed, still a scarce commodity for everyone, and they were furious at such profligacy.

Colonel Huling, already sensitive from months of complaints of lenient treatment and fraternization, stormed into Cline's office and, according to Cline, threatened him with a court martial "for encouraging good sentiment toward the prisoners of war." The threat, of course, was meaningless because Cline was a civilian. However, perhaps at Huling's demand, the following week's *Coconino Sun* clarified the issue, noting that the camp's sugar ration was according to regulations and amounted to a mere .68 ounces per man each day—describing it as "anything but lavish."[58]

There had been few problems with the prisoners of war by early summer. From their arrival in March until July 1, only two POWs had been officially disciplined, both for minor violations of regulations. One was punished with an extra hour of labor each day for one week because he was late getting to work. The other prisoner, Franz Mayer, was sentenced to one week in the POW camp jail for not saluting an officer. The jail, a small fenced enclave inside the POW compound, was sufficiently insecure to allow Papp to toss a sandwich or two over the fence to his friend.[59]

Discipline inside the POW camp began to break down in July. Prisoners stewed over an issue more solemn than mail, pay, or food—repatriation—and their discontent was quickly evident. As the prisoners finally realized they were not going home soon, they committed 6 disciplinary violations during the first two weeks of July, three times as many as during their first four months. They committed 16 violations by the end of the month. As they worked and waited anxiously for the invasion, there were 16 violations in August as well. The prisoners believed they were surely going home after the atomic bombs were dropped and the war in the Pacific ended. Yet, in early September there was still no hint of repatriation. They were irate. They committed 121 discipline violations in the first two weeks of September, three times all previous violations combined, threatening camp operations, security, and discipline.[60]

Captain Harley A. Edwards, who replaced Captain Paskiewicz, did not overreact. His staff and guards handled the discipline violations with an even hand—methodically and professionally. There is no indication that any serious problems occurred, that force was ever used, or that prisoners resented the punishments or treatment. Finally, the depressed prisoners hunkered down in late September for what seemed at the time an interminable sentence, having no idea when they would return home. There were no additional discipline problems.[61]

The prisoners of war, although not far from Flagstaff, never set foot in town. That was probably well and good, for the city had already accepted even more improbable strangers. This group of unlikely newcomers sailed onto the campus of Arizona State Teachers College in the summer of 1943. They were young navy men and marines from around the nation. They were officer candidates called apprentice seamen and they, along with thousands more, were needed quickly for what was rapidly becoming the largest navy in world history.

6

THE FLEET'S IN!

Aboard the USS *Flagstaff*

In the late summer of 1942, just eight months after Pearl Harbor, as engineers and workers raced frantically to build Navajo Ordnance Depot, Betty Jean Oliver settled into her sophomore year at Arizona State Teachers College (ASTC) at Flagstaff. For Oliver, the eight large red sandstone buildings, some decked with ivy, along with the trees, sidewalks, and tennis courts on the quadrangle spread an aura of permanence and prestige across the small college campus. That was comforting for the young woman from Patagonia, Arizona, whose family had been scattered across the country by the war.[1]

The school had weathered the Great Depression reasonably well. Public Works Administration projects between 1933 and 1938 renovated Bury, Taylor, and Campbell Halls, built North Morton Hall and the stone cottages, and turned Hanley Hall into a science laboratory. The government program also provided furniture and equipment, along with an overhaul of the heating plant. Additionally, the college was able to keep many employed by writing and publishing the Federal Writers Project book, *Arizona: A State Guide*.[2]

As war threatened, men first started to leave campus when Company I, 158th Infantry, Arizona National Guard, was activated in 1940. One morning, former student Laina Siniaho remembers, they were all gone, no goodbyes, nothing. She never saw any of them again. Shortly after the Japanese attack on Pearl Harbor—the most alarming wartime event for those on campus—the entire student body gathered in the Old Main auditorium to listen to President Roosevelt's declaration of war on Japan. Bill Cummings, like many others, was angry and immediately enlisted in the army. After Pearl Harbor, Estella Marie

Melton watched as friends departed almost every other day for the service. It was frightening, she recalls, for a scared nineteen-year-old girl far from home.[3]

In the fall of 1942, Betty Jean Oliver and other students noticed the change as soon as they returned to school. There were fewer men, women, and activities. There was an uneasiness in the air, especially among the remaining boys on campus. Many faculty and students, however, were involved in wartime activities such as home defense, first aid classes, air raid instruction, and rationing of food, fabrics, fuel, and tires. They were organized into thirteen civil defense committees responsible for everything from utilities and transportation to agriculture and recreation.[4]

Meanwhile, the college received its first wartime mission: the supervision of civilian flight training. The college had some experience with aviation programs from 1940, when President Thomas J. Tormey worked up plans for ground school pilot training, and even conducted some flight training at Koch field east of town. By late 1942, the Civil Aeronautics Administration needed help in training civilian pilots between the ages of twenty-five and thirty-six. With aircraft industries churning out thousands of planes each week, the government needed ferry pilots to fly the planes from the factories to their destinations. They also needed glider and instructor pilots. The CAA awarded contracts to four hundred civilian pilot training centers, including ASTC.

School officials began training the first eight-week class of thirty students in September 1942 at the field three miles north of Williams. The instruction was soon expanded to Clemenceau field at Cottonwood, in the Verde Valley, and included precombat and noncombat training for both the army and navy. Although planes and flight instructors came from Sky Harbor Airport at Phoenix, the college directed all activities and instruction. Revenues for ASTC from the civilian flight training gradually increased, and by 1944 it was a significant income-producing program.[5]

Some wondered about the future of the small college, which was quickly becoming a women's school. Enrollment had dropped by about half, and with more leaving each semester it would soon reach the

The Arizona State Teachers College Civil Aeronautics Administration flight training program was conducted at Williams field and Clemenceau field at Cottonwood in the Verde Valley. The program provided considerable income for ASTC, along with many new civilian pilots; those pictured are at Clemenceau field in 1944.

lowest point since 1925. Faculty, too, were released. Oliver, however, was only seventeen and the isolated campus seemed to have a life all unto itself despite the war. As the school year got underway, students and advisors looked to *The Pine*—the student newspaper and centerpiece of campus life—wondering how long the tiny staff could continue. It had been in publication for thirty years, since 1913.[6]

Student enrollment at Arizona's other colleges was also down, although some claimed that the Tempe figures were still inflated due to the high number of faculty, staff, and even groundskeepers that were enrolled as students. At ASTC there may also have been some fudging on enrollment. *La Cuesta*, the ASTC yearbook, shows an enrollment considerably smaller than that reported by the registrar's office. Although 243 students were listed in 1943, *La Cuesta* showed only 143. By the 1943–44 academic year, more than 500 former ASTC students—

called "Lumberjacks"—were in uniform, and *La Cuesta* showed enrollment plunging to 81, only 4 of whom were men. Some said the Arizona Board of Regents seriously considered closing the little college. One thing was certain: if the Arizona legislature cut funds to correspond with enrollment, ASTC would be in trouble, and perhaps never recover. If the school had to close, would it reopen? Some students were discouraged, fearing the school could not hang on much longer. When publication of *The Pine* was suspended in February 1943 for lack of writers and staff, the remaining students hunkered down for the worst.[7]

Meanwhile, across campus, President Tormey had been doing everything possible to attract the military to the sinking ship. Knowing that Flagstaff was in the federal sights with the army's ordnance depot close by, and that wartime programs were the only way to guarantee the school's survival, he and his staff churned away at government applications, reports, information gathering, and federal inspections, hoping to attract something to the mountain campus.[8]

National educators like Tormey had for some time tried to persuade the military services to conduct training on college campuses. In October 1942, President Franklin D. Roosevelt wrote to the secretaries of war and navy and encouraged them to use the nation's colleges and universities to stem their falling enrollments. In December the army and navy jointly accepted the invitation. The army components were the Army Specialized Training Program and the Army Air Forces College Training Program. The navy component, the Navy College Training Program, designated the "V-12" program, was created under authority of the Naval Reserve Act of 1938 to augment the service's existing V-7, V-5, and V-1 programs that were still not producing enough officers. Together, they would expand the naval reserve officer corps to command the world's largest navy ever, and much of the work would be done on the nation's campuses. In addition to these major training programs, the services used colleges and universities for other specialized training.[9]

The winter at ASTC passed without any word. Finally, in early March 1943, the War Department contacted Dean Tom O. Bellwood, who was acting as ASTC president following Tormey's departure on unpaid leave for wartime civilian service in California. Officials told Bellwood that the school had cleared several hurdles and was the only Arizona college under consideration for a navy V-12 program. Of the 1,600 colleges and universities that had applied, ASTC was on a third and final list that whittled the number of schools down to 238, about half of which would be selected for possible contracts with the navy to provide basic and specialized military training. The news, although not conclusive, boosted sagging spirits among the administration and faculty.[10]

A group of navy officials from San Diego arrived in Flagstaff on Friday, March 12, 1943, to examine the ASTC facilities. Their "rigid" two-day inspection left no indication of the navy's decision. Knowing full well the gravity of the situation as enrollment continued to fall, acting president Bellwood, administrators, and faculty waited anxiously until they finally received a telegram the following Saturday announcing the acceptance of ASTC for the navy's V-12 on-campus program. The *Coconino Sun*'s bold headline on March 26 trumpeted "College Accepted for Naval Program." It was finally settled. The college would survive after all.[11]

About the same time, Bellwood had responded negatively to the faculty's request for salary raises, noting that the stagnant state appropriation would result in a 15 percent salary reduction instead. He then attended a meeting in New York dealing with the V-12 program and soon learned that the navy would pay additional salary money of twenty dollars per man per month for instructional costs above and beyond other fees. With this good news, the state board of education moved quickly to raise the ASTC faculty salaries by 15 percent on June 21, and even agreed that further adjustments would be made in September.[12]

The college would train two hundred men at a time. The navy said the first contingent of apprentice seamen would arrive in Flagstaff on July 1, followed by another group on November 1. At the same time, however, the navy advised Dean Bellwood that the July contingent would be doubled to four hundred and remain at that strength for the duration of the war if the college would renovate the home economics rooms into a modern infirmary. The college immediately began work and notified the navy, thus ensuring the largest possible contingent of seamen.[13]

At the same time, the navy advertised the new V-12 program nationwide and distributed information and application forms to high schools. The army and navy gave entrance examinations on the ASTC campus on April 2, just two weeks after the college had been accepted for V-12 training. At Flagstaff High School, students like Howard Wren, then a junior, took note of the interesting opportunity to join the navy, enter flight training, and go to college a mile from home. He signed up with the V-12 program in January of his senior year. His older brother Laurance, however, entered the ASTC program with the first group of trainees in July.[14]

Secretary of the Navy Frank Knox recognized the enrollment drain at ASTC and other small colleges around the country. Confident that large state universities and privately endowed institutions would survive the war without aid from the federal government, or already had other military programs on campus, Knox pledged special consideration in dispersing V-12 programs to schools, like ASTC, that might otherwise have to close their doors. The secretary realized that careful distribution of the navy's 125,000 apprentice seamen, especially to the nation's suffering campuses, could keep these schools afloat until veterans returned from the war. The navy also took into consideration ASTC's excellent faculty, reputation in the sciences, vacant dormitories, and respectable facilities, along with the pleasant local community and huge depot project close by. President Tormey's earlier efforts to attract the military helped as well.[15]

Military training on an Arizona college campus would not be unique to Flagstaff. At Arizona State Teachers College at Tempe, an army air forces program trained 2,776 cadets and revived a sagging enrollment that eventually dropped below five hundred students. The University of Arizona, meanwhile, was soon in good shape with the navy's sixty-day indoctrination school for newly commissioned officers that, along with army and the Civil Aeronautics Administration programs, trained more than 11,000 servicemen.[16]

In the spring of 1943, the navy designated V-12 programs for every state west of the Mississippi except South Dakota, Wyoming, Nevada, and Utah. Two hundred and fifty-four trainees would report to Carroll College at Helena, Montana; 455 to the University of New Mexico at Albuquerque; 874 to the University of Texas at Austin; 542 to the California Institute of Technology at Pasadena; 260 to Willamette University at Salem, Oregon; and 421 to the University of Idaho (Southern Branch)—today Idaho State University—at Pocatello. Arizona State Teachers College at Flagstaff would receive 400 trainees, while thousands of other future navy officers would fan out to colleges and universities across the West.[17]

President Tormey drafted a statement from California assuring faculty, alumni, and state educators that the college would not turn over all of its facilities to the navy. Some of the curriculum and faculty would continue with the teacher-training mission, thus assuring ASTC a vital role in the long-range planning for Arizona education after the war. Conditions, he insisted, would remain as normal as possible, especially considering the fact that about 80 percent of the apprentice seamen would be coming from a college where they were already enrolled and familiar with campus life. Tormey returned to Flagstaff during the weekend of May 22–23 to assist with preparations already well underway.[18]

Commander Raymond Kaiser, a veteran of several naval campaigns ashore and afloat, arrived in Flagstaff on June 17 to organize ASTC's naval science program and set up the "ship's company," a self-contained naval unit on campus consisting of several officers and fifteen enlisted men and women—ten sailors and five marines, several of whom had arrived earlier. The ship's company handled the clerical details, the pre-officer training school, the physical education program, the daily and weekly drills, and assisted with the dispensary and the mail. The ship's company also included instructors, female commissioned officers and petty officers (WAVES), and medical and dental officers. Kaiser had experience in education, having established specialized training schools along with post-graduate naval institutions. He chose a motto for the detachment, "Factum, non verba" (Deeds, not words), in keeping with the navy's tradition of "results, not explanations." The executive officer, Lt. LeRoy Schnell, had seventeen years' experience working with colleges and had authored articles and textbooks on mathematics.

The navy contract with ASTC was negotiated on Friday, June 11, and included meals, tuition, health care, athletic facilities, and science and engineering equipment. The navy also paid the college for the use of dorms, the dining hall, administrative offices, and other facilities. Dorm rooms that otherwise would have gone empty were instead soon producing revenues. Trainees would be quartered in Morton, Campbell, North, and Taylor Halls, with the dining facility located in North Hall. Female civilian students were moved to Bury Hall but ate with the trainees in the joint dining facility that would serve 1,275 meals a day. Classes would be taught in the administrative and science buildings, while the Navajo Ordnance Depot hospital provided medical facilities.

Ration checks issued through the Bank of Arizona, Clarkdale Office of Price Administration, authorized the purchase of large quantities of rationed food for the ship's company, trainees, and civilian students. The OPA used a point system that could be adjusted for particularly scarce food items. One group of checks, for example, authorized 22,504 points for meats, fats, fish, and cheese, along with 51,004 points for processed foods, and 457 pounds of sugar. With the navy in charge of dining, the students soon reported a noticeable improvement in their meals.[19]

The sixteen-week, three-semester school year—the first in ASTC history—would enable new trainees to complete the four-year college course in two years and eight months. The program was very flexible, however, and those with several years of college could complete their studies in one or two semesters. The curriculum provided a liberal arts foundation with emphasis on science and mathematics, and included calculus, analytic geometry, engineering, engineer drawing, physics, chemistry, heat power, English, naval history, thermodynamics, and navigation. In addition to engineers, some of the students were following premedical or predental studies. Others, like Don Horner, were training to become naval supply officers, and some were even studying to become chaplains.[20]

President Tormey and Dean Bellwood began preparing the new curriculum. The administration immediately hired a dozen new faculty members, including eight math and science teachers, one of them Clyde W. Tombaugh, who as a young Lowell Observatory assistant had discovered the planet Pluto in 1930. Dr. Agnes Allen took over as acting head of the science department when Dr. Charles Hablutzel left to work on a top-secret project later revealed to be the proximity fuse. Tormey reminded the faculty that he expected them to maintain regular work and professional standards, pointing out that ASTC had been accredited for fifteen consecutive years by the American Association of Teachers Colleges and its instructors rated above average.[21]

As seen the previous year with the construction of Navajo Ordnance Depot, changes came rapidly. The college quickly turned the home economics rooms into an infirmary, at its own expense. College officials also ordered new kitchen equipment, with the navy furnishing many items that were in critically short supply. Dorms were readied and the curriculum coordinated with the faculty. Meanwhile, Commander Kaiser and Marine officer-in-charge Capt. Kirt W. Norton prepared to greet the trainees, acquainted themselves with the faculty and the Flagstaff community, secured the physical education program facilities, and made other last-minute arrangements.[22]

Finally, the day arrived. For Betty Jean Oliver and the other unmarried ASTC women, Thursday, July 1, 1943, is remembered along with Pearl Harbor, President Roosevelt's death, and V-E Day. That day, three hundred and seventy-four navy apprentice seamen and marines stepped off the trains at Flagstaff. With bags slung over their shoulders, the boys moved into formation. For the bustling army ordnance town high on the Colorado Plateau, it was a strange sight indeed.[23]

Those coming from northern California looked peculiar with their uniforms covered in soot from the railway tunnels along the route. For many of the young men arriving that day, the train ride was their first and an unforgettable experience. They were quickly marched to the ASTC campus, given a short military haircut, issued more uniforms and equipment, and assigned a room and roommate. They were then divided into four companies of about one hundred men each, with three platoons per company.

Some had never seen such a hodgepodge of American cultures, let alone live among them. Those from small towns, farms, and ranches had never been around so many men. The recruits reporting to their first assignment were startled by the petty officers barking orders at every turn. But, regardless of where they came from, everyone seemed to be hungry, all the time.

Those from cities like San Diego and Santa Monica were disappointed in the downtown that, strangely, was only a few steps from the station. Seamen from the University of Southern California were shocked that the navy would actually send them to "the end of the earth." Some talented students like Art Mehagian of Phoenix, who was later admitted to the U.S. Naval Academy at Annapolis, were hoping for a more distinguished school, like Harvard or Yale. They were all young and, like Jerry Garlock, ready to serve in the armed forces in any capacity, anywhere. They quickly noticed, however, that Old Main and the quadrangle of red sandstone buildings conveyed the "certain reverence" of an enduring institutional system where it would be difficult if not impossible to slide by unnoticed or untested. The sublime setting quietly articulated the upcoming academic and military challenges aboard the "USS *Flagstaff*."[24]

The landing of so many sailors and marines represented an extraordinary windfall for ASTC, and especially for the faculty whose jobs were on the line. With almost all Lumberjack men in the service, the trainees were enthusiastically welcomed by the college administration, as well as by the mostly female student body. The new arrivals came from across the United States, but primarily from California, Arizona, New Mexico, Nevada, and Utah. Some of the marines were older than the typical navy seamen, having seen action in the Guadalcanal campaign or elsewhere overseas. Some of these combat veterans showed signs of battle fatigue, along with malaria. Even though many of the eager servicemen resented being posted in the boondocks, they plunged into their studies and blended quickly into campus life.[25]

The navy published guidelines for their new program on the nation's college campuses—the *Manual for the Operation of a V-12 Unit*—which invoked John Paul Jones in setting the tone and objectives. "It is by no means enough that an officer of the Navy should be a capable mariner," Jones wrote in 1775. "He must be that, of course, but also a great deal more. He should be, as well, a gentleman of liberal education, refined manner, punctilious courtesy, and the nicest sense of personal honor." In this spirit, ASTC would provide instruction in the general sciences, naval science, and other prerequisites for the liberal education of a navy officer. The college could not, of course, provide blue water training.[26]

The navy's V-12 program was immediately well received across the nation because trainees were not required to undergo basic training before they were assigned to a college campus, and those who had already earned some college credits could continue with part of their civilian curricula. Students already enrolled in college could enter the V-12 program at their own institution, provided it had space. Unlike army trainees, the seamen were allowed to participate in the full gamut of campus activities and attended classes alongside civilian students.

In general, the V-12 program was more relaxed than the army programs. Some seamen having several years of college credits completed the course in two semesters. Although the navy insisted that apprentice seamen wear uniforms and conform to "strict naval discipline at all times," civilian women were also allowed to enroll in V-12 classes. A UC-Berkeley faculty member observed that army trainees marched to class in formation, whereas navy men strolled along with civilian students.[27]

Not surprisingly, the navy program quickly brought a military atmosphere to the Flagstaff campus. Classes began on July 12, and the pace picked up. Trainees marched and drilled frequently, and regularly presented the four-hundred-man unit in a review with the marching band. Uniforms were de rigueur—on campus, off campus, and even on dates, where approving women pronounced them "fabulous." Bugle calls announced the start and end of the day, and called the apprentice seamen to formation in between. Local children dressed in navy uniforms and saluted the flag at retreat ceremonies.

For Ruth Corbett, there was no question that the college was a navy base. Military customs even drifted across the streets to those

ASTC was home to 1,020 navy seamen and marines of the V-12 officer training program. The detachment, shown here marching on campus, maintained a strength of 400. Following ASTC, many continued with advanced studies at other universities or went on to boot camp or officer training courses.

who lived nearby. Not far from her home, at eight o'clock on icy cold mornings in 1943, a woman, dressed only in a cotton dress and apron, stood at attention on the porch of her small white house across from North Hall. As the last note from a bugle sounded across campus, she quietly withdrew inside her home, where the small American flag that hung in her window was adorned with one blue star, indicating that someone in the family was serving somewhere in the armed forces.[28]

Lest there be any doubt, the V-12 trainees were constantly reminded that they were sailors and marines. Eighteen-year-old Harold Elliott of Yuma was a case in point. Elliott, who had graduated from high school in midterm and completed a semester of junior college, arrived on campus with his hometown buddies Sam Dick III, Bill Parks, and Loren Peterson, among the first group of trainees, on July 1, 1943.

Yuma V-12 seamen from left: Sam Dick III, Loren Peterson, Bill Parks, and Harold Elliott. Eighteen-year-old Elliott arrived on campus with the first group of trainees on July 1, 1943.

But instead of classes and studies, Elliott was immediately put to work swabbing the deck in dorms left vacant by the departure of so many Lumberjacks for the service.[29]

Military discipline was readily apparent from the beginning. Most, however, were used to discipline, having grown up in an era when fathers would often add to any punishments administered by the schools. Howard Wren remembers that the navy "kept tabs on us twenty-four hours a day." A demerit system ensured trainees followed the rules and regulations. Those earning more than allowed were not granted liberty. Additionally, any seaman or marine who failed an inspection was punished immediately and required to run laps around the quadrangle. The austere dorm rooms were subject to daily inspections where officers checked that bunk corners were squared, the pillow and towel centered, the laundry bag tilted as only the navy demanded that it be tilted, and the bunk frame washed. Windows and locker boxes also had to be washed, the deck swept and swabbed, shoes shined, the clothes rack dusted, brass polished, and so on. In the process, the marines used more disinfectant than any other commodity, so much that it was reported a lonely germ would need an identification card just to get on campus.[30]

Trainees were required to obtain passes for any off-campus excursion, including church services, where many overlooked their souls in favor of the pretty girls in the choir. When a seaman got into trouble the entire platoon would suffer, and Victor Myers remembers he was "always" restricted to campus. Classes were held Monday through Friday, with Saturdays reserved for inspections, marching, and drill. A 10:00 P.M. curfew confined the sailors and marines to their rooms with lights out. The rigorous navy training never allowed enough time to study, forcing many to jury-rig electric bulbs in their closets for after-hours work. Overall academic performance was generally excellent because the stakes were so high—anyone who failed a course was immediately shipped out to boot camp or the fleet. Even so, some seamen could hardly wait to see action. During finals week of October 1943, for example, six men entered a classroom, signed their names to the exam books, and walked out. A few hours later, they were on their way to boot camp.[31]

The navy, like other armed services, recognized and valued leadership and selected the most promising seamen and marines to lead platoons and companies in the ASTC unit, regardless of their background or combat experience. Local Flagstaff trainee Howard Wren, for example, was a natural leader. He worked hard, had excellent grades, followed the rules, and was well respected by his peers. The ship's company selected Wren to command a trainee platoon of thirty or forty seamen.[32]

Two weeks following their arrival on campus, the trainees revived *The Pine,* and publication continued throughout the war. The change was noticeable immediately. Rich editorial columns provided elegantly written comments on a variety of subjects, including the war and the

Contrary to army programs around the nation, seamen and marines on the ASTC campus walked to class alongside female students.

postwar world. Other serious articles did not want in philosophy or scope. Additionally, the paper published letters from Lumberjack servicemen overseas, book reviews, poems, jokes, and light entertainment. The sports page kept track of intercollegiate games as well as intramural scores and league standings, and especially the navy-marine contests. *The Pine* announced navy uniforms, class and exam schedules, listed military orders along with departures and arrivals, changes to regulations and routines, and kept the campus abreast of the fighting.

Female students published their news and views in a column called "Bury It." Other columns, like "Scuttlebutt," "Impressions," "Giggles 'n' Gags," and "Shady Side," reported on almost all secrets of campus life, provided biographies of students, faculty, and seamen of interest, and kidded about steadies of the week. "As We See It," written jointly by a sailor and a marine, poked fun at the ship's company as well as other trainees. In short, everyone on campus could find something interesting and entertaining in *The Pine,* to include commentaries about themselves, their classmates, and even faculty.[33]

Just six weeks after stepping ashore the seamen and marines staged a fast-moving musical comedy, *Boots on Parade,* with an all-navy-marine cast of seventy-five that included former professional and amateur musicians and actors. The performance was dedicated to not only those who had died or would die in the service of our country, but also to those who were willing to die but would not. Seaman Vince Mancini's words in the evening's brochure articulated the difficulty of remembering such enormous sacrifice that "girds the hulk" of our society. He lamented that those who had given their lives for our freedom "will not forever live on in our memories." The blood which they shed is soon relegated, he wrote, "to the black ink" of our history books that only describe how it happened. To shear the inevitable consequence of time, Mancini dedicated the proceeds of the show to returning veterans' education at ASTC, celebrating the beautiful and noble achievements of those who love liberty and served in the armed forces.[34]

The program's original songs written (and reportedly copyrighted) by ASTC seamen Val Heegler, Kurt Miller, and Vince Mancini included "Only the Stars Remain," "Hit the Deck," "Now that I Care," "Flagstaff Hop," and "Over at the College Inn." The all-marine ballet *Dance of the Hours* was reportedly a sight to behold. Modeled after Irving Berlin's *This is the Army,* the show portrayed life on the ASTC campus and love of country.[35]

For those coming from big cities, the "hick town" high in the mountains of Arizona was a place to escape from, certainly not a place to stay. One anonymous seaman bided his time in Flagstaff by writing a poem:

> Somewhere in Arizona
> The snow is like a curse
> And each long day is followed
> By another slightly worse.
> The winds and rains blow thicker
> Than any desert sands—

And all the V-12 trainees
Wish for fair and warmer lands.

Somewhere in Arizona
The nights are made for love;
The moon is like a searchlight
And the clear-lit stars above
Sparkle as they do
On a balmy tropic night;
It's a shameful waste of beauty,
'Cause the girls are just a fright!

Somewhere in Arizona, yes
A pretty girl is seldom seen—
The sky is mostly cloudy,
And the grass is never green!
Each night when "lights out" rolls around
They don't have to count the sheep,
And the bugle's lusty squawk
Robs the men of needed sleep.

We seldom have a payday
So we never have a cent
We never miss the money, though,
'Cause we'd never get it spent.
Take me back to California—
The place I love so well—
For this God-forsaken outpost
Is a substitute for hell!³⁶

One goal of the navy program was to bring each student to top physical condition and keep him there. The basic physical education training required a minimum of six hours of exercise each week. Each day except Sunday began with calisthenics at 6:00 A.M., and often included running, tumbling, military drill, swimming, conditioning exercises, combat exercises, rope climbing, grass drills, deck exercises, weight lifting, games, or the obstacle course. On some days the seamen marched in formation through downtown Flagstaff and then ran back to the barracks, repeating the drill two more times. These activities were supplemented with the full gamut of intramural sports. These battles were especially lively when sailors squared off against marines. Additionally, ASTC was the birthplace for an unusual rough-and-tumble sport invented by one of the ship's company petty officers, Chief Specialist Paul Revere Ludwig.[37]

Ludwig, called "Dutch" by all but the sailors and marines, had graduated from Ohio University in 1927 as a three-year letterman and captain of the baseball team. He played semipro football and baseball for six years and coached for many years before enlisting in the navy as a physical education instructor in November 1942. Ludwig never lost his Ohio accent and seamen described him speaking with a heavy drawl, "Naow men, this mornin' we're gonna have a maael call . . . cause the maael's in."[38]

Although not a career navy man, Ludwig was a tough character, committed to sports and physical fitness, who quickly put his skills to use assisting the college physical education department and directing the navy's fitness training. Ludwig, called a mastermind in human torture by some trainees, took pride in "mass basketball," perhaps his most special creation. The game, also described by seamen and marines as "massacre on the hardwoods," was played on a regular basketball court. There was, however, one catch. There were no rules. Ludwig usually herded a company of about one hundred trainees to the court. He divided the men into two teams, issued fifty blue jerseys and fifty yellow, and placed a scorekeeper behind each backboard. Then he gave each man one boxing glove and tossed out about fifty basketballs. The objective, by any means possible, was to put the balls through the opposing team's hoop. Needless to say, all hell broke loose at the starting whistle and the melee often turned bloody. After a few wild minutes, however, they were all laughing so hard it was difficult to continue play.

Another one of Ludwig's creations was mass wrestling, where blue and yellow teams of ten men each squared off on a large mat. They faced each other, shoulder to shoulder on opposite sides, until the whistle blew. The goal was to drive the opponents off the mat any way possible, again with no rules. Ludwig also held mass wrestling bouts without dividing into teams—last sailor or marine on the mat wins. In this case, Earl Bay's idea seemed to work just fine. He dropped to the mat and held onto the legs of the biggest, strongest, and meanest sailor.

Some of the men described these sports as capital punishment. As *The Pine* noted, "Ludwig's conscience does not bother him for the cruelties he has wrought." In fact, Ludwig was rather pleased with these and his other creations, and even submitted them up the chain of command as games suitable for large groups. Grumbling aside, the men were young, healthy, and loved the combative free-for-all, along with their salty old petty officer Ludwig. Earl Bay enjoyed the rugged physical education training. It was interesting, diverse, and included much more than just daily calisthenics. He especially liked cross-country runs through the surrounding forests.[39]

Some seamen were successful at pulling pranks and avoiding the consequences. Sherman Payne of Prescott, who left his mother in tears when he joined the navy even though his first duty station was barely one hundred miles from home, was a case in point. During his first semester at ASTC, Payne roomed with a regular "salty dog" veteran, David "Boats" Neighbor, who had recently served with the Pacific fleet. Truth be known, Payne hoped that some of his roommate's old saltiness would rub off on the landlocked kid from Arizona—and it soon did.[40]

Boats had stepped ashore in Flagstaff fully equipped for campus life. In the bottom of his seabag he had stashed a long coil of rope, extra blankets, and watch caps—soft wool caps that could be pulled down over the ears in cold weather. Boats had special plans for their use. At lights out, Boats and Payne went to work. They rolled up their blankets to resemble human forms and placed them under the covers on their beds. They then removed the circular shades from their desk lamps, covered the shades with the watch caps to resemble human heads, and attached them to their rolled-up blankets. Confident that the impromptu dummies would pass the night watchman's bed check, the pair tied the rope to the radiator and lowered themselves from their second-floor dorm room to the ground, where they hightailed it for the action at the Black Cat Café. Getting back into their room past the night watchman patrolling up and down the dormitory hall was a little trickier, but they succeeded. Payne later recalled with a smile how the only time he jumped ship was in Flagstaff, Arizona.[41]

During his second semester Payne roomed with Art "Mousie" Mehagian of Phoenix. Art was "one smart kid," whom Payne credits with getting him through calculus. However, Mehagian had one minor character quirk. As his nickname suggests, he was deathly afraid of mice. Payne and some of the other seamen no sooner learned of the aversion than they began catching mice and tucking them securely under the covers at the foot of Mehagian's bed, whereupon "Mousie" would erupt from sleep as though shot from a cannon. Later, Payne and his friends discovered that they could produce the same effect by merely tucking a washrag under his sheets. Mehagian was a good sport, however, and took the pranks in stride.[42]

Pranks aside, within two weeks of the navy's landing the acting director of the physical education department and head football coach, Frank Brickey, was astounded by the athletic talent he saw marching around campus. Brickey, who was in excellent shape himself, quickly discovered he was incapable of outrunning the trainees or equaling their pushups, situps, or other exercises. Brickey had taken over the football team from Maurice Moulder after the dismal 1942 season, when the Lumberjacks won only one of six games and were outscored 93 to 18. The 1943 season was abruptly cancelled on March 3, due to loss of athletes to the service. In May, however, recognizing the potential value of army and navy programs to intercollegiate athletics, Border Conference officials voted unanimously to waive transfer rules for military athletes.[43]

By mid-July Brickey discovered that he had on campus—in the two-hundred-man marine detachment alone—between sixty and eighty football players, many of whom had played for colleges in the Pacific Southwest. Combined with veteran players from the two-hundred-man navy detachment, the "galaxy" of talent easily represented the greatest gridiron team in the history of the college. Brickey knew they "could whip anyone." Commander Kaiser agreed to let the seamen play. Acting president Bellwood was pleased if not eager to announce the resumption of intercollegiate football. College officials quickly searched for opponents, licking their chops at the thought of taking the field against the University of Arizona Wildcats or Arizona State Teachers College at Tempe. The biggest difficulty would be finding teams good enough to "afford real competition" for the Lumberjacks. The only obstacle to a rigorous regional schedule, however, was the navy's rule that seamen could not be away from campus longer than forty-eight hours.[44]

Brickey lived a coach's dream during the August 1943 workouts, finally selecting a starting squad with veteran players from Arizona, New Mexico, and Loyola Universities. The backfield was good enough to run a tricky single-wing formation with the fullback doing most of the work. The team also ran the double wingback and unbalanced line to the right, and even practiced the famous Notre Dame "T." They had great speed and size, and Brickey knew he could put all of their talents to work. With many former collegiate all-conference players and high school all-state stars, Brickey could concentrate on perfection, skillfully orchestrating his plays into synchronized, powerful movements guaranteed to roll over anything from Tucson or Tempe.[45]

The University of Arizona at Tucson and Arizona State at Tempe, no doubt aware of the powerhouse to the north, wisely passed on playing the Flagstaff superteam. The Jacks traveled to Yuma Air Base and drubbed the strong Gremlin team, also packed with college stars, by the score 25–0. By mid-September, however, the demands of the navy curriculum along with the loss of players to reassignment thinned the Lumberjack squad. They traveled to Albuquerque and played New Mexico, a team also loaded with V-12 college players, and lost 21–6.

Then the axe fell. Commander Kaiser notified coach Brickey that the apprentice seamen and marines who were doing poorly scholastically could not play football. That cut the roster from sixty-five men to thirty, and half of those remaining soon turned in their uniforms.

The dream was over for Brickey and Lumberjack fans and the remainder of the season was cancelled. For all, it was a difficult pill to swallow, as *The Pine* reported. Although seamen with passing grades could play ball the following two years, the Lumberjacks would not have a winning football season until military veterans returned to campus after the war. The 1943–44 basketball team, however, won its two games against Jerome. The 1944–45 squad, although posting five wins and six losses against teams that included college players at Kingman Field and Williams Field, won four of five games against Arizona and Arizona State, laying claim to the state college basketball championship.[46]

Campus social life blossomed with the arrival of the V–12 trainees. Most female students could scarcely believe their good fortune. Although some were miffed at being forced to move into the older Bury Hall, they quickly fell in step with the new campus routine. Some California students followed their serviceman sweethearts to Flagstaff; others, like Lorraine Inman of Anaheim, came alone. Still other women flocked to Flagstaff from surrounding states. Word that the navy had landed spread quickly. There were sailors on the ASTC campus—lots of sailors—and they outnumbered women at least five to one.[47]

The students were not the only women in town who noticed the navy's presence. One Saturday afternoon, a summer visitor saw a group of V–12 trainees on "shore leave." She rushed into the post office and up to the clerk's window demanding, "The fleet's in! The fleet's in! Where does it dock?"

"Fleet? Dock?" muttered the clerk vaguely, confused by a question having nothing to do with stamps or mail. Whereupon the woman snapped, "Certainly! I just saw with my own eyes scores of handsome young sailors out on the street but I haven't seen a sign of any ships or even water. Quick, my good man, which way lies the ocean?" Postmaster George Babbitt Jr., who had overheard the conversation, reportedly rushed goggle-eyed out into the street to see if, by some fluke, a ship had docked along the Rio de Flag.[48]

With their days chock full, many seamen found scant time for dating. Earl Bay treated women with the utmost courtesy and respect,

The social calendar included picnics and a wide variety of other activities.

meaning "they were mostly ignored." Other seamen, however, confronted with the draconian odds, turned courting into a fine art while displaying considerable chivalry and respect for the fair sex—anything else risked expulsion from the program. Delighted to be on the ASTC campus, relieved to not be slugging it out on Pacific islands, they cherished walks on campus, wrote poems, gave flowers, mingled at the soda fountain, and gathered around the Bury Hall piano for singing and talking. They ate their meals with the female students, and the dining hall became the daily meeting place. Free time was precious, and they enjoyed much of what little they had with the Lumberjack women.[49]

Under the circumstances, it was not unusual for female students to have several dates in the course of a single evening. Some lucky young women practiced "triple shift" dating—going out with a different navy man every two hours between 6:00 P.M. and midnight. Lorraine Inman recalled that she "always had a date and a wonderful time with the well-behaved" sailors. Local bachelors, understandably, had a different view. Jim Vandevier complained that he had to drive all the way to Williams—twenty-five miles west of Flagstaff—just to find a date. One Bury Hall student, dubbed "the stripper," made life excit-

ing by periodically removing her clothes in full view of gawking trainees directly across the way in Taylor Hall. Other Bury Hall women
regularly set sail from their first-floor windows to meet sailors and
marines for beers at the Hotel Monte Vista, north of the railroad tracks
downtown. If troop trains were at the station, they often took letters
from soldiers for mailing and exchanged addresses. Some enterpris-
ing students set up kissing booths in Ashurst Hall to raise funds for
various projects. Others, taking advantage of Sadie Hawkins Day, had
a wonderful selection from which to choose their date.[50]

Many women went "hog wild" over so many "handsome sailors"
on campus. Kathryn Custis, a student whose family lived in Flagstaff,
remembers a boatload of sailors dating "a trio of us town girls." Beverly
Bellwood, acting president Bellwood's daughter and a Flagstaff high
school sophomore in 1943, recalls that high school girls were "right in
the thick of it. It was wonderful." A few grew up too fast and got into
trouble. Two women were expelled after it was discovered that they
had spent the night in Oak Creek Canyon with some trainees. But for
the most part, wartime ASTC alumnae remember how much fun it
was having so many "bright, well-mannered, and friendly" navy men
buzzing around. The fact that a few were premedical and predental
students made them all the more interesting. "That was pretty exciting
for a girl right out of high school," Peggy Davern, a 1943 freshman, recalls. The trainees quickly adapted to the community, and Flagstaff families often invited eight or ten sailors to Sunday dinner. Patricia Herold,
still at Flagstaff High School, remembers her mother making waffles for
any and all V-12 men she brought home on Sunday evenings.[51]

With hundreds of seamen and marines on board, attitudes improved and activities flourished now that everyone had a date. Sorori-
ties, weakened by months of declining activity, soon bustled with people
and events. The trainees and female students flocked to the Club Win-
tertime Dance where a band played in a hall lined with fir trees. They
also went to the Sweetheart Ball, where each couple was introduced as
they walked through a large red heart. The women of Bury Hall hosted
an open house along with programs. Other events included the senior
ball, the Saturday night dances, bowling parties, dinner dances, snow

The Gamma Chi dance was just one of the many popular social events held on campus after the navy and marines arrived on July 1, 1943. The sailors and marines brought new traditions from California to ASTC, along with a vibrant campus life and rejuvenation of the college newspaper *The Pine*.

parties, and barn dances. There were faculty student banquets, teas, Saint Patrick's formal, church socials, the May Day Festival, and the Club Summertime Dance. During the balmy days of summer the excellent V-12 musicians—who were exempt from Saturday drill—held weekly outdoor concerts on campus. Trumpet player Vic Myers and others also organized a band that played on weekends at the Sahuaro Club.[52]

The navy influenced the traditional female dress standards on campus. Gowns, usually the rule at formal dances, were often ignored by students like Rose Titus, for example, who put on a skirt and sweater after work at the soda fountain and beelined straight to the formal where she was sure to find many navy friends who couldn't wait to dance with her, gown or no gown.[53]

The sailors introduced the latest dance craze from California, the "balboa," along with the lindy hop. The navy also brought USO shows, including entertainer Bob Hope. One show, however, was so risqué that acting president and Mrs. Bellwood walked out.

The seamen and marines even changed the language used on campus. They created affectionate nicknames for their favorite female students. Dorothy Schick, for example, became "Slick Chick Schick," and Betty Jean Oliver, the junior class and student body president with initials B. O., was confirmed as "Stinky." Women living on campus were the Bury Hall inmates. The seamen introduced a new lingo with words like scuttlebutt—meaning gossip—but which formerly denoted a water cask on a ship's deck with a hole in the top for dipping. They brought other navy terms, like hatch (door), sack (bed), bulkhead (wall), chow (food), deck (floor), swab (mop), ladder (stairs), knock it off (stop), bunk (bed), rest (a relaxed position rarely assumed), cork off (to shirk), and perhaps the most important, versatile, and underrated term in navy and marine parlance, gizmo—which covered much more territory than thingamajig, whatchamacallit, or dohickey. Gizmos were everywhere on campus. They could be carried, passed, held, eaten, slept with, worn, talked to, and even saluted—ad infinitum.[54]

"Scuttlebutt," the anonymous social columnist for *The Pine*, kept tabs on the comings and goings of the sailors and marines, as well as other student activities. In a poem dedicated to the women of Bury Hall, he plugged the marines while emphasizing unity among all the servicemen:

To the Girls of Bury

When you're feeling sad and blue
And you don't know what to do
Tell it to the Marines.

When the hour is getting late
And you just don't have a date
Tell it to the Marines.

If the situation's out of hand
And quick thinking is in demand
Tell it to the Marines.

Now to the girls of Bury Hall
Remember, this above all—
It's not what uniform we're in
Nor what we've seen, or where we've been,
But soldiers, flyers, macs, and mates,
We stand together—the United States.[55]

At the end of the first term in November 1943, twenty-eight sea-men and twenty-three marines of the senior class, all with several years of college prior to ASTC, became the first graduates of the navy's V-12 program at Flagstaff. As they gathered for graduation ceremonies and the reading of their orders, the men sat breathlessly awaiting their fate. Much was at stake and bad news struck like the shot from a six-teen-inch naval gun. They were headed to advanced studies, mid-shipmen's schools, boot camps, or officer training schools across the country. The lucky ones received orders for engineering or other ad-vanced studies at the University of Colorado, the University of South-ern California, Colorado College, or other universities around the West. The unlucky ones received orders to the marine's Parris Island for more training, to boot camp, Louisiana, the Great Lakes, or some god-forsaken place even farther from their beloved West like Asbury Park, New Jersey.[56]

For most of the seamen and marines, many of whom were right out of high school, nothing compares with their wartime experience at ASTC, where they recognized their good fortune in not going directly to the combat zones. Today, the history of World War II seems a "done deal" by many. For youngsters like Oliver Briggs, who were on cam-pus between 1943 and 1945, it was anything but a done deal. By mid-1943 the tide of war was finally turning, and Briggs and others fol-lowed the newspaper accounts of the horrible battles, knowing full well the undeniable effects on their own future. *The Pine* published action-packed letters from Lumberjacks and V–12 men at the front. It also gave accounts of those wounded in battle and the thirty-one Lumberjacks who were killed. As events unfolded, nothing was certain for Briggs and the other navy men at Flagstaff—they knew that most of the war's casualties were still ahead.[57]

Some of the women also followed the war closely. Lola Dunaway, for example, was studying late in Bury Hall on the evening of June 5, 1944, when Edward R. Murrow came on the radio. He was broadcasting live from a ship in the English Channel, describing the early morning attack of June 6 on the beaches of Normandy, France. She listened until 3:00 A.M., captivated by his vivid description of the events as they unfolded—rockets firing from hundreds of Allied ships, enemy shells landing not far away, and the fierce battles for the beachheads. At about the same time others in Flagstaff heard that the long-awaited invasion of Europe was finally under way. Police, ambulance, and fire engine sirens screamed along the city streets and the fire department and sawmill whistles blew at full throttle.[58]

The college and community settled in with the navy program. Similar graduation ceremonies, the reading of orders, joy, despair, sadness, and departures marked the end of each semester for seamen and female students alike. At the same time, more apprentice seamen arrived on campus to replace those who were leaving, keeping the detachment at around four hundred men. The *Coconino Sun* and *The Pine* saluted those departing and welcomed all arriving. For some, like Earl Bay, Flagstaff was just a brief stop en route to the Great Lakes, Fort Lauderdale, the Boston navy yard, Newport, aboard the cruiser USS *Huntington* based out of the Philadelphia navy yard, Guantanamo Bay, and San Pedro, California. Many of the female students had made friends or sweethearts during the brief period since the seamen arrived. The pace of campus life was so fast; time was so short; and then they were gone. With the constant arrivals and departures, some women plunged into their studies or work, reluctant to get too friendly. Others fell in love. Some even became interested in joining the navy.[59]

Most seamen considered the V–12 program a plum assignment. In turn, the navy, along with many others, regarded the trainees as the cream of the crop. Seaman Earl Bay remembers his ASTC colleagues as perhaps the finest people he ever worked with. One navy officer went so far as to recommend segregation of the trainees from other servicemen (mostly army) who might be passing through Flagstaff on furlough.[60]

The men were paid fifty dollars per month, more than double that of an army private. For a four-month semester, the total cost of a seaman's education at ASTC was $503.44—$200 in pay; $178 in food; $80 in college tuition and navy instruction; $6 for medical care; $32.96 for dormitories; and $6.48 for athletic equipment. Those coming from austere depression backgrounds happily adapted to the plush life, seen by some as a diet of "strawberries and cream." For others, the pay didn't quite match the $500 per month they had been earning at Lockheed. Many of the generous navy men shared their earnings with female friends. One seaman, a case in point, treated Rose Titus to a forty-five-cent banana split at the soda fountain—a considerable extravagance for the times, one that she has never forgotten.[61]

The infusion of government influence, money, and men onto the near-dormant campus kept the institution alive and probably stimulated the progress toward university status as well. In addition to the dozen new faculty members hired just before the navy's arrival, the college hired another science instructor and a history instructor, and added a curriculum research committee. The math department added Wednesday and Friday afternoon discussion seminars open for all interested in theories of abstract groups, differential equations, and continued fractions and their applications. They then added two new calculus and differential equations courses. The physics department also introduced a Wednesday afternoon seminar dedicated to the theory of relativity and wave mechanics. The history and social science department reorganized responsibilities, revised their curricula, and added new courses to better fit the needs of the students.

According to some, the faculty teaching load almost doubled. And, many of the students were very bright, having completed several semesters of studies at major universities, thus encouraging a talented and enthusiastic faculty to extend the depth and scope of their instruction. Likewise, the navy officers directing the studies program had all served at large colleges or universities and, knowing many seamen would be accepted for advanced studies, were not bashful in demanding rigorous engineering standards from the faculty.[62]

Navy training in Flagstaff continued throughout the war. The marines, however, were transferred after two terms, in early 1944, to Parris Island off the coast of South Carolina. The marine contingent was replaced by navy trainees who enlisted in the V-5 flight program, many coming from the University of Southern California. Commander Ralph B. Horner, a naval academy graduate, class of 1907, replaced commander Kaiser in August 1943 and commanded the ship's company until February of 1944, when he was replaced by Lt. LeRoy H. Schnell. Lt. Raymond C. Perry, who replaced Schnell in June, was a Stanford graduate and had earned a doctorate in education at the University of Southern California. He remained in command for the rest of the war.[63]

In the spring of 1945, "Stinky" Oliver and her roommate felt they needed to do something to help win the war. They too wanted to fight for their country. With the horrible battles of Iwo Jima and Okinawa providing an awful warning of what lay ahead in the invasion of Japan, they both joined the WAVES and shipped out for boot camp immediately following graduation.[64]

The navy program brought much-needed help to the school. Revenues, less the dining hall, for the year prior to the navy program (1942) were $263,094, of which $199,630 was the state legislative appropriation. Two years later, however, the total revenues more than doubled to $708,155, which included $110,980 for the navy program, $108,536 for the Civil Aeronautics Administration flight training at Cottonwood, and $159,236 for navy subsistence, along with the state appropriation of $199,000. The navy's rental of dorm rooms alone resulted in profits of $24,848 during their stay on campus, a considerable sum for the times. Acting president Bellwood noted that per capita costs did not increase during the war years, thanks to the navy, and that the situation placed the college in a good position to offer a general bachelor of arts degree to returning veterans.[65]

On October 9, 1945, the Women's Athletic Association sponsored a farewell ball for the V-12 unit with an "anchors aweigh" theme. On Saturday, October 20, the seamen participated in the traditional homecoming activities, the first since the fall of 1941 before Pearl Harbor. They accompanied the parade downtown and then watched the Lumberjack football team lose to the Luke Field Mustangs, 15–7.

Following the game, they departed by train and in private automobiles for eight days' leave, and then on to Albuquerque or the University of California at Los Angeles. As the seamen left town, most seemed to agree with petty officer Ludwig's lofty comment, "I don't care what yuh say—this place grows on yuh!"[66]

ARMAN PETERSON

The Fighting Arizona Colonel

No one knows exactly what happened to Col. Arman Peterson that day high in the skies above the Low Countries. His P-47 Thunderbolt—named *Flagari* for his beloved "old home town" of *Flag*staff, *Ari*zona—was heavily armored, equipped with cannons as well as machine guns and self-sealing fuel tanks that closed up when pierced by bullets. Although some complained that the Thunderbolt could not climb "worth a damn," Peterson, the former test pilot, veteran of forty-two combat missions, and an Army Air Corps rising star, knew how to make it climb by pushing the supercharged engine deep into the danger zone yet not beyond its limits.

Before dawn on the morning of July 1, 1943, the same day where back home the navy and marines would land at his alma mater, Peterson's Seventy-eighth Fighter Group lifted off from their base at Duxford, England, and headed for the Dutch coast. Peterson, as usual, led his men, the same as he had done on every mission regardless of how many planes were available from his three fighter squadrons—the Eighty-second, Eighty-third, and Eighty-fourth—totaling seventy-five planes.

Although Peterson could easily have sent his three squadrons out and remained back at base, he never did. Peterson strapped himself into *Flagari* and led the mission, whether it was a dozen, fifty, or, when other groups joined in, over one hundred fighters. He was not only the fighter group's twenty-eight-year-old commander of over 1,700 personnel, but he was also the base commander at Duxford Field and one of the youngest and most daring colonels in the United States Army, and by far the group's most experienced combat veteran at a time when pilots were often rotated back to the United States after twenty-five missions.

By the summer of 1943, Peterson not only had a third more missions than his most experienced pilot, but he also had twice as many missions as any other group commander in the Eighth Air Force. His reputation as the swashbuckling, cool, and courageous young commander of the American fighter pilots from Duxford was already widespread due to Associated Press and United Press dispatches, as well as accounts by his own men, who swore by him. His men not only *said* they would follow him anywhere, they did. He was a leader of the finest caliber and demonstrated courage, beyond a shadow of a doubt, that made him an idol. Peterson was described as "brilliant," setting an inspiring example of leadership for all members of his command.[1]

Peterson was one of those rare souls who had all the right stuff and every member of the command knew it. The younger pilots, especially, worshiped him. There was something about their colonel that eased the stress and tension of daily battle. When Peterson downed one German fighter and was asked how he did it, he replied, "Aw, he just floated along with his head under his arm and I shot him." Returning quietly from another mission when his plane had been hit but limped along with a gaping hole in the fuselage, Peterson, asked why he didn't call mayday over the radio, replied, "I was doing all right. It cut down my speed a little, that's all."[2]

Peterson, along with most of his pilots, preferred the air-to-air combat over other missions, especially when they went out searching for the Luftwaffe in "rodeos" or fighter "sweeps." They also pulled bomber-escort duty, along with strafing missions—perhaps the most dangerous due to enemy anti-aircraft artillery firing from the ground. Fighter pilots took great pride in their ability to test their skills against the Luftwaffe in one-on-one air combat. Dogfights were exciting and dangerous, and the confident young pilots eagerly sought the life-and-death struggle.[3]

Early on the morning of July 1, 1943, Peterson led not only his entire group of between 50 and 75 planes, but also the Fourth and Fifty-sixth Fighter Groups, for a total of 129 aircraft.[4] Every pilot

Arman Peterson graduated from ASTC in 1936 and became a fighter pilot and a test pilot before commanding the Seventy-Eighth Fighter Group at Duxford, England. He was shot down and killed over the Netherlands on his forty-third mission on July 1, 1943.

recognized his radio call sign, "Kingpost Leader." On this mission they were hunting for the Luftwaffe, not escorting bombers. Many earlier sweeps had failed to get the German fighters to come up and engage. The enemy pilots often preferred, instead, to husband their aircraft for the Allies' eventual land assault on the continent. On this day, however, the Germans came up, in numbers about equal to the Americans.

The three groups were at twenty-nine thousand feet doing 210 miles per hour as they flew just south of The Hague, near Hoek van Holland. Peterson's men spotted the enemy and were the only group to engage the Luftwaffe. The German Focke Wulf FW 190 fighters were below and to the west, placing the Thunderbolts in the glare of daybreak, an ideal attack position. Peterson called out, "There they are. They're Huns, lads. I am making a ninety-degree turn and going down. Give 'em hell! Here we go."

Leading a flight from his Eighty-fourth Squadron, Peterson ordered two pilots to tail him as he drove his fighter down violently to attack and break up four FW 190s. He immediately took out the lead plane and then climbed back up from his dive to get into attack position. The two tail men lost track of him in the sun's glare as Peterson made his Thunderbolt climb faster and higher. At the same time, he commanded his pilots to stay in pairs and attack the disarrayed Germans before they could regroup.[5]

In the huge dogfight of around one hundred fighters, someone heard Peterson saying, "Is anybody down here with me?" and others saw him fly into a cloud. Some saw parachutes that were probably German. As Peterson went into his second attack dive he did not have a wingman for cover. He was, according to one pilot, probably killed instantly by an unseen enemy fighter who attacked from above. In a few brief, violent minutes, the Americans shot down four German fighters, perhaps forced another down, and seriously damaged five others.

When the group finally landed back at Duxford, the men sat around waiting anxiously for all aircraft to return. One after another the planes came in, all but their commander, Colonel Peterson. Time stood still, and each minute seemed like an hour. Men drifted away from the softball game and began asking when was the last time anyone saw him. Finally, they could wait no longer. Acting without orders, hardly a spoken word, and almost in unison, every crewman and pilot refueled the Thunderbolts and the entire Seventy-eighth Fighter Group took off again looking for "Pete."

They made two sweeps of the day's combat zone, hoping to find their colonel, or any Germans who dared come up and fight again. It was a long shot, but they hoped he had bailed out, ditched into the Straits of Dover or the North Sea and was rescued, or landed on the continent and was captured by the enemy. Finally, running low on fuel, they returned to Duxford and the mess where Peterson had presided over the head table, and had talked about this or that with casual ease despite dangerous missions scheduled within the hour. That night there was a haunting stillness in the mess hall and a vacancy at the head table—but no mourning. American fighter pilots don't mourn.[6]

The news spread quickly. Hugh Baillie, head of United Press, released a dispatch from London, "Heroic Col. Peterson Lost in Air Scrap with Nazis." The Associated Press and *Stars and Stripes*—the armed forces newspaper—provided details of the story.

There were other theories on what happened to Peterson. He may have been hit by friendly fire, again, as happened the month before while escorting B-17 Flying Fortresses ("Forts") on their bombing runs over France and Germany. Peterson accepted the risk and held no grudge, saying, "It's just part of the job to protect the Forts and I got too close."[7] On his last mission, however, Peterson and his men were out hunting, not escorting bombers. His oxygen system may have malfunctioned at thirty thousand feet when he pushed the plane into a violent dive as he chased the German Focke Wulfs. Or, perhaps least likely, he may have been hit by anti-aircraft artillery.[8]

Back home, the July 9 *Coconino Sun*'s bold headline "Col. Arman Peterson Missing in Action" shocked the Flagstaff community. Peterson was the town's shining star, someone destined to not only become one of the army's youngest general officers, but after the war perhaps an Arizona or national leader as well. It ran in the family.

His father, Andrew C. Peterson, for whom Northern Arizona University's Peterson Hall is named, was an Arizona pioneer, part of the Mormon migration that crossed Lee's Ferry in 1878, settled at Saint Johns, and watched the Atlantic & Pacific Railroad cross Arizona Territory. He served in the Spanish-American War, graduated from Brigham Young University, and earned a master's degree from the University of Utah. He returned to Utah as high school principal and district superintendent at Spanish Fork, where Arman grew up until age nine. He then took the family to Arizona, where he served as a prominent educator and was active in politics, becoming speaker of the house in the Fourth Arizona Legislature. Known as "A. C.,"

Peterson was also professor of political science and sociology at ASTC in Flagstaff from 1927 until his retirement in 1944.[9]

At Flagstaff High School there were hints that Peterson's son Arman was different—that somehow he was not made like the rest. Not only was he an unequivocal extrovert who thrived around others, but he also had many close and lasting friendships. He was a good recreational tennis player and an accomplished violinist who gave recitals at a young age. Despite numerous activities, he was one of the kids who always worked after school. He landed a job at Schmidt Jewelry Store when he was in the eighth grade and worked there through college. He also worked at the Webber Brothers service station, delivering gasoline to their underground tanks. Although he played varsity basketball and was on the track team in high school, his jobs prevented him from practicing with the teams.

Peterson took studies seriously and always held an A (4.0) average. He was high school class valedictorian, and at ASTC, where he was elected student body president twice, he was active with the debate team, served as manager and editor of the student newspaper, and received the coveted Lowell Award for outstanding scholarship. He majored in mathematics, with minors in history and political science. He was also somewhat of an entrepreneur, bottling water from Leroux Spring at a time when Flagstaff's reservoir was low and polluted by too many salamanders, and selling the five-gallon jugs to ready buyers. He used the profits to pay off the loan for his "snazzy" Ford Model A roadster convertible.[10]

As a youngster, Peterson saw a World War I biplane and was hooked. He later flew as a passenger and decided aviation was definitely for him. Following graduation from ASTC in 1936, he joined the Army Air Corps. Peterson earned a regular army commission as a second lieutenant after completing aviation training at Randolph Field, then called "West Point of the air," and Kelly Field at San Antonio, Texas, where he graduated third in a class of several hundred. He was selected to lead the graduation ceremony's grand flight review and eventually passed the difficult hurdles to become a "pursuit" or fighter pilot.

At Peterson's first duty station, however, it appeared that his luck might have changed. He was summoned by a board of investigating officers at Barksdale Field, Louisiana, where the best pilots in the American army were tenaciously recruited by both sides of the war in Spain. Peterson had been caught violating regulations—flying his plane upside down, in a formation of three, just a few feet above the cotton fields. The punishment, however, was minimal and Peterson's brief career remained intact.

In 1938 Peterson married a beautiful ASTC schoolmate from California, Juliet "Julie" Osborn, who had previously been selected college homecoming queen by movie star Andy Divine. A skilled seamstress, Julie made her own depression-era wedding gown out of silk that Arman had salvaged from old or unserviceable parachutes. In 1939 the young army couple was posted to Moffett Field, near San Jose, California, and began a series of assignments that would catapult his career to high command.[11]

Peterson was selected to be a test pilot for the new Curtis P-40— a Curtis P-36 with an improved engine—at Wright-Patterson Field in Dayton, Ohio. The new engine changed the aerodynamics, and the army wanted to test the plane in dives at terminal velocity, a dangerous experiment.

Peterson's first test flight did not go as expected. The P-40 would not come out of its dive. As the plane plunged out of control toward the earth, Peterson tried to bail out but the cockpit canopy was stuck. He radioed back to the base and told them they needed to fix that on future models. Meanwhile, he tried various combinations of movements on the controls without success. As the plane hurtled downward he unstrapped his safety harness and crawled as far forward in the cockpit as possible, hoping the shift of his body weight might cause a change in the plane's attitude. No luck. He then reached up under the cockpit and cranked the control for the stabilizer fin that was hinged to the elevators. Nothing. Suddenly, the plane, on its own, came out of the dive and even started to climb. Peterson managed to regain his seat despite heavy gravitational forces, and finally took control of the wild aircraft. After landing, Peterson discovered that pulling out of the dive had bent both wingtips up about a foot.[12]

The Petersons were posted to March Field at Riverside, California, where he flew Lockheed P-38 Lightnings and commanded a squadron for over a year. On one flight, his nosewheel would not come down as he approached the field. Despite various measures, nothing worked. Peterson regained altitude, circled the area, and flew out his remaining fuel. Meanwhile, the newspapers and radio stations got wind of the emergency, flocked to the field, and turned the situation into a media event as Peterson carefully brought down his plane for the first P-38 belly landing.

The young pilot often took advantage of cross-country trips to drop into Flagstaff and visit his parents and friends. Peterson, sometimes bringing along a fellow pilot, would circle the town before landing. His parents recognized the plane and would head immediately for the air field and bring them home. On one trip, however, Peterson was stranded at the Flagstaff field with engine difficulties. Pilots were strictly forbidden from working on their aircraft. Hence, his brother Dale repaired the propeller gear mechanism in the plane's nose and Arman eventually took off.[13]

After Pearl Harbor, the Petersons were posted for a second time to Hamilton Field north of San Francisco, where Arman was assigned coast patrol duty. The *Oakland Tribune* did a multipage story about Peterson's squadron that included photos of Arman in his cockpit, instructing his pilots, taking off, and in the air. In May he was selected to command the new Seventy-eighth Fighter Group of P-38 Lightnings that had been activated in February 1942 at Baer Field, Indiana, and moved to Hamilton Field. Two months later, after already losing one child in birth, his wife Julie gave birth to Susan Julie on July 18, 1942. Peterson, meanwhile, rushed to train his pilots and ground crews, losing about one pilot each month in fatal crashes. The new group, with their motto "Above the Foe," sailed from New York to England on the *Queen Elizabeth* on November 24 to join the Eighth Air Force. Julie returned to Flagstaff to be with Arman's family.

Peterson's group was stationed on the east coast of England at Goxhill, about 150 miles north of London. In February 1943 he lost most of his pilots and P-38 Lightnings to the Twelfth Air Force for support of Operation Torch, the invasion of North Africa. Peterson

Peterson stands in front of his Curtis P-36 Hawk at the Flagstaff air field. Peterson and his friends often took advantage of cross-country trips to drop into Flagstaff and visit his parents.

then received the first operational P-47 Thunderbolts, along with new pilots and crew. Once again he rushed his men through training on a new plane. After they were combat ready, all 1,700 personnel and seventy-five aircraft moved on April 1 from Goxhill to Duxford, nine miles southeast of Cambridge, where the grass runway two thousand yards long and sixteen hundred yards wide allowed mass takeoffs and landings.[14]

Pilots who served with Peterson remember that he thrived in advance planning, whether it was bore-sighting the guns, improving gun sights, compasses, or other parts of the planes, or having the command give up two weeks of rations to feed local children. When commanders met at the Air Ministry, Peterson was always a step ahead of the others.

Colonel Peterson's advance planning extended to other areas. Before leaving the states, Peterson and his men carefully packed and shipped several crates of American liquor, which was enjoyed at Christmas when he spoke to the group saying, "Like you all, I would rather be at home with my family, but failing that I am with those I'd next rather be with, the men of the Seventy-eighth." Two months later the remainder of the booze was used to bid farewell to their North Africa–bound comrades in a raucous ceremony at the officers' club, marked by flying glasses and liquor bottles, "bombing" of the ceiling lights, use of all available fire extinguishers, and general buffoonery bordering on debauchery that only those exposed to the daily wages and perils of war can fully understand or appreciate.

At Duxford, word of Peterson's skills began to get around. He led fighter sweeps on April 8. Then, on April 13, just four and a half hours after returning with his Eighty-third Squadron, Peterson took off again for France leading his Eighty-second Squadron, along with a squadron from the Fourth Fighter Group and one from the Fifty-sixth Fighter Group. He led missions on April 15, 17, 21, and 29, and the group settled into what was to become a routine pattern of operations with Peterson leading his three squadrons of sixteen planes each.

As his group's striking power developed and they engaged the Luftwaffe more frequently, Peterson's star also rose as he skyrocketed through the ranks, promoted from lieutenant to full colonel in just over a year. As the Eighth Air Force struggled with aviation theory and the best role for their bombers and fighters, the effectiveness of Colonel Peterson's Thunderbolts helped reassure leaders that the bomber escort concept was sound. In record-breaking bomber raids, Peterson's group flew escort over Antwerp and Kiel in mid-May, getting their first kills. Peterson soon shot down his first Messerschmitt ME 109—although some reports credited him with three. The group also continued fighter sweeps searching for the Luftwaffe.[15]

In June, the Allies' Combined Bomber Offensive over Nazi–occupied Europe officially started. At the same time, it was obvious that Peterson's Seventy-eighth Fighter Group was the most successful of VIII Fighter Command's three groups, due to the courageous and energetic young commander who was called "the fighting Arizona colonel" and led every mission in *Flagari*, regardless of the target or dangers involved. Morale was high. The pilots and ground crews were comrades in arms and reportedly "grinned easily." Radio broadcasts to the United States were made from Duxford Field and press dispatches glorified the army colonel. Media personalities flocked to the base—including Walter Cronkite and United Press director Hugh Baillie, both of whom came to meet Peterson and have their photos taken with a true warrior. William Randolph Hearst Jr. came to Duxford, along with Gladwin Hill of the Associated Press.

Some newsmen even listened in to Peterson's wireless during air battles as he warned of "bandits at two o'clock," or told his men that he was going down to keep the Luftwaffe away from airmen bailing out of a doomed B-17 bomber. They listened as Peterson put his Thunderbolt into a dive and instructed his pilots to "Keep your eyes open now, check your gas gauges, and head for home when low."

Peterson was not only a warrior, but he was also charming, fun to be around, and endeared himself to those he came in contact with. Capt. Eddie Rickenbacker came to Duxford, as did the "father" of the Royal Air Force, Viscount Trenchard. Generals Hap Arnold, Ira Eaker, and Jacob Devers visited Peterson. James Cagney, Bing Crosby, and singer Frances Langford came to his base, as did King George VI and Queen Elizabeth, and Sir Anthony Eden, the British minister of foreign affairs, who even invited Peterson to play some tennis. The charismatic colonel handled the dignitaries—and the generals who tagged along—with ease, as well as anyone else who came to see one of America's best-known airmen of mid-1943.

Peterson also knew how to deal effectively with his superiors. Despite a severe shortage of aviation fuel in June, he dispatched his pilots on various missions to salvage parts and supplies needed for his aircraft and men, as well as on a few unauthorized "social calls." When Peterson received a curt order from Eighth Air Force Headquarters telling him to comply with guidelines on fuel conservation, he reflected for a moment and then casually told the caller that the commanding general's airplane had flown to Land's End to purchase fresh crabs for a Sunday dinner. Peterson heard nothing more about fuel restrictions.

Between June 18 and 23, and a mission over Huls, The Netherlands, Peterson wrote his last letter to his wife and family in Flagstaff.

He responded to their previous comments on ASTC affairs, the recent cold snap in town, the difficulty of gardening, and asked for a photo as proof that Flagstaff victory gardens could grow anything at high altitude. He mentioned that he had shot down another enemy fighter on June 22, adding a second German flag to the tail of his Thunderbolt, preferring to leave the details until he returned home.[16]

Following the loss of Col. Arman Peterson on July 1, the group's pilots continued to conduct search patrols over the battle zone. When Bob Hope performed at Duxford two days later, on July 3, morale was so low the Hollywood comedian admitted he had never had such difficulty getting a laugh. Hope said it was one of his toughest USO shows, as pilots and crews got up and left to take their turns on search patrols. Eventually, the officers gathered at the officers club and conducted their ritual eulogy for missing pilots—a pyramid of men hoisted someone up to the vaulted ceiling and wrote Peterson's name in candle soot. Although an unusual ceremony, for the men of the Seventy-eighth Fighter Group it bore almost mystical significance.

The Peterson family was notified that Arman was missing in action on his forty-third mission. They were not aware, however, that the Germans had recovered his body from recently harvested farmland near the coast of Ouddorp, Holland, where his parachute had malfunctioned and he died on impact from a broken neck. One witness, however, reported that a German soldier had fired at Peterson, perhaps the cause of the damaged parachute. *Flagari* crashed into nearby shallow waters.

The Peterson family and Flagstaff community prayed for Arman's return, hoping that he was still alive somewhere. Finally, on August 6, after five dreadful weeks, the German government reported Peterson's death to the International Red Cross, and the army informed Julie the same day. The *Coconino Sun*'s bold headline of August 13 announced the loss of a favorite son. The Germans released the body to the Dutch Red Cross for burial in the local cemetery.

In October, army representatives presented Mrs. Peterson his medals, among them the Distinguished Flying Cross, the Silver Star, the Air Medal with three Oak Leaf Clusters, and the Purple Heart.

Officers of the Royal Air Force sent a large silver cup, and the Soviets awarded him the Order of the Patriotic War First Class for his work in helping clear the skies for Soviet ships in cold seas below. Peterson was one of fifty-one recipients of a Soviet medal—General Dwight D. Eisenhower another. Sir Anthony Eden had taken a personal liking to Peterson and sent a letter expressing his deepest sympathy. The Arizona legislature passed a concurrent resolution expressing "great pride" in one of the state's best-known airmen, and conveyed sympathy to his father, the Hon. A. C. Peterson, ex–Speaker of the House of Representatives, and to his mother, widow, and daughter.[17]

Some probably wondered if Col. Arman Peterson hadn't done enough after twenty-five or thirty missions, especially considering that he had a wife and daughter back home. As the group commander he did not have to lead every mission. Of the Seventy-eighth Fighter Group's seven wartime commanders, Peterson was the only one killed in action. Arman Peterson, however, was not the type of commander who could send others into harm's way and kick up his heels back at the field.

The death of such a popular, promising, and heroic young man brought the horror of World War II to the heart of the Flagstaff community, where people were stunned by the loss. Almost everyone in town knew or had heard of him. Peterson's story, however, is but one example from the scores of other courageous Flagstaff boys and men who fought far from home and whose history is yet to be told. More were reported missing, killed in action, or held as prisoners of war. Seventeen servicemen from Flagstaff and fifty-one from Coconino County died in the war, and many others returned seriously injured. The loss of Col. Arman Peterson, however, seemed especially tragic to the community.[18]

8

A TOWN ON THE MOVE

Flagstaff at War

The loss of seventeen Flagstaff boys should have been enough for the small mountain town, but there was more. With no place for the new workers to stay, the Flagstaff housing shortage became critical, if not chaotic. For women, new tensions accompanied the new opportunities. Racial and labor unrest surfaced, and juvenile delinquency took an alarming turn. Meanwhile, military airplanes all too often crashed into the San Francisco Mountains.

The housing shortage quickly became a major crisis in 1942 when about fifteen thousand construction workers and family members descended on Flagstaff, a town of only five thousand. City planners expected about seven of the eight thousand workers to be the contractors' problem. The contractors, however, primarily Atkinson-Kier, housed only about a thousand in the barracks on the work site. Indian Village helped, where over three thousand workers and family members soon settled.

Flagstaff officials had planned, based upon the fact-finding trip to Fort Wingate, to provide housing for only five hundred depot employees who would remain for the permanent wartime labor force—in itself a difficult task. The city's limited space was quickly taken with the arrival of the first engineers in January 1942. Consequently, with nothing available, many disgruntled people camped around Flagstaff, Bellemont, and Williams. In the end, at least five thousand of the fifteen thousand men, women, and children remained in Flagstaff looking for homes, apartments, hotel rooms, or just about anything. Relief was not forthcoming from the private sector because resources and labor needed to build homes were scarce.[1]

Most residents opened their hearts and homes to the newcomers, but a few took advantage of the "wild times" that were not dissimilar to the gold rush. In the summer of 1942, however, the gold came from pockets of desperate workers in the form of rent money. Although an increase in rents would be expected, the wild orgy of price gouging by some was unprecedented.

Many renters who lived in Flagstaff before the onslaught and were not employed at the project quickly found themselves out of money or out on the street. One family renting a home near 111 North Beaver Street for thirty-five dollars per month was suddenly moved to a back-lot "shack" and paying eighty-five dollars. Jesus Gil noted that if some-one had an old woodshed that needed burning down, it was high time to rent it out in 1942. A bootblack in town paid two rent raises in two months, but when asking for a receipt was told to pay up or get out. Many rents doubled or tripled—even for rooms with an outside toilet, no electricity or running water, bad floors, leaks, and bedbugs. Mrs. Harrison, at 19 North Park Street, squeezed many renters into one room and raised the rent at the same time. Some poor souls even paid rent just to set up their tent on someone's property. Almost all of the city's seventeen tourist courts charged exorbitant prices, one as high as one hundred dollars per month—a month's pay for a common la-borer.[2]

Some greedy landlords were unusually creative. Mrs. Moran, who owned the Tour Inn at 9 West Phoenix Avenue, locked the rest rooms and shut off the hot water to force her old renters out. She then jacked up the price for depot workers flush with cash and willing to pay boomtown rates. She even locked one renter out of his room and then charged him five dollars just to get back in for his things. Mamie Bradford rented her dirt-floor garage at 112 Mike's Pike to a family. One landlord of eight properties, Manuel Vasquez, never gave receipts. Vandevier's Lodge and Auto Inn hiked the rent fifty cents every day. Complaints of gouging flooded the chamber of commerce and law enforcement offices faster than they could be addressed.[3]

The situation deteriorated and Maj. Demmie Cox, the project engineer, warned that he would report unfair landlords directly to

Washington. Nevertheless, rents continued to soar out of control, despite the fact that Flagstaff was listed as a defense rental area and prices were frozen as early as March 1, 1942. Questions and answers concerning federal rent control appeared in the *Coconino Sun*. The local War Price and Rationing Board met in the Masonic Building and issued its "last warning" to those unwilling to comply with federal regulations.

Despite the warnings, rents continued to climb and some landlords raked in outrageous profits. Chamber of commerce secretary Leo Weaver, hoping to deflate the scandal, finally appealed directly to the Arizona Office of Price Administration for the establishment of a local rent control office. The OPA commissioned the U.S. Bureau of Labor Statistics to conduct a thorough inspection of the notorious Flagstaff situation. The complaints proved justified. Frank Gold, a local attorney and chairman of the rationing board, assumed duties as district attorney for federal rent regulation enforcement, and W. E. Jolly, justice of the peace, resigned and assumed duties of rent examiner.[4]

Even as officials attempted to enforce more rental laws, which went into effect on October 1, 1942, it was obvious that the situation was spinning dangerously out of control. The coming of winter threatened to jeopardize the defense project because many families were without permanent shelter. Hundreds of people camped around Flagstaff and Bellemont in tents, huts, and lean-to shacks. Some lived in their cars, parking across the street from a school, and mothers would hang blankets on fences to dry in the sun while children were in class.

Finally, on October 15, the National Housing Agency declared Flagstaff a "critical war site" and approved the emergency construction of ninety-six new double-family duplex dwellings under Title 6 of the Federal Housing Authority Act. The $575,000 project (about $6 million today) would consist of two hundred temporary units costing $2,000 each. Additionally, the NHA approved forty-six permanent homes costing a total of $175,000. Architectural work would be done by the Lescher & Mahoney Company of Phoenix, and the entire project would be federally financed. Although Flagstaff could not tax the federal property, a portion of the rent would be paid to the city in lieu of taxes. As with the January 1942 announcement of the ordnance depot construction, the addition of two hundred housing units was theretofore unimaginable, and once again staggered and delighted local citizens and desperate workers.[5]

On Wednesday, November 11, the San Francisco office of the FHA dropped another bombshell. They notified Major Myrick by telegram of an even larger emergency housing program for Flagstaff and Navajo Depot that included the two projects already announced in October, plus four additional projects consisting of more houses and dormitory apartments, renovation of the Veterans CCC camp on the Fort Valley Road, and thirty houses for the depot.[6]

Nationwide, efforts to solve the housing crisis moved slowly until President Roosevelt consolidated sixteen different housing organizations into the National Housing Agency in February 1942. Once underway, and despite concerns by New Deal reformers who wanted to use public housing to revitalize cities and confront social ills, the government rapidly spent $2.3 billion in a massive construction program, some of which was destined for Flagstaff.[7]

As cold weather arrived in late 1942, however, there was no sign that the homeless workers, wives, and children would find relief. The Lescher & Mahoney plans for the projects were delayed and bids were not taken until January 1943, when the contract for the two hundred temporary units was awarded to the Del E. Webb Company of Phoenix for $511,569 (about $5.3 million today). It would provide lodging for about eight hundred people—about one-sixth of the city's prewar population, or about two decades' worth of growth.

The NHA placed the remaining five projects on hold, expecting the worst of the crisis to soon be over; officials believed the two hundred new units would be adequate to meet long-term needs as depot construction workers left the area for other top-dollar jobs. The Del E. Webb Company began work on Wednesday, January 27, just days after winning the contract. Meanwhile, homeless workers and families burrowed into any corner or niche that offered shelter for the remainder of the winter.[8]

Del Webb had started a Phoenix contracting company in 1927 and prospered during the Great Depression. He was already familiar with Flagstaff, having renovated Taylor Hall at the Arizona State Teachers College on a PWA project. By 1941, Webb had established himself as one of the largest contractors in Arizona. After Pearl Harbor the government looked to Webb for work on a list of projects, including major construction at Williams Field, Fort Huachuca, Luke Field, and the Japanese-American Relocation Camp at Parker.[9]

The Del E. Webb Company wasted no time. They were given one hundred days—until April 17—to complete the work, and they expected to be on time. Construction continued through May, however, due to shortages in all kinds of metal products. A desperate housing situation grew even worse when sixty families were forced to vacate the ASTC stone cottages on June 20 to make room for students attending the summer session. Meanwhile, ten boxcars of FHA furniture arrived in mid-June. Families finally began moving into Flagstaff's new federal homes—War Housing Project No. 2221—in July.

War Housing Project No. 2221 was located northwest of Antelope Spring and today's Flagstaff monument adjacent to Flagstaff Middle School. The project was named Clark Homes in honor of pioneer John Clark, who formerly ranched on the site. Clark Homes, as a federal project, was first occupied by ordnance and other war workers along with army and navy personnel. With two hundred units and hundreds of children, it soon became a village unto itself.

Eventually, everyone from college administrators and professors to depot laborers lived in Clark Homes. For some it became "the place to live" in town and they couldn't wait to move in. For others "it was a pit." The homes resembled military barracks with thin walls that did little to keep noises out or warmth in. Fumes from kerosene used in heating and cooking were especially unpleasant.[10]

Flagstaff, as with the other new ordnance and military cities scattered across the trans–Mississippi West, found the war at its doorstep just weeks after Pearl Harbor when the depot project engineers arrived in town. There was little time to mobilize the public and organize for war. Although far from western ports and large military training bases, Flagstaff was immediately caught up in the determination of a nation at arms. The struggle demanded patriotism, economic mobilization, sacrifice, and the shaping of public opinion.

The *Coconino Sun* was the most effective instrument used to influence local public opinion, with articles on battles overseas, rationing, civil defense, victory garden bulletins, depot news, war bond drives, the meat shortage, and hundreds of other war-related topics. Publisher Columbus Giragi unleashed his contempt for the Axis hordes in a column "Sparks from the Grindstone." The army's ordnance department saw Flagstaff as an "ordnance town" and provided regular public relations releases. These articles not only gave depot workers and local citizens the big picture in the nationwide manufacture, shipping, maintenance, and storage of ordnance and hardware similar to that found at Bellemont, but they also provided information about how the munitions were being used against America's enemies around the world.

Colonel Huling frequently used the *Coconino Sun* to address Navajo Depot problems, disseminate ordnance department bulletins, ask for help, recognize achievements, and provide a history of military subjects. The *Coconino Sun* also followed servicemen like Arman Peterson, soldiers with Company I and the "Bushmasters," announced draft calls, listed those drafted along with volunteers, welcomed returning veterans, congratulated those cited for bravery, and reported those missing and killed in action.

For Flagstaff women, the war was a milestone as well as an enormous challenge. The women who were not employed were expected to work with the Red Cross, in civil defense, or on other war-related projects. There was much to be done. For those who had jobs at Bellemont, the war opened many doors and provided opportunities previously unavailable and unimaginable.

Hundreds of local women, along with Navajo and Hopi women from the reservations, found their first good-paying jobs at the depot, where they joined thousands around the country as "women ordnance workers," or "WOWs." Even before entering the war, the percentage of female employees in the ordnance department had risen from 11.5 percent in the summer of 1940 to 17 percent by July 1941. The War

Department initially encouraged heavy defense industries to use women only after all available men in the area had been employed. In Flagstaff, however, everything changed instantly after Pearl Harbor, not so much because of the departure of men for the service, but rather because of the eight thousand construction jobs created overnight at Bellemont. Even after depot construction was completed, the two thousand permanent depot jobs were far more than the city's prewar or wartime population could effectively support. Due to the chronic depot labor shortage, Flagstaff women were not just encouraged to work at Bellemont, they were desperately needed, and they knew it. It was a nice feeling.[11]

By 1942, the ordnance department, as well as other government branches, media, and industry, organized aggressive recruiting campaigns to persuade women to enter the workforce, achieving an extraordinary degree of intervention in the American economy as well as shaping social attitudes and values. The War Manpower Commission searched for women in areas where laborers were few. The Office of War Information also targeted women, promising patriotic and exciting work for high wages.

In October 1942, the manager of the U.S. Employment Service in Flagstaff stated that race, age, and sex were no longer barriers for defense work. He warned those women not yet working in the war effort to pick their job in a defense industry before they were assigned something. The ordnance department goal for employing women climbed to 60 percent, and the percentage of female workers peaked at 47.6 percent in the spring of 1945. At Navajo Depot, however, the number of women employed fluctuated between five and seven hundred, and probably remained close to one third of the labor force due to the limited number of women in the area.[12]

After steadily courting women for eighteen months, the ordnance department publicized a 1943 survey that reflected attitudes of the period rather than any serious examination of working women's issues. The survey stated that women had greater finger dexterity than men, greater patience, and greater enthusiasm. It also said women took instructions far more personally than men, that they were patriotic without cynicism, and that they did not mind getting their hands and faces dirty. On the other hand, it also reported that women wanted their jobs glamorized and the lack of beauty shops in town could cause serious problems. The survey also noted that women would accept 99 percent of the responsibility for a task, but they always wanted "to receive a final O.K. on their work from a man."[13]

American women responded to the call to work with enthusiasm. Their numbers rose from 14.6 million in 1941 to 19.4 million by 1944, when 37 percent of all adult women were employed. By the end of the war, women held 38 percent of all federal jobs. The greatest change for Flagstaff women, as well as for women across the nation, was the employment of large numbers of married women. Before the war the average working woman was young, single, and usually not in search of a permanent position. During the war, however, married women accounted for almost three-quarters of the increase in women's employment rates, and for the first time in American history married workers outnumbered single workers.[14]

Many American women worked at monotonous and routine jobs on assembly lines where hours passed slowly. These jobs had often been redefined from male to female work. This was not the case at Navajo Ordnance Depot, where women were immediately employed in a variety of areas that included driving heavy semitrailers, checking munition lot numbers, drop-testing fuses, and cleaning, stamping, painting, inspecting, and shipping ammunition. They worked on assembly lines and they also maintained, modified, and repaired serviceable and damaged ammunition. They operated forklifts, managed road and rail traffic, repaired vehicles, ran the mail room, and became logistics specialists. In far more dangerous work, they salvaged the explosive charge (TNT) from unusable or outdated shells. Although women were also employed in administration, many of the depot jobs were dangerous and required specific training. With women working at almost everything except heavy lifting, it was not uncommon for them to be involved in serious accidents requiring hospitalization.[15]

Lois "Fergi" Ferguson (Price) was a Navajo Depot telephone operator who lived in a Victory Village barracks for telephone operators,

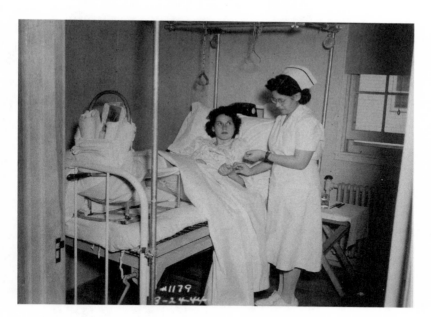

Trini Lopez attends to an injured employee at the depot hospital. Navajo and Hopi women along with Flagstaff women made up about one-third of the depot's labor force. They were employed in all areas of work except for heavy lifting and serious injuries were not uncommon.

where there was also a housemother in residence. Her family, typical of many, was separated by the war. Her mother remained in Socorro, New Mexico; her brother was in the navy; and she followed her railroad-worker father to Bellemont, where he lived in the section house. Ferguson was young and wanted to go home to her family, but there was no home to return to. She took some pleasure in watching the frequent trains loaded with guns, equipment, and troops passing through Bellemont, with soldiers hanging from the windows asking "Where are we? What town is this?" and "What's the price of whiskey here?" For Ferguson, the locomotive's whistle conveyed a certain sadness. The work as a depot telephone operator was often very lonesome.[16]

Before the war, many of Flagstaff's Hispanic girls and women worked for middle- and upper-class families as maids. Their pay was usually low and their duties often included laundry, baby-sitting, and preparing meals. After Navajo Depot opened, however, many of these women left domestic work and took more meaningful and challenging jobs at Bellemont where the pay was much higher.[17]

For nineteen-year-old Jessie Jimenez (Alonzo), depot work meant "doing a man's job" and bringing home a "man's" paycheck. She worked at a variety of tasks, including stenciling, inspecting, and loading and unloading grenades and ammunition. For the first time in her life she felt involved in something significant. The job and good pay were very important for her and other depot employees from Flagstaff's thriving Hispanic community at Plaza Vieja, at the Old Town Spring, and Plaza Nueva, or "little Mexico," south of the railroad tracks and east of Beaver Street. She was proud of the uniform that was offered to depot employees for voluntary wear in town. Eventually, several of her children would be born at the depot hospital.[18]

Flagstaff was on the move, and some of this was attributed to women at Navajo Ordnance Depot working round-the-clock shifts in jobs they never could have imagined. Women—Navajo, Hopi, Hispanic, and Anglo—who had never held a rifle were doing just about everything with ammunition except the actual firing. Women who had never seen an explosive were now cleaning, painting, and stenciling everything from a grenade to a one-thousand-pound bomb.

Navajo Ordnance Depot was but one of many organizations competing for the services of local women. When the Civil Aeronautics Administration's campaign to create more pilots proved effective at ASTC and across the country, the army announced a similar program in December, 1943, to recruit "air minded" women for the Women's Army Corps. The "Air-WAC" program advertised 155 aviation-related jobs available to women—almost everything except actually flying the plane. Flagstaff recruiters entreated, "Every woman . . . has a job waiting for her in the Army Air Forces" where she could demonstrate "her courage and loyalty, and have an opportunity to obtain valuable training for peacetime employment." The army's Air-WAC office in the Flagstaff chamber of commerce building assured women there were

Jessie Jimenez (Alonzo) was one of many in Flagstaff's Hispanic community who left their jobs in town for work at Navajo Depot. Jimenez loaded grenades, checked ammunition for damage, and stenciled and painted ammunition. Women at Navajo Depot were issued a uniform for voluntary off-duty wear.

jobs in the air corps for those from nearly every field of business and industry.[19]

Some Flagstaff women signed up immediately. For single women like Earlene Ellsworth, the Air-WACs was appealing. She enlisted, as did Althea Ragsdale, head librarian at ASTC, who surprised faculty and friends alike when she joined up, stating that her association with the V-12 apprentice seamen and marines on campus convinced her she could serve her country best by joining the service. As with the Navajo Depot jobs, air corps positions also appealed to married women like Theresa Sarabia, who had worked at Babbitts, and Jane Drye, daughter of the Flagstaff chief of police. Caroline Blahnik was Flagstaff's first woman to be accepted by the regular WACs, saying she was willing to do anything to be of assistance in "this man's army," also noting that the first WAC to land on foreign soil was an Arizona woman. Mrs. Blahnik was soon followed into the WACs by another married woman, Hazel Power.[20]

The other services also wanted Flagstaff women. Three sisters, Vivien, Edith, and Isabelle Brooksby joined the WASPS, hoping to become ferry pilots. Flagstaff's first WAVE, Annice McGinley, a librarian and teacher at Flagstaff High School, signed up in February 1943. Maryann Granan and Beatrice Herring also joined the WAVES, as did ASTC homecoming queen Katherine Kramer and student body president "Stinky" Oliver. Billie Weaver, Leo Weaver's daughter, became an army nurse, as did Aline McCoy and several others.[21]

World War II resulted in an unprecedented mobilization that touched all women in Flagstaff, whether they worked at home, in town, at Navajo Ordnance Depot, volunteered for the armed forces, or helped with everyday activities that were suddenly deemed critical to meet the social needs of American wartime society. The ordinary trappings of daily life were no longer available—they were used to fight the war. Consequently, Flagstaff women salvaged, saved, and recycled metal toothpaste tubes, tin cans, shoes, and paper. They carefully used their ration coupons to get small portions of scarce supplies of meat, gasoline, coffee, cigarettes, and sugar. They collected scrap metal and tires and served as chairmen of salvage and clothing drives.[22]

Flagstaff women also grew some of their own food in victory gardens. They enrolled for "active service" in numerous civil defense duties and signed up for first aid, rescue, ambulance, casualty, and decontamination squads, and also learned how to combat gas and air attacks and fire. They ran "victory book campaigns" and collected hundreds of volumes for shipment to servicemen overseas. They volunteered for War Relief Fund drives, bond drives, and many other fund-raisers. Some formed a local unit of the Women's Motor Corps to drive trucks, ambulances, and cars for the emergency evacuation of civilians. Women volunteered as nurse's aides and helped staff the locally funded servicemen's center at Hotel Monte Vista and the USO on Leroux Street. Some worked as Red Cross volunteers in dozens of areas, to include knitting and sewing. Others did clerical work for parents of missing servicemen and parents of servicemen killed or taken prisoner.[23]

The women of Flagstaff were also called upon to help feed some of the thousands of soldiers and sailors passing through town on the constant stream of westbound trains. Teeming with troops, munitions, and equipment, the trains roared into Flagstaff day and night, many making brief stops. The American Red Cross provided city women a one- or two-day advance notice of feeding requirements, along with the trains' arrival and departure times. Some of the times were not convenient. One group organized by Ethel Sechrist fed 225 sailors, beginning at 7:30 P.M. on a Saturday night.[24]

Even proper feeding and care of the American family was promoted as an important part of defense work, something that should receive the attention of every Flagstaff "housewife and mother." In addition to the hardships of food shortages and rationing, long and grueling hours of work at home or in the shop, office, or at Navajo Depot, Flagstaff women were told that proper care was not being given to domestic health. The employment of female workers, and especially the entry of large numbers of Flagstaff mothers into defense work at Navajo Depot, was cause for alarm, according to the secretary of the local welfare board. In Flagstaff, as elsewhere across the nation, all available single women were hired by 1943. This resulted in the hiring of housewives and mothers and was viewed by some as "even more disturbing." Nursery day care and even foster homes were suggested as solutions for Flagstaff children, although neither was implemented. The Red Cross sponsored courses in nutrition and adequate diet to enable women to prepare well-balanced meals, something that would become more difficult as the war progressed.[25]

Juvenile delinquency was also attributed to working women. According to city officials, the volatile combination of Flagstaff's boom-town conditions, acute housing shortage, lack of teenage supervision and day care facilities, and especially the employment of the city's women—notably mothers with children—contributed to the social ills and enormous domestic difficulties that were rampant by the summer of 1943. The city's juvenile delinquency rose by 50 percent from the previous year, and rose 75 percent in three years. Serious juvenile crimes increased by 100 percent in just one year.

Coconino County superior court judge H. K. Mangum warned the community about juveniles with nothing to do but get into trouble, and the "appalling" number of youngsters under the age of thirteen who committed offenses. Most offenders, however, were between the ages of thirteen and sixteen, and their crimes included disturbing the peace, petty and grand larceny, carrying concealed weapons, assault and battery, and even rape. The Flagstaff youth, according to Sheriff Peery Francis, were spending their time in pool halls, bars, and on the streets. The city magistrate imposed a 9:00 P.M. curfew for all under the age of sixteen, and fined parents or proprietors twenty-five dollars for infractions. With few choices remaining, Mangum requested more funds for additional space at the state reformatory.[26]

Teenage delinquency notwithstanding, it was difficult for Flagstaff women to not be gainfully employed in the war effort. *Coconino Sun* editorials told women, "Do not try to be the old-fashioned housekeeper that you were during peace times," reminding them that the war effort was more important than dust under the bed or cobwebs on the ceiling, and urging them to "Enlist in some phase of war work." Flagstaff women already had a full plate when Columbus Giragi reminded them their most important role in the war was the giving of sons, brothers, and husbands for battle. By the summer of 1943, the *Coconino Sun* reported that Flagstaff women were simply too busy with depot work, rationing, salvage, or Red Cross and civil defense work to participate in the community's social clubs. At the same time, the newspaper searched for any idle female hands that might be put to use.[27]

By early 1943 it was already apparent that the war influenced Flagstaff women beyond their daily labors. Judge Mangum, taking the manpower shortage into consideration along with his personal convictions, heartily recommended to the state legislature that women should have equal rights—to include sitting on his jury. Before the war's end the law was changed and local women served on a county jury, resulting in what is believed to be the first conviction reached with women jurors in the state's history. There were also indications—resulting in part from the enormous increase of women in the Flagstaff labor force—that local interest in women's rights was growing. City attorney H. C. McQuatters discussed the "legal status of women in Arizona" before members of the ASTC chapter of the American Association of University Women, and Mrs. Horace Evans discussed the Equal Rights Amendment before members of the Business and Professional Women's Club.[28]

Meanwhile, almost two thousand workers reported for duty at Navajo Ordnance Depot every day in round-the-clock shifts, many taking buses from downtown Flagstaff. Enlisted soldiers assigned to Navajo Depot came to the city on passes, frequenting the USO as well as local saloons and cafés. Military recruiters searched for anyone not already taken. Hundreds of apprentice seamen and marines at ASTC came into town at every opportunity, as did Navajos and Hopis from Indian Village. In evening presentations before the Rotary Club and other organizations, Colonel Huling and his representatives outlined the role of Flagstaff depot workers in the war. For those still uninformed or uninvolved, the *Coconino Sun* ensured nothing was overlooked and passed along requests for volunteer services.[29]

There were other developments in town. Liquor dealers declared "unrelenting warfare" on the infestation of bootleggers who preyed on Native Americans and threatened to cripple manpower at Bellemont. Flagstaff's well-dressed men learned that the army needed wool—suit-coats had to be shorter. Vests were prohibited, as were cuffs, pleats, extra trousers, and patch pockets. Women's hemlines went up and their swimming attire became skimpier, reviving the two-piece suit. Other government regulations banned sliced bread, told butchers how to cut meat, and limited the number of ice cream flavors and shoe colors.[30]

In some areas of town, however, the government didn't have much to say. The Paso del Norte, a two-story hotel and apartment building at the corner of South San Francisco Street and Benton Avenue, while looking respectable on the outside, had a secret. The recessed windows and Southwest-style architecture welcomed customers who climbed three steps and entered the front door of the busiest brothel in Flagstaff.

Prostitution thrived during the war, especially during the year of depot construction. Both Paso del Norte and Pearl Polk's place on South O'Leary Street did a booming business, despite competition from Bellemont and the Wagon Wheel Inn close to Williams. The Paso del Norte was notorious, remaining open from the 1920s until the 1960s, and everyone knew it was a whorehouse. Prostitution and gambling were illegal in Flagstaff, but tolerated as long as they remained under control and did not involve serious crime or flaunt the payoffs. Slot machines, however, had been shut down by the sheriff's election platform in December 1940.[31]

As the town swelled with construction workers, many recognized that some newcomers from Oklahoma, Arkansas, and the mountains of the South were very different from themselves. Frank Brooks ran a grocery store and rented out fifteen small cabins on west Railroad Avenue. When his new renters asked for credit until they were paid, Brooks gladly obliged. He couldn't understand their failure to pay, however, after several weeks of work had passed. Finally he confronted those "fellahs in bib overalls, the watch pocket kind." They complained about the lack of pay, pointing only to crumpled up slips of paper in their pockets which seemingly had no value. It was immediately apparent that they had never seen a company check.[32]

Fred Metz, a longtime resident of Flagstaff, was downtown one day when some "weird characters" came out of a store. The couple wore overalls tucked into their boots and railroad-style caps. While gazing into the window of a shoe shop, the wife stated that she had never owned a pair of store-bought shoes and wondered if she could buy a pair for two-and-a-half dollars. Her husband exclaimed, "Sure, go in and help yourself. I just paid fifteen dollars for a gee-tar."[33]

The children of these newcomers entered Flagstaff public schools at an alarming rate. In September 1942 the elementary school enrollment climbed 54 percent from the previous year. High school enrollment jumped 9 percent. The flock of new students added to the crisis caused by the departure of many teachers and administrators who took higher paying jobs at Bellemont or were drafted. By midmonth the school board had changed the faculty roster three times. The board was also forced to temporarily discontinue bus service to Bellemont, as well as service for all students who lived more than two miles from school, due to the lack of buses and the exploding enrollment in town. The cancellation compounded the hectic and dangerous traffic conditions already present along Route 66 from Flagstaff to the construction site.[34]

As the war progressed and Flagstaff's population reached ten thousand, the city had not witnessed such feverish activity since the summer of 1882 when thousands of tracklayers made Flagstaff "Terminus, Atlantic & Pacific." Along with the prosperity, however, came racial and labor unrest.[35]

In the spring of 1942, with boomtown conditions well entrenched, two hundred African American soldiers from Company D, First Battalion, 368th Infantry Regiment, from the all-black Ninety-third Infantry Division at Fort Huachuca, came to Flagstaff to be trained as military policemen. Other companies fanned out to Sanders, Seligman, and Winslow. The regiment, formerly part of the all-black Ninety-second Infantry Division during World War I, was activated in March 1941 at Fort Huachuca, a post which had traditionally housed African American soldiers because it was "far enough away" from civilian communities to minimize local protests. The 368th Regiment served as a nucleus for expansion of the Ninety-third Division and its military policemen in Flagstaff. The division had black officers in junior grades, but was otherwise commanded by white officers.

The arrival of black soldiers in Flagstaff corresponded with a mass migration of blacks out of the South in 1942. Confined to menial jobs in defense industries, Southern blacks also suffered from declining cotton prices and increased mechanization. Lured by the growing labor shortage and enormous employment opportunities, blacks fled the South in great numbers for meccas like Los Angeles or the Bay Area where decent jobs were guaranteed.[36]

The military police company settled into the Mount Elden CCC camp, which had formerly housed men employed on CCC projects at

In early 1942 a 250-man company of African American soldiers from Fort Huachuca came to Flagstaff to train as military policemen. The army converted the Mount Elden CCC camp into a training camp, where they remained until October.

Wupatki, Sunset Crater, and Walnut Canyon National Monuments. Camp Elden, located between the Peaks Ranger Station and Christensen Elementary School, was closed in March 1942 and reopened for the army shortly thereafter. The military police company was not the only African American unit assigned to Flagstaff. In 1944, one hundred black troops in the "NOD Detachment" helped move munitions.

The army turned the Mount Elden CCC camp into a training base. The site, as with most former CCC camps, contained about twenty-four buildings for two hundred men. The African American soldiers, with their vehicles, equipment, and weapons, along with the ASTC marching band and the Flagstaff High School drum and bugle corps, paraded through downtown Flagstaff on Army Day, April 6, 1942. Afterward, the camp was opened for inspection to the Flagstaff public.[37]

African Americans were not new to the San Francisco Peaks area. The 1851 Sitgreaves expedition included an African American man, Moses Gibson, as camp cook. The first to remain in the newly created town of Flagstaff probably came as a result of the railroad and lumber businesses in 1881 or 1882. By 1920, fifty-three African Americans lived in Coconino County, and by 1923 the Saginaw & Manistee workforce included a small "black squad" of at least seven. Blacks entered the local lumber industry in greater numbers following the 1924 purchase of the Flagstaff Lumber Company by the W. M. Cady Lumber Company. Cady brought African Americans from Louisiana, where he had considerable experience employing minorities. By 1930 the black population of Coconino County had grown to 115. A few black mill workers lived on the northeast corner of "Little Mexico." Their homes were small, unpainted, smoke-blackened frame houses, occupied primarily by those from Louisiana. Blacks were relative newcomers to Flagstaff, however, compared with Hispanics, who had always been part of the town.[38]

For the black military policemen in 1942, life in northern Arizona left much to be desired. Leo Weaver expressed a typical Flagstaff attitude for the times toward black soldiers when the commanding officer of twelve hundred "colored troops" visited Fort Tuthill looking for a temporary training facility for his regular army soldiers. Weaver immediately wrote Governor Sidney P. Osborn expressing his deep concern, stating that the city did not want colored troops in Flagstaff. Governor Osborn replied that Flagstaff's objections were similar to those made by other communities. He reminded Weaver that the country was at war, and that the army had asked to use Fort Tuthill temporarily and could proceed to take the facility by other means. In the end, the army selected another site.[39]

Flagstaff's simmering racial unrest was evident in some local cafés and restaurants. Captain Beverly G. Hayes, an officer stationed at Camp Elden, brought a black noncommissioned officer into town for a cup of coffee and was refused service. In June of 1942, Doc January assaulted a black man in the Bellemont Inn, and later Doc and his friends opened fire on the homes of black workers who lived near the cinder pits. The Grand Canyon Café shoot-out in July 1942 was even more serious.[40]

On July 10, 1942, army private Jesse Smith and four other black soldiers stationed at Camp Elden came into town. Trouble started just before midnight as they made their rounds of restaurants and bars where they were often refused service. After they attempted to break into a home, one of the soldiers was caught at the Jackrabbit Café, "a Negro restaurant," and taken to the city jail. The others, allegedly drunk, returned to Camp Elden, confiscated two submachine guns and a riot gun—a twelve-gauge shotgun—returned to town and forced officials at gunpoint to release their jailed friend. After being refused service at several all-night restaurants, they headed to the Grand Canyon Café on Route 66 where they threatened customers, the dishwasher, and the cook.[41]

Sheriff Peery Francis and a dozen deputies and officers surrounded the café. Around 3:30 A.M. private Jesse Smith cocked the firing bolt of his machine gun and, as the *Coconino Sun* reported, declared, "To hell with you . . . we're going to fight this out." Smith then shoved the machine gun barrel past the café's screen door, and swung it toward the deputies. Merrill Schremp, a deputized off-duty Arizona motor vehicle division officer, with deputy sheriff Pete Michelbach kneeling in front, fired one round and killed private Smith. Officers in back of the café fired one round to warn the soldiers of their position. Three soldiers surrendered and one was found hiding under a table. The investigation absolved Schremp of blame. Several soldiers were tried by court-martial at Fort Huachuca and some were transferred to other camps.[42]

Following the shootout, the army restricted soldiers to certain sections of the city, and black soldiers coming into town were always accompanied by a white officer. By fall, however, the atmosphere improved considerably. The Camp Elden soldiers not only trained effectively, but worked hard gathering scrap metal, even convincing some that they were the best military men stationed in Flagstaff. At a retreat ceremony on October 10, 1942, the recruits became full-fledged military policemen. The ceremony also signaled the end of military police training for black soldiers at Camp Elden.[43]

Racial unrest in Flagstaff continued, however, and there were signs of trouble resulting from the town's explosive growth rather than problems from soldiers or sailors. Judge Mangum, who had already warned the town about the serious juvenile delinquency problems, warned the community that unless the gang fights between whites and Hispanics on the south side were curtailed, Flagstaff could break out into a deadly race riot similar to those at Los Angeles and elsewhere around the nation. Mangum's appeals to the board of supervisors, city council, and school system failed to curtail the fights, and none of the town's nineteen civic organizations took any serious action.[44]

Labor unrest in Flagstaff was nothing new. In July 1894 the town council passed a $45 gambling license fee on all games. The "sporting element" of the "skylight city" objected, boycotting the town and discontinuing all games. The bartenders joined the strike, and the musicians and chophouse waiters also threatened to tie up the town. A few decades later the Flagstaff lumber industry was forced to make changes when loggers went on strike in June 1917 and Flagstaff mills closed in August in advance of a pending strike. After two decades of poor economic conditions, union organizers returned to Flagstaff logging camps in 1937, and workers went on strike against Arizona Lumber and Timber in August 1938. Union activities in the summer of 1940 extended to Kayenta where they threatened filming operations of the Edward Small Productions.[45]

Labor problems surfaced in May of 1942, when state representatives of the Culinary Workers and Bartenders Union moved into Flagstaff to organize employees. With cafés, restaurants, and bars jammed full—often with men standing elbow-to-elbow the entire length of the bar—the situation was ripe for union organizers as well as the exploitation of workers. Although Arizona was generally calm during the war, the labor movement in Flagstaff was one of many propelling the nation's union membership from 8.7 million in 1940 to 14.3 million five years later. The problem in Flagstaff, however, fueled tempers and threatened violence.[46]

In early 1942 labor organizers moved quickly into the Bellemont project, where it became a 100 percent American Federation of Labor (AFL) closed-shop job. Atkinson-Kier's personnel officer, Wade

Church—later the acknowledged spokesman for the labor movement in Arizona and president of the state's AFL—agreed, based on efforts by Leo Weaver, to give 25 percent of the Atkinson-Kier jobs to Native Americans. Many complained, however, that reaching the goal was unfair and difficult because Indians first had to pay $26 (about $270 today) just to join the union. Others objected to being laid off or departing for military service without any refund in dues. Additionally, the union forced subcontractors to deal only with union wholesalers in Flagstaff. The Babbitt store and non-union meat companies were prohibited from delivering meat or lumber to the depot project or Bellemont restaurants. About the same time, union leaders in both Flagstaff and Williams sent four hundred workers on strike for a week at the Saginaw & Manistee mills.[47]

Trouble began in early May, when labor organizers moved into town and marshaled forces for a closed shop in eating and drinking establishments where standing-room-only crowds were common and lines often extended outside and down the street. Recognizing that union coffers might rake in dues approaching a quarter-million dollars at Bellemont alone, the AFL looked to city bars and restaurants as another lucrative target. The union's best came to town—A. H. Peterson, an organizer from Los Angeles, along with C. P. Flynn, state secretary of the AFL. The worst also came—including a notorious international racketeer. More than fifty merchants, perhaps sensing trouble, formed an association on May 11 and voted in favor of an open shop, vowing to resist union efforts "to the end."[48]

Members of the state Culinary Workers and Bartenders Local 631 of Phoenix took action on May 13 when they called all union members out of a nonunion Flagstaff restaurant and left bills unpaid. The Local 631 began to organize café and restaurant employees and force closed-shop contracts. The union claimed that the city was infested with business wolves, underpaid workers, and exploited employees. Considering the boomtown conditions, there was probably some truth to their accusations. Union officials reported to the Associated Press that Flagstaff merchants charged the highest prices and paid the lowest wages of any city in the state. C. P. Flynn asserted that Flagstaff prices had risen from 25 to 100 percent on food, clothing, and other items, and that butchers were paid half the wages of those in Phoenix.

Proprietors were alarmed when picket lines shot up around town. Tempers flared when pickets actually followed customers into restaurants and bars and then argued their case. By Tuesday evening, May 26, after two weeks of heated confrontations, the owners of bars, cafés, and restaurants had seen enough. They closed their doors and locked up. And then, unexpectedly, all of the town's retail and wholesale stores jumped into the fray and followed suit. All of Flagstaff's merchants went on strike. Thousands of newly arrived workers and family members did without or drove to Williams, no doubt wondering what type of crazy town they had landed in. Meanwhile, the situation deteriorated as more people arrived each day looking for housing, food, and construction jobs. An American Legion official called upon Governor Osborn to declare martial law, as did Joe C. Dolan, acting chairman of the merchants' association, who twice asked the governor to place the city under martial law so the heated dispute might be settled without violence—or, as Dolan saw it, in favor of the owners.[49]

The aggressive union tactics continued, adding to public discontent caused by the inability of thousands of depot workers (as well as local families) to buy, sell, drink, or eat anything in town. The picket lines themselves became even more controversial when a Navajo depot worker in front of the Hotel MonteVista explained he had to picket just to keep his construction job, because union leaders at Bellemont required the Native American construction workers—all new union members—to put in one day of picket duty. Leo Weaver, who had made great efforts to get Indians jobs at Bellemont, expressed his outrage in telegrams to John Collier at the Bureau of Indian Affairs and to Senator Hayden.[50]

The lockup in Flagstaff seriously threatened progress at Bellemont just as the project shifted into high gear. Confrontations on the picket lines were frequent and almost came to violence. The situation finally culminated in a bizarre escort out of town for some of the union organizers. According to the June 5 issue of a Phoenix paper, the *Arizona Fax*, a Flagstaff mob a hundred strong stormed the hotels and boarding houses and ran the union men out of town in the company of a police escort. The *Fax* called the incident "the Flagstaff deportation," comparing it to another infamous Arizona labor dispute: "Following in Bisbee's slimy footsteps, Flagstaff takes her place in the hall of infamy as Arizona's—and perhaps the nation's—first scene of the forcible deportation of union men and women in World War Number Two."[51]

At the *Coconino Sun,* however, Columbus Giragi saw it very differently. He reported that fewer than a dozen Flagstaff residents asked the organizers to leave town in the company of a police escort, which was unnecessary but had been "foolishly granted." Any thugs in town, according to Giragi, were "very recent arrivals."[52]

Letters supporting the Flagstaff Chamber of Commerce and Merchants Association poured in from Arizona, Utah, New Mexico, Oklahoma, California, and Hawaii. Morgan Coe of the *Santa Paula Chronicle* (Santa Paula, California) stated that no community in America was sufficiently organized to confront the union with such success and accomplish anything similar to Flagstaff's remarkable feat. A photo in the *Honolulu Star Bulletin* showed tourists in Flagstaff locked out of a café, with the caption "Open Shop Town 'Strikes' Against Union."[53]

Flagstaff businesses remained closed from Tuesday to Sunday, May 30, when it was revealed that union officials at Bellemont requested normal operations. The merchants' strike was slowing down depot construction and threatening the prosecution of the war. Merchants quickly voted to open their stores and keep them open. A compromise was reached with the union whereby one particular organizer would not be allowed to return to town, and negotiations would begin immediately concerning the union's future with the city's restaurant and café workers.[54]

Around the nation, wartime strikes were not unusual, and they frequently interrupted military production and inflamed public opinion. The Flagstaff city strike of May 1942, however, was very unusual, if not unique, because merchants and owners locked their doors and refused to come to work or sell their products. The strike briefly threatened construction at Bellemont. If continued, however, it would no doubt have diminished the army's ability to get bombs and munitions to forces in the Pacific.

The city's united stand soon cracked. According to Leo Weaver, it was defeated by one Greek restaurant that "did not have the backbone to hold out." By the end of July seven restaurants signed an agreement to accept a closed shop contract if 51 percent of their employees joined the union. Negotiations continued until September 1945, when most of the eating and drinking establishments signed up, agreeing to a closed shop if 51 percent of their workers joined a union and voted accordingly.[55]

In addition to these ground-level struggles, the war came to town from above. The Flagstaff public was repeatedly reminded of the risks in military aviation as bomber after bomber slammed into the San Francisco Peaks or nearby forests during bad weather. Even before Pearl Harbor, a B-18 twin-engine bomber crashed on Mount Agassiz during a blizzard on October 2, 1941, taking the life of the brother of Marie Morfeld (Rolle). Then, a B-17 Flying Fortress trapped in a snowstorm smashed into Mount Elden in March 1943. In April 1944, a twin-engine navy transport crashed and burned on Anderson Mesa, killing eighteen. In June 1944 three airmen parachuted from a doomed B-24 Liberator over the Grand Canyon, and on September 15, 1944, another B-24 Liberator crashed into Mount Humphreys. Three days later yet another B-17 Flying Fortress slammed into Fremont Peak. In between bomber accidents were crashes of various light military planes, trainers, and a Corsair, on either the peaks or in the forest.[56]

Eleven aircraft accidents took a total of fifty-six lives. Situated east of Kingman Field, west of Winslow airport where some ferry or instructor pilots were trained, and with Davis-Monthan Air Base, Williams Field, and Luke Field to the south, Flagstaff witnessed more than its share of military air crashes. Many were due to the high altitude of the San Francisco Mountains and unpredictable weather along the Mogollon Rim. For Flagstaff officials and volunteers who removed the airmen's remains from charred crash sites on the peaks or in the forests, as well as for local residents, the casualties of war struck at home as well as far away.

Early on Monday morning, July 16, 1945, Flagstaff residents were awakened at 4:45 A.M. by the rattling of dishes and windows. Although the disturbance appeared to be a strong earthquake, army officials said an ammunition bunker had accidentally exploded at Alamogordo, New Mexico, five hundred miles away. This was not comforting news in Flagstaff, considering that eight hundred similar bunkers chock full of munitions were nearby at Bellemont. The *Coconino Sun* described the effects from the distant blast.

At the same moment when windows rattled in Flagstaff, the cruiser USS *Indianapolis* waited in San Francisco harbor to set sail across the Pacific Ocean on a top secret mission. The *Indianapolis* had a huge wooden box, thirty by thirty feet square, lashed to the deck. The unusual looking crate was under armed guard and cordoned off by red tape. The skipper, Captain Charles McVay, anxiously awaited word from Alamogordo before sailing to Tinian with "Little Boy," the atomic bomb destined for Hiroshima.

Meanwhile, also at the same moment, thousands of miles to the east across the Atlantic Ocean at the Potsdam Conference, President Harry Truman waited for news from Alamogordo. It was late afternoon, and he was on his way to Berlin when he stopped the convertible to receive honors from the largest armored force in the world, the U.S. Army's Second Armored Division, which was deployed along one side of the highway for his inspection. Truman stepped into an open half-track reconnaissance car and passed down the long line of men, wheeled vehicles, and tanks, as far as the eye could see, taking twenty-two minutes from beginning to end to review the division.[57]

At Alamogordo, one of the men exclaimed, "My God, the damn thing worked!" More than three weeks later, on August 10, the day after the second atomic bomb was dropped on Japan at Nagasaki, the War Department disclosed that the July 16 blast that shook Flagstaff was the "Trinity" atomic test at Alamogordo.[58]

The war ended quickly, but perhaps not soon enough for soldiers, sailors, and airmen from Flagstaff who were preparing for the invasion of Japan. A few minutes after 4:00 P.M., on Tuesday, August 14, 1945, almost all of Flagstaff listened to President Truman's radio message announcing the surrender of Imperial Japan and the end of World War II.

The announcement triggered a "mammoth celebration" downtown. Within minutes, automobile horns were blowing and the mill whistles blew at full blast for hours. The city fire truck raced around town loaded "high and deep" with servicemen and other celebrators. Bars closed immediately, as did almost all other stores, and churches opened. The *Coconino Sun* launched an extra edition of fifteen hundred copies that hit the streets less than an hour after the President's speech. The *Sun* turned out another run of fifteen hundred copies before dark.

An enormous crowd gathered and all seemed to be yelling and waving flags. The closing of bars didn't seem to bother some. One depot worker was so drunk that when friends loaded him into the back seat of a car and drove off, he crawled out the other door and tumbled onto the ground as they continued down the road. A cowboy at the intersection of San Francisco and Aspen tried to step up onto the sidewalk, missing the curb every time. A soldier home on leave stood in the middle of Route 66, offering to share his big open bottle of whiskey with anyone who wanted a swig. Thousands sang and cheered until late in the evening. The sheriff's office was pleased that bottled cheer was not available from the bars, because it was evident that "hell could have popped—easily."[59]

From Navajo Ordnance Depot, Colonel Huling asked all employees to return to their depot jobs promptly, as there were many boxcars of munitions to unload the next day. He reminded workers that Navajo Depot was a permanent establishment, and that any reductions in force would be accomplished through normal turnover rather than involuntary separations. Huling thanked all depot personnel, both military and civilian, for their "splendid" service, and announced that operations would immediately follow a standard forty-hour workweek.

The day after the President's speech, the government terminated Flagstaff rationing of canned fruits and vegetables, fuel oil, oil stoves, and gasoline—which had been rationed since December 1, 1942. Other items, such as meats, fats, butter, sugar, shoes, and tires, remained on the rationed list. The housing shortage in town had not improved much, despite Clark Homes. Mayor Arnold Bledsoe requested authority from the FHA to build an additional fifty homes as soon as possible to make room for returning servicemen.[60]

9

CONCLUSION
Crossoads for Change

Flagstaff was Arizona's war town. Although others welcomed more servicemen, no Arizona town received federal projects that stirred such diverse economic, social, and cultural forces.

World War II was a watershed event throughout the American West, transforming sleepy communities into bustling cities where life was viewed differently after 1941. Flagstaff was no exception. Business flourished as the federal arsenal triggered changes and problems that pushed the city into the modern era. In short, Flagstaff grew up as it struggled through a critical juncture in the city's history, bidding farewell to prewar complacency and jumping on a new train of fast-moving events.

At Navajo Ordnance Depot, the train was led by a tough and talented career ordnance officer, Col. John Huling Jr., who arrived in mid-1943 when the new depot was in serious trouble with deteriorating labor and morale problems. With efficiency at its worst and a deadly munitions bottleneck looming, Huling set out immediately to correct the situation, turning his attention from one crisis to another. If one method didn't work, he tried something else; if someone had a better idea, he used it. By 1945, however, Huling, with the help of his civilian personnel officer Ernest H. Eickmeyer and staff, turned the depot around.

The most significant and noticeable effect of the war was economic. World War II brought extraordinary prosperity to Flagstaff. The undeniable difference from prewar years was, of course, the massive $30 million munitions depot ten miles west. The war stimulated numerous local companies, service industries, and tourism. The opportunities created by these industries set in motion the prosperity and expansion of the following decade.

Much of the depot's 1942 multimillion-dollar payroll from the eight thousand construction jobs went into Flagstaff pockets, dwarfing the town's prewar income. During the war, much of the annual payroll for the average force of around fifteen hundred workers also went to Flagstaff, $3.1 million for 1944 alone. All together, Navajo Depot brought about $42 million (almost a half-billion in today's dollars) in construction and salaries during the war and much of it remained in town. Despite deductions for war bonds, withholding taxes, and contributions to fund drives, depot workers realized a "huge amount of spendable income." At Arizona State Teachers College, the navy's V-12 program and the Civil Aeronautics Administration's Civilian Pilot Training program also brought about $750,000.[1]

Depot construction payrolls and the purchase of local goods and services by contractors and workers energized the Flagstaff economy. By mid-1942, county and city revenues had increased so much that a property tax rate reduction was possible, despite more county and city employees at greater salaries, and even after a 10 percent reduction in property values was allowed. In local forests, the demand for wood to help build the depot, along with the arsenal's requirements for dunnage and ammunition crates for storage and shipping, brought record-breaking revenues of two hundred thousand dollars to the Coconino National Forest in the fiscal year ending June 30, 1943. About 25 percent of this money went to county schools and 10 percent to forest road maintenance. Local sawmills were operating at maximum production, and were regulated more by the availability of manpower than by facilities or raw materials.[2]

With thousands of new residents and many new businesses in town, the city collected more revenue than was expected or budgeted. The magistrate court, for example, planned to collect $6,000 in April 1943, but instead, with juvenile delinquency soaring, collected $19,872, triple their original estimate. In April 1944 the city planned on $14,000 from private sales taxes, but instead collected $18,544, a 33 percent windfall. The same month new business licenses were expected to bring in $11,000, but instead yielded $13,172, a 20 percent increase.[3]

Although the cost of city services increased, the expanding tax base revenues exceeded expenditures. In April 1944, for example, the budget recapitulation showed a net gain of $58,087. Considerable gains were not uncommon, such as that for April 1943, when tax revenues of $46,943 represented a 355 percent increase from the previous year and contributed to the month's net gain of $82,491. All told, the county and city budgets were solidly in the black.[4]

Although tourism declined during the war, the depot fueled a diversification of the Flagstaff economy and reduced the city's long-term dependence on lumber and visitors. The 1942 depot construction and fifteen hundred permanent depot jobs benefited not only service industries such as restaurants, bars, and laundries, but stimulated utilities, transportation, and ranching, as well as retail trade in hardware, clothing, steel, construction materials, lumber, and other goods. Babbitt Motor Company, for example, increased their assets by 36 percent despite wartime fuel rationing and automobile restrictions.

The economic effects of the depot extended to the reservations, where Native American workers returned frequently with full pockets and usually spent some of their disposable income. At the Babbitt and Roberts Antelope Springs Trading Post close to Jeddito, net gains surged from $702 in 1941 to $5,892 in 1945.[5]

The war's second significant impact on Flagstaff was the boomtown population explosion and acute housing crisis that resulted in the construction of War Housing Project No. 2221, Clark Homes. During Flagstaff's first sixty years, 1882 to 1942, growth remained slow but constant with an economy based primarily upon lumber, ranching, and tourism. The depot construction quickly doubled the town's population. Demographic charts for Flagstaff during the 1940s are often misleading, and should reflect the population leap to 10,000 in 1943, followed by a gradual postwar decline to 7,663, as reported by the 1950 census.

In addition to those in town in 1942 and 1943, another ten thousand people were scattered across the forests or living in Bellemont, Indian Village, and the construction site. This enormous influx forced residents to look beyond their own means to solve the problem. The depot project boosted Flagstaff residential housing significantly, from prewar years when fewer than twelve homes were built per year. The 1943 construction of Clark Homes alone squeezed at least two decades of Flagstaff growth into just a few months—not including the new apartments and dormitories at Navajo Ordnance Depot and Indian Village.

Flagstaff received more than 10 percent of the 1,960 homes allocated around the state by the National Housing Agency in 1943. Thirty-five similar projects were underway in thirteen other Arizona cities—Yuma, Kingman, Morenci, Miami, Bisbee, Warren, Tucson, Gila Bend, Wickenburg, Glendale, Mesa, Douglas, and Patagonia—totaling $6 million worth of federal housing (about $62 million today).

The effects of the war were not all economic or housing related. By 1943 the departure of men for the service almost destroyed Arizona State Teachers College at Flagstaff, formerly one of the largest employers in town if not the most lively institution. The navy came to campus in the nick of time and saved the struggling college.

After the navy landed in July 1943, the next two years were anything but a period of retrenchment, stagnation, and financial strain as found at many of the nation's colleges. On the contrary, by late 1943 the navy program pushed student enrollment beyond that of the prewar years. The student newspaper, *The Pine*, described a rich campus life filled with challenging classes, naval training, ski club outings, weekend dances, Grand Canyon hiking, and many other activities.[6]

The navy years at ASTC were in many ways the best of times because of the war. The campus buzzed with activity. Even the food service improved. For trainees who arrived in Flagstaff from duty in the Pacific, campus life was a glorious blessing. For young seamen and marines who had yet to experience combat, every day seemed precious. For veterans and fresh recruits alike, life was there to be lived to its fullest before they headed overseas or across the country. For students like Lorraine Inman, it was "the best of college life."[7]

With the departure of the navy V-12 men, campus life became less interesting and certainly less exciting. For the female students who remained behind, the change was sad, if not troubling. Letters mailed to navy friends and sweethearts often returned with a stamp indicating that the addressee was posted elsewhere. A few were reported missing or killed in action. Most of the California students and many others left ASTC for a new start at another school.

According to local legend, a woman named Cathy committed suicide in North Morton Hall after learning that her fiancé had been killed in battle. Although there are no official records of the suicide and many versions of the story, one thing is certain—there have been numerous legitimate reports of ghostly happenings, strange noises, electrical malfunctions, doors unlocking and lights turning on by themselves, and other inexplicable phenomenon in North Morton Hall, perhaps a lingering testimony to the turbulent World War II years for campus women as well as men.[8]

Of the 125,000 apprentice seamen enrolled in the navy's V-12 program nationwide, sixty thousand completed the course and many became national leaders, such as Warren Christopher, Howard Baker, Jeremiah A. Denton, Robert F. Kennedy, and Melvin Laird.[9]

Many seamen and marines eventually rose to flag rank. After the war, the program gave the nation mostly educators, lawyers, and engineers—although medicine, dentistry, industry, sports, fine arts, politics, government service, and business were also well represented. Many became college or university presidents, deans, professors, high school principals, teachers, and coaches.[10]

Flagstaff's V-12 program, one of 131 nationwide, succeeded because of the "warm and intelligent" leadership provided by the college administration and an enlightened group of navy officers. Distinguished V-12 alumni from ASTC at Flagstaff include U.S. District Court Judge Earl H. Carroll, San Diego State University chemistry professor and graduate dean James W. Cobble, California Canners and Growers vice president William C. Gruber, Associated Press assistant general manager and assistant to the president Robert H. Johnson, Walt Disney Company vice president Luther R. Marr, Arizona Public Service chairman Keith L. Turley, and prominent Arizona educator Harold L. Elliott. The only V-12 marine trainee to reach four star rank, Kenneth McLennan, was educated and trained at ASTC.[11]

During the war, 1,020 apprentice seamen and marines participated in the Flagstaff V-12 program. Some, like Victor Myers, believe they were very lucky to be able to mature in such a "good environment." Of all V-12 programs nationwide, the ASTC unit was average size with a four-hundred-man detachment. The largest program was Dartmouth with nearly two thousand trainees; the smallest was sixty-eight at Webb Institute of Naval Architecture in New York City.[12]

In Flagstaff, the navy program brought the war home and instilled a greater sense of patriotism. Several former students and local women eventually married navy men. Many generous Flagstaff families "adopted" sailors and kept in touch with them long after the war. The experience also influenced young women to join the WAVES, WACs, Air WACs, or WASPS.[13]

But perhaps most important, the navy came to Flagstaff just in time to save the struggling teachers' college. The V-12 program boosted enrollment, eased the wartime financial strain, and injected new life into the almost dormant institution. Before the navy arrived, some science students like Rose Titus (Davis) thought the science faculty lacked qualified instructors. After the navy landed, however, "that all changed," because the navy demanded top-level instruction. The college curricula improved and the faculty relished the opportunity to expand the depth and scope of their instruction. Students like Marycarol Pryor (Bazacos) and Iola Aston (Sanders) were convinced that the navy men, with their high goals and diverse interests, talents, and abilities, helped raise the general academic standards of the college. The sailors left behind new traditions, along with enduring memories of a vibrant academic and extracurricular life.[14]

Other newcomers, the Austrian prisoners of war at Navajo Depot, brought out some of the best and worst of Flagstaff. Although local interest in the prisoners of war waned after the war ended, the Austrians continued to work away. Some even volunteered to move munitions after V-E Day. They hoped to return home any day but that was impossible.

The camp again reached its full complement of 250 prisoners after some returned from agricultural work around the state. In late September 146 prisoners were transferred to Florence to assist farmers. Flagstaff residents hoped that the move would open up jobs for returning veterans and local workers and it probably did. The labor shortage, however, continued through February 1946 and the flow of munitions did not stop. Colonel Huling requested more prisoners of war and even ran ads in the newspaper for ammunition handlers, stating that the depot would continue to move munitions until "peacetime status" was achieved the following year—projected for September 1946.[15]

The prisoners continued to labor through an uneventful fall while waiting for repatriation. They nourished the idea that they should go home first, as they were Austrian, not German. One prisoner, Karl Schilhan, died from natural causes, but otherwise nothing out of the ordinary interrupted the calm routine. Certainly the Bellemont prisoners of war experienced none of the harassment that occurred at other POW camps around the U.S. following the end of the war. The prisoners occupied their spare hours in many endeavors, one of which was to fill the camp with numerous small Austrian flags—more flags than one visitor had seen at any other camp.[16]

Prisoners expected to be home by Christmas, but the holidays arrived and they were still at Bellemont. In Europe, more than five million captured German soldiers and millions of dislocated civilians caused enormous logistical problems for the Allies, who were unable to provide food and shelter for all. The situation became critical as winter approached. With much of the European agricultural base destroyed and millions of persons displaced, sending POWs back to Europe in 1945 would have added to the problem. Additionally, American farmers protested vehemently against losing their prisoner labor, ultimately forcing President Truman to announce a delay in their repatriation.[17]

Another International Red Cross inspection team arrived on January 24, 1946, noting that Bellemont was a good camp, although somewhat spartan compared to others—probably because prisoners expected to return home any day and had little enthusiasm for improving the barracks with new furniture. Mail had improved since the first inspection in June 1945, as had the food ration. The inspection team noted some Austrians were voluntarily loading munitions. Many of the improvements promised by the camp commander, however, had not been made, such as providing a copy of the Geneva Convention, creation of athletic fields, and making a sick bay available.[18]

The winter snows came to Bellemont, no doubt reminding Austrians of their homeland. An additional 116 POWs arrived in February 1946 to relieve the labor shortage. Local preoccupation with the prisoners ended and no additional articles appeared in the newspaper. The camp was finally deactivated on April 17, 1946, and the prisoners returned to Florence. Between March 1945 and April 1946 they contributed 52,805 man-days of labor to winning the war against Imperial Japan and reorganizing munitions for peace.[19]

Papp, Grünberger, Gastgeb, Gröbner, and the other Austrians from Navajo Depot soon boarded trains for Camp Shanks, New York. They then traveled by ship to Le Havre or Cherbourg, France. Former Navajo Depot prisoner Heinrich Mueller was 39 years old when he finally arrived in Vienna. He wrote back to Ernest Harris, a friend from the depot, stating that his home was standing but completely empty except for some old hats and shoes. Everything else was gone. Conditions were terrible. Mueller lived on just 1,550 calories, which he described as "too small for living and too much for dying." Mueller, who was used to smoking twenty cigarettes per day at Bellemont, lamented that he was now lucky to scrounge one. Mueller was still wearing his prisoner of war uniform because clothes and shoes were not available. Mueller longed for the prisoner life and wished he could return to Flagstaff for "the good time again."[20]

Repatriation of the prisoners of war ended an extraordinary chapter in the history of Navajo Ordnance Depot and Flagstaff. The buildings were soon sold and moved away. The large stone monument built by prisoners in 1945 eventually toppled over, lying on its side, alone among the pines for decades but marking what was once the camp's chapel along the northern fence line.

There was no other camp in the nation where enemy prisoners of war worked on a daily basis with large numbers of Native Americans.

Many Austrians worked side by side with Navajos and Hopis inside the Indian Village camp and elsewhere at other depot tasks. They enjoyed the experience, especially the contact with Indian children. The native cultures fascinated the Europeans. Many Austrians formed friendships with Navajos and Hopis, often exchanging photographs and other memorabilia. In some respects, both the Austrians and Indians were refugees with common problems.

Many Flagstaff residents criticized Colonel Huling and the POW camp administration. Some flocked to Bellemont, taking pleasure in glaring at the prisoners, often asking rude questions. Many protested against the lenient treatment, especially following proof of Nazi atrocities overseas. Some bemoaned what they believed to be the prisoners' unlimited access to rationed items.

In retrospect, Flagstaff probably accepted the prisoners of war no less enthusiastically than any other American town where prisoners were not employed for the direct benefit of local farmers or industry. At a time late in the war when reports indicated that many American prisoners in German hands were being poorly treated, some Flagstaff residents grumbled but did not interfere with depot operations.

The war also made Flagstaff more racially diverse. Before 1942 the town was mostly Anglo and Hispanic with a small African American community—except, of course, for the annual pow-wow days that drew thousands of Native Americans from the nearby reservations as well as from across the West. The war brought the first large groups of African Americans to town. First came the company of black military policemen from the 368th Infantry Regiment from Fort Huachuca, who trained at Camp Elden during much of 1942. Then, in 1944, one hundred black soldiers were assigned to Navajo Ordnance Depot to help move ammunition. Throughout the war troop trains of black soldiers also stopped in town.

Racial prejudice in Flagstaff was probably less than other Western towns of the same size, due to the presence of both Anglo and Hispanic communities from the beginning. Regardless, city leaders were not pleased when it appeared that black soldiers would be coming to Fort Tuthill. Black military policemen were sometimes refused service in town. Beginning with the war, however, depot employees labored in crews that included Hispanics, Navajos, Hopis, whites, blacks, and Indians from other tribes. Most of them, at one time or another, came into town. Depot workers then and later reported no racial discrimination at Bellemont. Perhaps influenced by this unique experience, the city eventually recognized the black soldiers' contributions to the war effort and the community. Racial prejudice in Flagstaff appeared to be declining by 1945.[21]

For Native Americans, the war was a turning point that affected racial diversity in Flagstaff in both the short and long term. Of 8,530 Navajos employed in July 1943 as reported by the Navajo Agency, about 1,000 were at Navajo Depot, 1,500 on the railroads, 2,000 in the armed forces, and 100 in the WACs and WAVES. The remainder worked in mines, sawmills, plants, and agriculture. Ultimately, about 3,600 served in the armed forces and about 10,000 to 12,000 in industry, with Navajo Depot representing about 10 percent, the largest single concentration of Native Americans at one location dedicated to the prosecution of the war.[22]

The establishment of Richardson's Trading Post at Navajo Depot in 1943 was critical, and allowed the 3,500 Navajos and Hopis of Indian Village to purchase the things they needed and enjoyed. Instead of quitting their war work and going home, they stayed. Trader Billy Young knew exactly what favorite foods and necessities were required to keep them on the job. The trading post provided the stability necessary for the thriving Indian community where, by war's end, most residents lived in wooden homes, although many tents and hogans were still used. With the trading post, life became simpler than before, allowing many of the Indian Village residents to come into Flagstaff for leisure shopping, restaurant meals, recreation, or, for a few, alcohol. Billy Young, who spoke fluent Navajo, also opened a market in Flagstaff and provided a warm welcome in town for friends from Bellemont. When periodically returning to the reservations during lambing season, for ceremonies, or to visit relatives, the Indian Village families again traveled through Flagstaff.

The employment of Native American workers and the relocation of their families to Indian Village proved a success. They quickly became vital to Bellemont operations. Navajo men, who made up the majority of the heavy laborers, moved approximately eight hundred thousand tons of ammunition by hand and did much to help win World War II. Hopi men did much of the skilled craft work.

The Native American women were no less significant, working in many areas of the depot. Some Indian women traveled by themselves across the reservation or the state to the unknown hub of Bellemont, others followed their husbands. The working women were also part of the enormous cultural experiment brought about by the good-paying army jobs. For many Indian women, depot work forced them to change their way of dress, when pants, work shoes, gloves, and a hat were required. The many cultural implications were evident as they moved around Indian Village from traditional hogans, to tents, and then, in a matter of months, to apartments.[23]

The Navajo Ordnance Depot experience provided, for the first time, good wages to many Navajo and Hopi workers and exposed them to a different life beyond the reservations. At Shonto on the Navajo Reservation, for example, before the war not more than six men in the community had ever earned wages except on temporary projects. None had served in the armed forces. Of seventy men at the end of the war, two had been in the army, many did seasonal agricultural work in Utah and Idaho, but at least fifty had worked at Navajo Ordnance Depot or on the Atchison, Topeka, and Santa Fe Railroad. Unlike work on the railroad, however, the army jobs at Bellemont were not far from the reservation and did not require moving about. Plus, families could live together at Indian Village.[24]

For Indian Village children, the exposure to English was a significant legacy from Navajo Ordnance Depot. Colonel Huling and his officers strongly encouraged English language instruction and schooling for the youngsters. The Navajo and Hopi children who rode buses to Flagstaff schools were immersed in a new language. Some of these children believe today that this sink-or-swim challenge gave them advantages over those who went to BIA schools. Soon, some village children were teaching their parents English, graduating from Flagstaff High School, and earning college degrees.[25]

Navajo leadership over Navajo people was a unique consequence of depot work and Indian Village. The army promoted those with language skills and many laborers recognized, for the first time, the importance of learning English. Bilingual Navajo and Hopi foremen quickly became spokesmen and supervisors. The first Native American foremen, Maxwell Yazzie and Julius Begay, eventually held tribal or chapter positions of responsibility, as did James Maloney, Frank Luther, Dudley Yazzie, and Mark Begay. Doc Scott, a forklift operator and later a Navajo Code Talker, became president of the Tuba City Chapter, a political subdivision of the Navajo Nation. Village youngster Larry Atcitty went on to become administrative assistant to Tribal Chairman Peterson Zah, and another, Larry Kee Yazzie, later served as tribal prosecutor.

The custom of elected representatives, although not new to Navajos and Hopis, became more meaningful to their cultures because of the enormous stakes involved at the arsenal. The army depot helped form excellent leaders because they were required to handle a multitude of difficult problems on a daily basis. The depot experience, according to O. Tacheeni Scott, played an important role in modernizing the Navajo people by providing a communal living environment with good-paying jobs requiring specialized training that also included advancement opportunity, thus setting a "mold" away from the reservation for those qualifying to lead their people.

Years later, Raymond Nakai, for example, was one of those tribal leaders. Nakai was known for his eloquence and intelligence, and rose rapidly through the depot leadership ranks, making many lifelong friends. At the same time, he became a celebrity on his morning Navajo language radio program, *Sunrise Serenade*, on KCLS in Flagstaff. A natural leader, Nakai was eventually elected tribal chairman in 1963, and served until 1971. He brought into tribal government other former depot employees who had learned leadership, English, and customs of the off-reservation world at Bellemont.[26]

For many Native American families, Bellemont was just a stopping point on their migration from the reservations into nearby Flagstaff. One thing was certain—the Navajo Ordnance Depot experience opened up vast new horizons for many Navajos and Hopis, during

World War II and afterwards. As the depot workforce gradually dwindled, those leaving Bellemont were faced with a monumental decision: Should they return to their people on the reservation, or should they move into the new world of Flagstaff? An increasing number of Navajo workers moved into town by 1950, and the majority were former employees of the depot. As Indian Village housing improved with modular homes and utilities, it also filled to capacity and some workers were forced to rent apartments or homes in Flagstaff. Some were able to purchase their own homes, due in part to a history of excellent credit at Richardson's Trading Post.[27]

Although Flagstaff was a border town adjacent to the Navajo and Hopi Reservations, most residents had never seen a Native American child in a Flagstaff school. By 1943, however, Indian children were bused to city schools and Indian families gradually moved into town.[28]

The migration of Native Americans into town seemed only natural. There was always a quintessential early West flavor to Flagstaff that was readily apparent in the border town adjacent to the Indian reservations. Sheep and cattle ranching, the railroad, and the lumber industry seasoned the pot. After 1942, with Navajos and Hopis coming into town on weekends or moving into town permanently, Flagstaff became even more Western. Events took an interesting turn at the Orpheum, the city's movie theater, where Anglo, Hispanic, and Indian viewers watched the traditional "cowboy and Indian" films and the audience chuckled, hissed, and even booed as the screen Indians lost battle after battle to the cowboys and cavalry.[29]

Navajo Ordnance Depot meant more than just a steady, good-paying job for the thirty-five hundred Indian Village residents at peak employment. Although several hundred Navajo Code Talkers fought bravely in the Pacific Theater and several thousand Navajos served during the war, James M. Stewart, Indian Service Superintendent at Window Rock, was convinced that the years of backbreaking work, positive attitude, courage in the face of dislocation and hardships, and the unequivocal determination displayed by Navajos at Bellemont best "symbolized the war spirit of the entire tribe."[30]

The prodigious physical effort exerted by the depot's Navajo ammunition handlers spoke for itself. They would go wherever the government needed them, stating, "We will work, we will go without things to which we have grown accustomed." They declared they were "fighting for our land and for our way of life, the free way that we have known." They were fighting for their homes and for their children. For Navajos especially, the war was their personal battle and it had to be won. They would help win it best at Bellemont.[31]

The war influenced the town in other ways. Flagstaff's labor unrest was part of the nationwide growth in union membership that unfolded during the war. Around the country strikes were not unusual—14,471 occurred between Pearl Harbor and V-J Day—but the city lockup was extraordinary. The disturbing 1942 confrontation between labor and Flagstaff business did not go unnoticed around the West. It perhaps represented the first shot in the "right to work" battle that was finally brought to the Arizona Legislature in January 1945. On November 5, 1946, perhaps due in part to the Flagstaff affair, the Arizona Legislature passed the Right to Work law, which protected workers against discrimination based upon their union status or lack thereof.[32]

As Charles Ynfante noted in his study of the *Coconino Sun* for the war years, the initial burst of patriotic enthusiasm disappeared by 1943. Local news and social activities were replaced by sobering reports of the war's progress, and bulletins from state and local governments. People gave unselfishly to war bond drives, a bomber was named for the county and a Victory Ship for the city. The toil of war, soldiers like Arman Peterson who were killed or missing in action, rationing of food and resources, and the weekly call of men for service "muted whatever spontaneity the people of the city might have had." They were "trapped in a 'patriotic routine.'"[33]

Things were changing, however, as juvenile delinquency startled the community, eventually forcing Flagstaff leaders and organizations to expand recreation and clubs. Despite the grind of war and depot work, a small group of citizens cultivated new associations to help recover Flagstaff's vibrant life. Flagstaff women, both single and married, grew accustomed to good jobs at Bellemont, joined the service, or volunteered for Red Cross and civil defense work. More notice was given to the future and potential of women in town.[34]

In some respects, the wartime boom created a schism in Flagstaff. The Hispanic women who left domestic work for Navajo Depot jobs never had it so good. After the war, with tourism growing, many also went on to work in motels and restaurants and never returned to domestic work. For the middle- and upper-class homes that lost their help, it was the end of an era.[35]

According to John G. Babbitt, Navajo Ordnance Depot "pepped everything up" and Flagstaff was "rocking along." For Agnes Allen, the depot, soldiers, and Native Americans speeded up the change in the growth of the community. For Olive McNerney, Flagstaff first began to really grow during the war, as the school children and population were constantly moving. Workers were needed at the depot. It remained short-handed throughout the war.[36]

In summary, the impact of World War II on Flagstaff was breathtaking, reaching the very heart and soul of the community. The city became, almost overnight, an "arsenal of democracy" where hard work and discipline were required and expected from all. The town did, indeed, go to war. Cherished frontier values endured, but by 1945 the mountain town was different. Many changes were good, some not. Although citizens looked to the federal government more than ever before, they also nourished a confidence that came from becoming a major player on the national stage. National policy, after all, had come to town. Flagstaff people, and their economy, culture, and society had evolved. Local high school graduates no longer just migrated to the lumber mills or tourist courts for jobs. Expectations increased. Native Americans no longer came to town just for the pow-wow. Things were different.

In the broader context of American history, however, the Flagstaff story represents just one example of what happened across the land in hundreds of other towns and cities. Flagstaff's war experience marked a turning point and set the stage for the prosperity of the 1950s, when its population grew 138 percent, the largest increase of any decade in city history.

Three events were critical in sparking this growth. The depot construction and wartime operations brought about $42 million through town in one way or another. Then, the navy V-12 program saved the struggling college. And finally, Navajos and Hopis began moving into town, more comfortable with the small step from Bellemont's Indian Village into suburban life. Without the navy program, the school probably would have closed in late 1943 or early 1944 and, once closed, ASTC might not have reopened after the war when thousands of returning servicemen flocked to cities where they had received military training during the war—ASTC at Tempe and the University of Arizona at Tucson. Flagstaff today, without the depot's wartime launch, Northern Arizona University, or the native community, would probably resemble other small towns along the railroad line, towns like Holbrook, Winslow, Williams, and Kingman.

Despite the enormous celebrations of V-J Day, one question lingered in everyone's mind: Would Navajo Ordnance Depot remain open?

10

EPILOGUE
An Old Army Post That Didn't Fade Away

The army kept Navajo Ordnance Depot open after the war. Twenty-five of sixty similar depots were closed. The decision was no doubt influenced by the Ordnance Department's study in August 1945 that designated Navajo Depot as the most effective of all ordnance installations in the United States. The achievement was due in no small part to the first Indian Village foremen Julius Begay and Maxwell Yazzie, the Navajo and Hopi heavy laborers, employees from Flagstaff, and the leadership of Colonel Huling and his staff.[1]

Although Colonel Huling announced the first reduction of one hundred employees just weeks after V-J Day, the hectic demobilization required the continuing movement of munitions as the army reorganized for peace. No ammunition handlers were let go.

With perhaps 750,000 tons of munitions and explosives in igloos, magazines, and outside storage after the war, every corner of Navajo Ordnance Depot was full when the arsenal assumed another mission that would last almost fifty years—the destruction by explosion (demilitarization) of outdated or unserviceable ammunition. The blasts began to shake Flagstaff on a regular basis until 1994, much to the annoyance of some local residents. In addition to surveillance, maintenance, repair, and destruction of munitions, depot workers also salvaged TNT by "washing it out" of shells and bombs, another extremely dangerous operation.

Outside depot fences, the population of Bellemont began to decline as residents moved into Flagstaff or away. A 1946 shooting left three Blevins men dead when they tried to forcibly enter the home of Henry Singleton, a depot guard. Ernest, Henry, and Leroy Blevins were violent characters with criminal records. Singleton was tried for murder and acquitted.

A bizarre but humorous incident occurred in 1948 when rumors drifted around town that the Navajo Depot commander, Col. Arthur B. Custis, had turned the base into a private hunting reserve for himself and fellow employees, and had stashed a mountain of meat in depot lockers. State officials, however, believed they—not Custis—should control the game because nine thousand acres of the depot came from Arizona lands. In the rush to build the base it seems the jurisdiction over wildlife was never finalized.

Colonel Custis, the first West Point graduate to command the depot, was a somewhat cadaverous-looking individual. He was also described as "Pope-like," someone who wanted folks "to kiss his West Point ring." On September 23, in what must have been an extraordinary sight, a bevy of officials from not only Arizona Game and Fish and the sheriff's department but also the U.S. Marshall's Office and the U.S. Fish and Wildlife Service raided the federal arsenal—an extraordinary act by itself. Custis was furious when officials rousted him out of bed. He demanded to know "who in the hell" reported him. Custis was described as "very officious" and looking for a fight. Others said he was the most disagreeable person they had ever met. It probably didn't help when Custis called the officials "yokels," and said everything on the depot was under his control and he could have them "shot for coming in [there]."[2]

After a heated discussion of wildlife ownership, poached game in depot lockers, and federal versus state jurisdiction, the conversation improved dramatically when officials showed Custis a search warrant. Reports of the incident reached General Omar Bradley, the Army Chief of Staff at the Pentagon. Custis soon retired, and federal and Arizona officials signed an agreement in late 1949 marking the beginning of extensive cooperation on depot wildlife issues. Later, cooperation expanded with the Forest Service when a full-time forester was hired to oversee the woodland management plan.[3]

Another peculiar but dangerous incident occurred in 1949, when an igloo containing thirteen tons of munitions blew up after rats chewed through electrical wiring. The gigantic explosion sent a towering column of smoke soaring high into the thin mountain air—the scene somewhat resembling an atomic blast. Fortunately, it happened on a Saturday and no one was injured. The explosion, however, catapulted the huge one-ton steel door into the sky directly toward Indian Village about a half-mile away where one worker sat relaxing on his front porch. Witnesses said he watched in disbelief and amazement as the smoke signal rose to the heavens and the massive steel projectile arched into the sky and hurtled toward his home, landing just a few hundred yards short of the village. He then began to mutter something about the "crazy white man" and quickly packed up his family and belongings in a truck and left Indian Village, never to be heard from again. Depot finance personnel had no luck finding him on the reservation to present his last paycheck.[4]

Despite the shocking effect of the igloo explosion, the Indian Village community remained vibrant with more than one thousand residents. Meanwhile, Katherine Beard and Imo Wardlow, founders of the Flagstaff Mission to the Navajos in 1948, began two decades of "furiously paced" ministry to the Navajos at Indian Village. First they needed permission from the new depot commander, Col. Joseph Kaminsky, who, according to nurse Sarah Brown, could not put two sentences together without swearing. When Beard and Wardlow entered his office, Kaminsky leaped up from behind his desk and pounded on the desk top, saying, "I'm Catholic and I'm going to remain a Catholic." Nevertheless, he gave them permission to begin their work, and the Indian Bible Church was built just a few hundred feet south of Richardson's Trading Post.[5]

Postwar reductions cut depot employment by more than 50 percent, to seven hundred by end of the decade. Everything changed immediately, however, when North Korea invaded South Korea on June 25, 1950. Isabel Simmons and Scott Franklin, in the depot personnel office, began "hiring like mad"—saying to hell with the civil service regulations. Navajo Ordnance Depot once again provided critical support for a war in the Pacific. The labor force jumped to over one thousand within months as trains stuffed with munitions again rolled through Flagstaff, across the Arizona Divide, and into Bellemont. Unlike World War II, however, many seasoned employees were either already in place or readily available in Flagstaff and familiar with eighteen-hour workdays.

The influence of the Korean War extended to the Flagstaff economy. The number of depot employees reached 1,450 in 1953 and the payroll climbed to $6 million, four times that of the interwar low of about $1.5 million. Payroll and operating costs came to about $9.5 million, almost all of which was spent in the state and locally. New construction in 1952 included $2.5 million for warehouses, new rail tracks, and other improvements. In 1953, sixty-nine homes were built adjacent to the old prisoner of war camp under authority of the Wherry Housing Act, named in honor of U.S. Senator Kenneth S. Wherry from Nebraska. Victory Village was torn down and sold. One hundred homes were built in Indian Village, and construction employed five hundred workers, many of whom were local.

As during World War II, women once again answered the call as more jobs were opened to them. Perhaps one-quarter of the employees were women. About 600 of the 1,450 employees were Native American, to include Navajos, Hopis, Apaches, Tohono O'odhams, Hualapais, and a few from other tribes. Additionally, many Hispanic and a few African American workers joined those already on the force. All together, they helped the depot move eight hundred thousand tons of munitions during the Korean War.[6]

The postwar reduction in force cut the number of employees to 841. Good news came, however, when Navajo Ordnance Depot was declared a permanent Department of the Army installation in 1954. Employees rejoiced knowing their jobs were finally secure. The community in Wherry housing began to flourish.

Children like Bill Horbaly loved Wherry housing, where paved roads with names like Grant, Lee, and Sherman Streets came to homes with real front yards, porches, driveways, and shrubbery. Wherry housing was created in the image of a company town, not dissimilar to those found around the West in mining and manufacturing centers. The depot commissary, hospital, and recreation center provided most necessities. At Wherry, fathers and sons hunted turkeys in nearby woods and fired up thousands of rounds of the depot's condemned small arms ammunition in target practice. It was a place where fishing, catching snakes, swimming, and camping were a priority. They hunted jack-rabbits on the parade ground, and in winter snuck into the depot's restricted area to slide off the igloos with their Flexible Flyer sleds. Too far from Flagstaff to receive television, the children of Wherry housing lived in a delightful and isolated world.[7]

Perhaps due to the relative isolation, alcohol remained an impor-tant part of life for many at the depot. One night, the post safety officer, strangely unconcerned about his personal well-being, closed an evening's revelry during the walk home by re-living his army para-trooper days. For an airborne "jump" he needed height. Seeing a ga-rage, he climbed up onto the roof and, using his umbrella for a para-chute, jumped. The safety officer landed hard, breaking a leg.

With a reputation for drink already well established at Bellemont, some doctors at the post hospital helped keep the whiskey flowing by prescribing large amounts of bourbon for many of their friends and patients. The prescriptions actually called for quarts of whiskey or-dered through official channels to be used outside the hospital in "self-treatment" for disorders such as diarrhea, food poisoning, and "or-ganisms unknown." Reports of the "great whiskey caper" eventually reached the Pentagon.

In nearby Bellemont, Johnny Whipp's bar was the scene of fre-quent brawls, where officers and depot men found women and booze available on Friday nights and black eyes and broken noses were not uncommon on Monday mornings.[8]

The depot's post–Korean War inventory consisted of 404,386 tons of explosives in December 1955. New strategic materials added to the mercury, rubber, and tannin already in stock included more crude rub-ber bales, 366 tons of goose feathers for sleeping bags, quinine, asbestos from the Globe-Miami area of Arizona, and aircraft ejection devices. Shortly after the Soviet Union launched *Sputnik* in 1957, Nike-Ajax missiles and Honest John Rockets were added. The commander, Lt. Col. Harry L. Field Jr., said the missiles "saved our necks" as the manpower erosion slowed temporarily. The missiles, however, elevated Navajo Ordnance Depot to the dubious honor of becoming the number three Arizona target on the Soviet's nuclear target list, behind the Tucson missile sites and the Phoenix air bases.[9]

By 1958, the depot still remained a significant economic force in Flagstaff with a payroll of $2.5 million, larger than all in Coconino County, except for the construction of Glen Canyon Dam. Additional funding at Navajo Depot added $1.5 million, much of which was spent locally.

The number of "long hairs"—non-English speaking Indian workers at Navajo Depot—dropped to twenty and the interpreter position was finally deemed unnecessary. One hundred twenty of the six hundred employees were Native American. In 1958, all the occupants of Indian Village moved to attractive new quarters a few hundred yards east, with Hopis in the eastern section of the camp and Navajos in the west.[10]

Native Americans remained an important part of the workforce into the 1960s, when new Indian leaders were appearing at the depot. The first leaders, men like Julius Begay, Maxwell Yazzie, and Guy Multine, were true pioneers. By the 1960s many had moved on, were retiring, or were close to retirement. Raymond Nakai took several leaders with him after his election as Navajo Tribal Chairman in 1963. By 1962 only forty-four of around one hundred homes were occupied, and Indian Village was officially closed in June 1964, although a few housing units held tenants until the buildings were sold in 1970. The end of Indian Village closed an extraordinary chapter in the history of Navajo and Hopi peoples of northern Arizona, as well as that of Flagstaff.[11]

The number one depot civilian employee, "Henry" Eickmeyer, had arrived in 1943, and according to one commander was "worth his weight in gold!" He was replaced in 1960 by another civil service professional with almost twenty years experience, Ward C. Olson, known by some as "Mr. Ordnance." They, along with hundreds of other career civil servants, ensured the depot ran smoothly and efficiently, capturing numerous awards and commendations for the base.[12]

For a few weeks in 1961, Flagstaff's Municipal Airport hummed with activity due to one peculiar item stocked at Navajo Depot—clay targets. Apparently the targets used by all services for shotgun training and skeet and trap shooting had for years been funneled to Bellemont. In March 1961, when the Pentagon finally declared the depot's ten million "Targets, clay (skeet and trap)" to be excess, the rush to Flagstaff was on. Within days large air force and marine transport aircraft landed to pick up their share of the targets during the month-long "Operation Clay Pigeon." Flagstaff had never seen such air power, military or civilian. On one day alone, four marine C-119 "Flying Boxcars," four air force C-123 cargo transports, and one C-47 set down. They were soon joined by large C-130 transports. Flagstaff was, for a while, the "clay pigeon capital" of the United States.[13]

The destruction or shipment of all of Navajo Depot's chemical weapons began slowly after the Korean War. At its largest inventory in the mid-1950s, the number of chemical weapons probably reached about sixty-eight thousand bombs in various configurations of phosgene (CG), cyanogen chloride (CK), and mustard gas (H). Some phosgene and cyanogen chloride bombs were demilitarized by using a charge to crack the end of the bombs, letting the contents dissipate into the air. Despite the hazardous nature of these operations, there were no injuries or incidents. In 1958 the mustard bombs were shipped to the Naval Weapons Station at Concord, California, and loaded aboard the SS *William Ralston*, which was then towed out to sea and scuttled. The remaining stockpile of phosgene and cyanogen chloride was shipped to Rocky Mountain Arsenal in 1965 and 1966.

With the passing of years, and despite the depot's continuing economic influence, some Flagstaff residents began to resent the hazardous materials close by. Cracks appeared in the formerly robust military-civilian partnership as some expressed their disgust with the smoke rising from the depot's prescribed burns and munitions detonations, suggesting the need for more environmentally acceptable solutions. Others said the taxpayers got few government rewards from the busloads of depot schoolchildren who were brought into town, many of whom were Native American. Others complained about the free medical care given to depot employees and families, saying that it was taking away valuable patients from Flagstaff just as an addition to the hospital was underway.[14]

Accidents involving ammunition were uncommon at Navajo Depot. In 1953, however, powder flared up inside an igloo containing tons of munitions. The heroic and quick reaction of Ed F. Dallago and Simon P. Prado, both war veterans, prevented the loss of life. They disregarded their own safety in the face of imminent explosion, entered the igloo, and rescued five badly burned workers whose clothing had caught fire. Dallago and Prado were awarded the Commendation Medal for Meritorious Civilian Service for their heroism above and beyond the call of duty. The only fatality from an explosive occurred in 1955 when Eddie Scott, a thirty-three-year-old munitions handler, was killed when working with a "dud" that exploded.[15]

Tragedy struck again in the mid-1960s, however, when Robert H. Cline, the only son of Platt and Barbara Cline, entered a depot reservoir to retrieve a drum of herbicide that had fallen from a small boat to the bottom of the pond. Cline, a diver, was to be paid a small sum for his public service. As he looked for the drum, his wife and two sons and others watched from the bank. After two dives, however, Cline did not come up again. To the horror of all on the bank and the Flagstaff community, Cline had become tangled in weeds at the bottom of the pond and drowned. His widow and Platt Cline sued the government for failure to provide adequate safety measures and were awarded $389,390, the largest Arizona settlement up to that time for a single death.[16]

As the arsenal celebrated its twentieth anniversary in 1962, the name was changed to Navajo Army Depot and it was assigned to the U.S. Army Materiel Command.

When the United States entered the war in Vietnam, the *Arizona Republic* described Navajo Army Depot as one of America's "insurance policies" for uncertain areas of the world. The number of employees doubled to 845 in 1967, and the depot's loading docks and igloos once again buzzed with activity. More than 548,000 tons of ammunition and bombs were received and shipped between 1965 and 1971. The payroll soared once again to about $4.7 million, and many Northern Arizona University students worked night shifts.[17]

For employees like Isabel Simmons, the Vietnam war years were an especially harrowing experience because the depot, unlike previous

wars, was responsible for notification of the next of kin when a northern Arizona soldier was killed. Many of those were Native American,
thirteen from the Tuba City area alone. Depot employees often knew
the families. For administrators like Simmons, a disagreeable call from
an irate family member was not nearly as heartbreaking as muted calls
from others. For those doing the notifying, it was a nerve-wracking
job which often carried them to desolate spots on the reservations.
Many widows and family members from forty-one death notifications
or survivors assistance cases came to the depot, where they were presented the deceased's medals in solemn ceremonies.[18]

Unconfirmed rumors in mid-1970 pointed to the end of active
status for Navajo Army Depot. The Flagstaff community worried about
the future of one of its largest employers. By August the dreaded news
was official—the depot would be downsized drastically to 110 employees and given a reserve status mission to store and monitor about
250,000 tons of war reserve ammunition worth about $200 million.
Active service for Navajo Depot was over, and the payroll plunged
from $4.7 to $1.1 million by March 1, 1971. The commander, Col.
Albert N. Abelson, NAU President J. Lawrence Walkup, and state
officials sought government help in finding jobs for the 439 employees
released.[19]

The end of the federal presence at Navajo Depot resulted in a
total of 735 workers laid off since 1967, of which more than 400 were
permanent employees. More than 2,000 lives were suddenly in disar-
ray in the community of 26,000 residents. The name was changed again,
to Navajo Army Depot Activity, and the base was placed under the
command of Pueblo Army Depot, and later Tooele Army Depot. Few
took stock, however, of the depot's history outside of providing jobs.

Navajo Depot had supported many organizations and projects over
its years of active service: the FBI; scientists who measured electrical
storms, mapped cloud physics, and worked with satellite photogra-
phy; high altitude vehicle testing projects; and as a storage area for the
lunar mission development vehicle. Youngsters from northern Arizona
were put to work at the depot under President Johnson's Youth Employment Project. The base stored Coconino County civil defense

materials and supported the sheriff's department. It supported active and reserve units from all services as well as the U.S. Naval Observatory, the U.S. Astrogeological Survey, the U.S. Weather Bureau, the National Science Foundation, and the U.S. Forest Service. Additionally, the depot supported local fire departments along with the police, Route 66 vehicle accident victims, search and rescue, and emergencies during winters when only tracked depot vehicles could move through heavy snows.[20]

Navajo Depot had been an extraordinary partner with the community, many of whom worked at Bellemont. Most commanders took an active civic role, especially Col. Oscar A. Ramnes, and Lt. Col. Harry Field Jr., who was honored as Flagstaff's Boss of the Year and later became city manager after he retired from the army.

Navajo Depot employees, although in reserve status, continued to monitor, repair, and store several hundred thousand tons of ammunition as well as destroy unserviceable or outdated ammunition and bombs. The Arizona Army National Guard began to use some depot facilities in 1975. Flagstaff residents heard little from Bellemont other than an occasional blast. Publicity was minimal and the work force small. Some began to wonder what was going on "out there." Others suspected that the base was a little too quiet—perhaps guarding terrible secrets. In reality, operations were continuing as before but on a smaller scale as the newly activated 1057th Ordnance Company of the Arizona Army National Guard received hands-on munitions training.[21]

Suddenly, Navajo Depot once again hit the news, part of a statewide controversy that erupted in September 1979 when Arizona Governor (and Flagstaff son) Bruce E. Babbitt sent National Guard troops to seize radioactive tritium from the American Atomics Corporation. The tritium was leaking from their plant in downtown Tucson that was also adjacent to the school district's main kitchen. The tritium, a gas and radioactive isotope of hydrogen, was used as an energy source to cause other materials to glow in luminous clocks, watches, and signs.[22]

The Guard placed the 1.5 ounces of tritium in a leased 7.5-ton nuclear materials carrier called a "Super Tiger" that came from Washington state. It was then loaded onto a 25-ton tractor-trailer for shipment to Bellemont, probably the most secure and protected storage site in the state. In Flagstaff a protest demonstration fizzled and the tritium arrived without incident at Bellemont where it was stored under guard.[23]

When the dust settled, the price tag for the tritium affair cost Arizona taxpayers dearly. Governor Babbitt's concern for Tucson safety appeared legitimate, however, based upon a Nuclear Regulatory Commission report of dangerous conditions at the plant and coming just months after the Three Mile Island partial core meltdown. Letters to the editor of the *Arizona Daily Sun* objected angrily to the move. One imaginative NAU senior likened tritium storage to "putting a bomb on your head and waiting for it to go off."

Experts on radioactive material flocked to Flagstaff—including a past chairman of the U.S. Atomic Energy Commission, and officials from Arizona's AEC. Using community forums, they tried in vain to persuade citizens that the chances of contamination were negligible. One expert admitted, however, that the 1.5 ounces of tritium would be dangerous if swallowed, but otherwise could be stored safely in a sandwich bag. Their supplications, however elegant, contradicted the essence of the governor's emergency order. Despite lingering doubts, the tritium was stored at Navajo Depot until July 1980, when it was shipped to Ohio.[24]

Some blamed Navajo Depot for the tritium affair. The years of quiet followed by the outburst of publicity spawned rumors that all kinds of terrible, exotic tools of war were stored at Bellemont. One creative reporter described the apparent serenity as a "superficial facade" and branded the depot as a "site of mysteries." Others claimed the arsenal was "shrouded in secrecy." By the 1990s these perceptions and other wild rumors would fuel a Sedona cottage industry of bizarre tales and personal accounts linking the isolated post to a wide variety of nefarious activities.[25]

Meanwhile, back in reality, Col. Robert B. Pettycrew, the chief of staff for the Arizona Army National Guard, convinced state officials that an ordnance battalion could be recruited from northern Arizona communities, trained at the depot, and then used to operate the base and save money for the Defense Department. The concept was eventually approved and Col. John L. Johnson Jr., AZ ARNG, set up an office at Navajo Depot in March 1981 to begin coordination for the transfer of operations. Although the Guard would run the depot and assume responsibility for the maintenance and destruction of the ammunition, the property and munitions would remain on federal books.[26]

Although new buildings went up at Navajo Depot, most ammunition shipments were outbound—not a good sign for those like Gus Florez and Earl Hedges, who had moved munitions for decades. In 1988 the Department of Defense Commission on Base Realignment and Closure (BRAC) targeted the depot for complete closure by 1995. One of the commission's alternatives was to return the land to the Forest Service.

The Forest Service had good reason to want Navajo Depot, where the scenery along the southern boundary was described as something out of Yellowstone National Park. "Every evening about dusk, hundreds of elk beat a well-worn path from the confines of Navajo Army Depot to drink at nearby Rogers Lake."[27] The scene was possible, however, due in part to the limited and controlled hunting on the depot in combination with years of Defense Department conservation and wildlife preservation.

Just as the BRAC report was released, Lt. Col. Larry Triphahn, AZ ARNG, took command of the threatened depot and began searching for alternatives to keep it open. Although by 1991 most munitions had already been transferred to Hawthorne, Nevada, or elsewhere, the depot once again supported a war. During Operations Desert Shield and Desert Storm the base shipped sixty-eight boxcars of air force 750-pound bombs as workers put in ten-hour shifts.

The battle for ownership of Navajo Depot heated up. The army wanted to keep the base in military hands and Arizona officials certainly did not want to lose the best National Guard training facility in the state. The struggle for ownership of the base reached the highest levels of the first Bush Administration, pitting the Department of Defense against the Department of Agriculture in a tug of war. The

Forest Service threatened lawsuit. Congressional hearings were finally scheduled for March 26, 1992, before the Subcommittee of National Parks and Public Lands.[28]

Many in Arizona were concerned about the hearings. The end of the Cold War spelled shrinking defense budgets for the state as Williams Air Force Base closed and others were reduced in size. Congressional plans to reduce weapons systems manufactured in Arizona made the state the third most vulnerable in the nation for economic dislocation.[29]

As expected, most of Arizona's elected officials fought vigorously to keep the base, to include Senator John McCain, Congressman Bob Stump, Governor Fife Symington, former Governor Rose Mofford, and State Representative John Wettaw. Edward Z. Fox, Director of Arizona's Department of Environmental Quality (ADEQ), testified that the depot and ADEQ had developed a plan to address all areas of environmental concern.[30]

The congressional hearings were inconclusive, but by summer it appeared Arizona and the army had won the battle. Ownership of Navajo Depot was transferred to Arizona in 1993. The name was changed again, to Camp Navajo. Completion of the $6.4 million regional training complex for six hundred soldiers gave the base a training capability in addition to storage.

The depot commander, Larry Triphahn, along with Tom Galkowski and Tim Cowan created a plan for marketing the depot's enormous storage and training facilities in the post–Cold War world. Triphahn traveled across the West to secure contracts, winning customers with both the air force and navy.

The congressional hearings raised environmental questions. Contamination from "chemical canyon" and the demolition area had been an army concern since the depot's first environmental assessment in 1979. More than a dozen environmental studies were conducted in the 1980s and 1990s and a master environmental plan was finalized in October 1993.

Tim Cowan lobbied for the depot's share of limited cleanup funds that were designated for the army's 1,877 sites with environmental hazards. Camp Navajo sites, however, were low in priority because they posed limited danger compared to others like Rocky Flats and Rocky Mountain Arsenal. Unlike decommissioned bases elsewhere, Triphahn and Cowan believed keeping Camp Navajo open was the best way to obtain scarce funds needed for a sound, long-term environmental program. Many projects have been completed, and the government has spent over $16 million in Camp Navajo cleanup.[31]

The decades of blasts from destruction of ammunition that ended in 1994 did not lack for interesting moments. Cowan, then public affairs officer, received phone calls from those angry about noise caused by the explosions. One woman complained that the blast had knocked her canary "off its perch." Another noted that Cowan was no longer a major and chortled, "They promoted you?" She was "shocked" and then hung up the phone. One caller claimed his entire home had suffered from the noise and needed to be replaced. Depot officials went to one Forest Highlands home and gave a formal briefing to the disgruntled resident.[32]

The unprecedented negotiations that resulted in the Strategic Arms Reduction Talks (START) and treaty with Russia in 1991 called for the reduction of Russian and U.S. strategic nuclear forces. The air force began removing Minuteman II intercontinental ballistic missiles from duty in underground silos scattered across Missouri, Montana, and South Dakota. In 1992 the air force began shipping the missile motors to Hill Air Force Base in Ogden, Utah, for disassembly and then on to Camp Navajo, where crews led by Tom Shimonowsky prepared the motors for long-term storage in igloos that had been modified for temperature and security requirements.

In 1998 the navy, likewise, began removing Trident I ballistic missiles from their submarines at the Bangor submarine base in Washington state and shipping the motors to Camp Navajo for storage. In both cases, the nuclear warheads went elsewhere.

Camp Navajo and its Cold War weapons were the focus of considerable international attention in March 1995. General Major Viacheslav Romanov, the fifty-year-old chief of the Russian National Nuclear Risk Reduction Center, and his ten-member team from Russia, Kazakhstan,

Stage II of a Minuteman intercontinental ballistic missile motor is lowered to a storage cradle on a flatbed trailer. Each igloo has been modified for temperature and security requirements and holds several motors. Camp Navajo stores over a thousand intercontinental ballistic missile motors along with other strategic materials.

Ukraine, and Belarus arrived at Camp Navajo to inspect the United States stockpile of strategic missile motors stored in the World War II-vintage igloos in accordance with the START Treaty. The camp was under Romanov's orders and it was only the second U.S. base to be inspected under the treaty. Romanov and his crew counted and inspected the missile motors to ensure there were no fakes.[33]

Camp Navajo storage of intercontinental ballistic missile motors continued to increase to well over a thousand motors, bringing a multi-million dollar business to Flagstaff and northern Arizona. Construction of the missile motor transfer facility and upgrades for 152 igloos alone cost approximately $43 million. Today, about sixty thousand tons of the nation's strategic weapons and other materials valued at about $3.6 billion are stored at Camp Navajo, making the depot one of the most important sites for the Russians who have inspected more than a dozen times since their first visit in 1995.

Many interesting people were part of the story of Flagstaff and Navajo Ordnance Depot during World War II. Colonel Huling retired from the army after his son's death at the end of the war. Huling had served twenty-nine years, including two world wars. He departed with his family for Lafayette, Indiana, where they planned to look after their farm in Warren County. Major Myrick was promoted to colonel and retired to Scottsdale, returning to the depot for the twentieth reunion in 1962. He died in 1977. Lucile Michael, who came from Fort Wingate to Bellemont with Myrick's staff, lives in Flagstaff.[34]

Leo Weaver, a pioneer of the Arizona guest ranch industry and secretary of the Flagstaff chamber of commerce who did much for Native American workers in 1942, moved to New Mexico and then to Tucson where he died a poor man—as he probably wished and most probably would have expected—in 1951.[35] Beloved Indian trader Billy Young, who ran Richardson's Trading Post and operated Young's Market in Flagstaff, was honored in 1970 by the Southwest Parks and Monuments Association and the National Park Service for fifty years of service on the Navajo Reservation and at Bellemont. Young also served Flagstaff in many responsibilities. He died in Mesa on May 23, 1990.[36]

Jim Boone, the big, strong, and infamous foreman who became a legend himself, retired and returned to the Navajo Reservation in 1959, but not before he bought his home at Indian Village and brought it along. John Billy, one of the first members of the depot's Navajo council and the son of Hosteen Nez, the first chief of the Navajos living on the depot, retired in 1964 and planned to build a new home at White Cone, on the reservation, where he was going to "just lay around like the rest of the guys." John Billy died on March 9, 2003.[37]

Former Austrian prisoners of war Josef Papp and Friedrich Gröbner live close to Vienna and retain fond memories of their time at Bellemont. Walter Gastgeb died in 2002. Papp returned to Flagstaff in 1998, and again in 2001 when he dedicated the prisoners' monument, recently restored by Stan Cornforth and the Flagstaff Route 66

Car Club. Little else remains from the camp. Rusted lengths of barbed wire, small pieces of black asphalt roofing, and fragments of siding are scattered among the grama grass and pine needles. A thick pine forest has crowded out what was once a camp for enemy soldiers, marked today by only the monument and concrete foundations at the former entrance area.

Col. Arman Peterson, who was first buried in a local Dutch cemetery and then the National Cemetery in Belgium, was returned to Arizona where he was buried with full military honors at the Peterson family plot in the Thatcher cemetery. Bob Hope, shaken by the experience of performing before Peterson's men at the time of his loss, launched a movie in the 1950s about the "fighting Arizona colonel."[38]

This story of Flagstaff and Navajo Ordnance Depot ends on the second floor of the Camp Navajo headquarters building where Sergeant Mary Lynch, a fifteen-year veteran of the Arizona Army National Guard and granddaughter of Navajo Tribal Chairman Henry Taliman, performs her duties as transportation specialist. Sergeant Lynch, a thirty-four-year-old Navajo soldier with long black hair tucked up neatly above the collar of her army uniform, is one of a dozen Native American employees at the camp.

Lynch came from a family of seven girls and three boys at Oak Springs on the Navajo Reservation, about ten miles north of Lupton, Arizona, where they ran four hundred sheep, three hundred head of cattle, and twenty horses on almost one thousand acres. She learned to rope, herd, tend, brand, and butcher both sheep and cattle, chop wood, and hunt. Lynch laughs when she thinks of army basic training. The army was not hard—living on the reservation was hard.

Lynch has spent more than ten years at Camp Navajo, where she enjoys her job and the National Guard. She is proud to wear the army uniform, to be a Native American woman working to succeed, and to set the example for her children. She likes working at the base of the sacred San Francisco Peaks, and often leaves the building to take in the mountain view from Volunteer Prairie and pray. Lynch is very aware of her people's rich history at Camp Navajo and is especially proud of the name. She is saddened that many Navajos, as well as non-Navajos, have no idea why the name was chosen, noting that "my people too have forgotten." Lynch knows many who lived in Indian Village where she often walks among the old roads, sidewalks, cement foundations, and ponderosa pines. For her it is a special place. She respects Indian Village "as a place where my people lived," and says "I get a feeling that my people are still here."

Although a half-century apart, Lynch has much in common with the Navajos and Hopis who first migrated to Indian Village in 1942. Lynch came because she needed work. For her, Camp Navajo marked a starting point in finding a good job, much like her people before. The change has not come easily, however. Richardson's Trading Post is long gone and she has few with whom to speak her native tongue. She misses the reservation dearly and longs for the open spaces where extended family take part in daily life. Lynch has learned many skills at Camp Navajo and hopes to someday take them home, just like Julius Begay, Maxwell Yazzie, Guy Multine, Jim Boone, John Billy, Raymond Nakai, and the many other Navajo men and women who came before.[39]

NOTES

Preface

1. Cline, *Mountain Town*, 2; *Arizona Daily Sun* (Flagstaff), March 22, 2002; Locke, *Book of the Navajo*, 68.

Introduction. An Armed Camp

1. Sheridan, *Arizona*, 272; *Arizona Republic* (Phoenix), December 3, 1978.

Chapter 1. Summer 1941

1. Griffith, "In love"; *Coconino Sun* (Flagstaff), June 30, 1939.

2. *Coconino Sun*, June 27, July 11, 1941.

3. Cline, *Mountain Town*, 298; *Coconino Sun*, June 7, July 5, 1912, July 3, 1931, July 7, 1933, July 6, 1934, July 3, 1936, July 2, 1937, July 8, 1938, June 23, 1939, July 5, 1940, June 27, 1941; conversation with Richard Mangum, September 17, 2002; miscellaneous documents, folders 1, 2, 16, Flagstaff All-Indian Pow-Wow Collection, MS 51, Northern Arizona Pioneers Historical Society, Special Collections and Archives, Cline Library, Northern Arizona University.

4. Griffith, "In love"; *Coconino Sun*, July 3, 1936, July 2, 1937, July 5, 1940, June 27, 1941.

5. *Coconino Sun*, July 2, 1937, June 28, 1940, June 27, July 4, 1941.

6. *All Indian Pow-Wow*, 18; Griffith, "In love."

7. *Coconino Sun*, July 5, 1940; Griffith, "In love."

8. *Coconino Sun*, July 5, 1940, July 4, 1941.

9. Ibid., July 5, 1940, August 15, 1941; Griffith, "In love"; *All-Indian Pow-Wow*, 3; conversation with David McQuatters, September 12, 2002; Mangum conversation.

10. Walter J. Hill prisoner files; Tinker, *Northern Arizona*, 22; Haskett, "History," 20–22.

11. Haskett, "History," 21–22, 29–30, 46; Tinker, *Northern Arizona*, 22–24; *Arizona Champion* (Flagstaff), January 1, 1887.

12. Conversation with Al Richmond, January 8, 2002; Myrick, *Santa Fe Route*, 7–8; Peterson, "Cash Up," 205–6.

13. Cline, *They Came to the Mountain*, 134.

14. *Arizona Miner* (Prescott), August 25, 1882; "Bellemont, Arizona," History of the Santa Fe Coast Lines, 1940, 28, Santa Fe Railway Archives, Kansas State Historical Society, Topeka.

15. Haskett, "History," 21–22, 29–30; Tinker, *Northern Arizona*, 22–24.

16. Mangum, "Pioneer Doctor"; *Arizona Champion*, November 24, 1883; Cline, *They Came to the Mountain*, 119, 136.

17. Cline, *Mountain Town*, 17.

18. Coconino is a Hopi name for the Havasupai Indians who live at Supai in the western section of the Grand Canyon. Cline, *Mountain Town*, fn 18, 22.

19. Cline, *Mountain Town*, 27–28.

20. For more on Hill's story see the author's article, "Boom to Bust in Bellemont: The Tragic Story of Northern Arizona Pioneer Walter J. Hill," *The Journal of Arizona History*, 41, no. 2 (Summer 2000): 181–96; Ashworth, *Biography*, 33.

21. Cline, *Mountain Campus*, 358.

22. Cline, *Mountain Town*, 105; Mangum, "Flu."

23. Cline, *Mountain Town*, 241, 263, 273; Westerlund, "Boom to Bust," 190.

24. Putt, *South Kaibab National Forest*, 168; Mangum, "The CCC"; Cline, *Mountain Town*, 298.

25. Steinbeck, *Grapes of Wrath*, 160; interview with Sally Coddington, May 12, 1999; Scott and Kelly, *Route 66*, 61–62; Cline, *Mountain Town*, 298.

26. Cline, *Mountain Town*, 307; Mangum, "The Underpass."

27. Stein, *Logging Railroads*, 13–18; U.S., Bureau of the Census, *Fifteenth Census of the United States: 1930*, Arizona, vol. 4, Coconino County, Bellemont Precinct.

28. Plopper, "Requiem," 15; interview with A. P. "Pete" Michelbach, Sedona, May 17, 1998; "Official List of Officers, Stations, Agents, Station Numbers, etc., no. 50," January 1, 1942, 108, Santa Fe Railway Archives, Topeka; Arizona WPA Writers' Project, *Arizona: A State Guide*, 319.

29. Arizona WPA Writers' Project, *Arizona: A State Guide*, 319; Michelbach interview; interview with Gregorio "Curly" Martinez, November 1, 1998.

30. Thorstenson and Beard, *Geology and Fracture Analysis*, 5, 10–12, 24, 41; interview with Don Thorstenson, December 1, 1998.

Chapter 2. Wild Times

1. Reilly, *Lee's Ferry,* 345–46; *Coconino Sun,* December 19, 1930; Hazel B. [Weaver] Jordan to P. T. Reilly, November 18, 1964, and Billie W. Yost to Reilly, October 22, 1964, both in folder 423, box 30, series 1, P. T. Reilly Collection, MS 275, SCA, CL.

2. Ibid.

3. Reilly, *Lee's Ferry,* 345–46; various documents, folders 423 and 424, Reilly Collection.

4. Reilly interviews with Hazel [Weaver, Jordan] Bray, June, 1976, and various documents, folders 423 and 424, Reilly Collection; Reilly, *Lee's Ferry,* 411; *Arizona Daily Star* (Tucson), April 10, 1951.

5. Reilly, *Lee's Ferry,* 390–95; Reilly interview with Hazel Jordan, December 22, 1964, and other documents, folders 423 and 424, Reilly Collection.

6. Cline, *Mountain Town,* 314, 332; idem, *Mountain Campus Centennial,* 509; Vance, "Lumber and Sawmill Workers," 83–84; *Coconino Sun,* March 7, 1941; "Report on the City of Flagstaff, Arizona," February 17, 1942, Defense, Housing, and OPM, 1942, folder 2, box 10, series 2, Flagstaff Chamber of Commerce Records (hereafter FCCR), MS 193, SCA, CL. Later in the war, the Flagstaff lumber industry employed 596 workers at peak production in 1944. "A Survey of Flagstaff, Arizona, and Coconino County," September 1944, 5–6, Post War Planning Reports, General Correspondence, 1943–44, box 26, Governor Sidney P. Osborn Collection, RG 1, Arizona State Archives, Phoenix.

7. "Navajo Ordnance Depot, vol. I, Basic History thru 31 December 1942," exhibit 3, RG 156, National Archives. Also see the author's article, " 'U.S. Project Men Here': Building Navajo Ordnance Depot at Flagstaff," *Journal of Arizona History* 42, no. 2, summer 2001.

8. Thomson and Mayo, *The Ordnance Department,* 360–78.

9. Thomson and Mayo, *The Ordnance Department,* 360–63, 368, 371–78; "Board Report on Selection of Site for Ammunition Storage Depot, Flagstaff-Prescott Area," December 30, 1941, RG 156, National Archives, hereafter Site Board Report 109.

10. Site Board Report 109; Senator Carl Hayden to Governor Sidney P. Osborn, February 16, 1942, Ordnance Depot, Bellemont, 1942, box 19, Osborn Collection; Thomson and Mayo, *The Ordnance Department,* 367.

11. Hayden to Osborn.

12. "Navajo Ordnance Depot, vol. I," exhibit 3; Site Board Report 109.

13. Weaver to Hayden, February 2, 1942; to Capt. [Ernest W.] Thomas, December 31, 1942; C. M. Wesson to Hayden, December 27, 1941, all in Navajo Ordnance Depot, 1942, FCCR, MS 193, SCA, CL.

14. Igloo Area History Committee, *Igloo,* 6–7.

15. *Coconino Sun,* January 23, 1942.

16. *Coconino Sun,* January 23, 1942; telegram, Hayden to Weaver, January 21, 1942, FCCR.

17. Interview with Martha Mulnix, January 19, 2001; with A. P. "Pete" Michelbach, Sedona, May 17, 1998.

18. Weaver to Hayden, 28 January 1942, FCCR.

19. *Coconino Sun,* January 30, February 20, 1942; July 27, 1945.

20. *Coconino Sun,* January 30, 1942; interview with Shelton G. Dowell Jr., March 27, 2002.

21. *Coconino Sun,* January 30, February 13, 1942; Navajo Ordnance Depot, 1942, files, FCCR.

22. Weaver to Thomas, December 31, 1942; to Ernest McFarland, February 3, 1942, both in FCCR; "Navajo Ordnance Depot, vol. I," 5; "Final Project Map, Navajo Ordnance Depot, March 10, 1952," Los Angeles District Real Estate Division, Records of Projects Affecting Mineral Resources, 1944–1957, Records of the Office of the Chief of Engineers, RG 77, National Archives Pacific Southwest Region, Laguna Niguel, California; Thomson and Mayo, *The Ordnance Department,* 367, 378; Office of the Chief of Engineers, "Owned, Sponsored and Leased Facilities," December 31, 1945, 311, copy at U.S. Army Military History Institute, Carlisle Barracks, Pennsylvania.

23. Ashworth, *Biography,* 132, 167–79; interview with Henry Giclas, January 7, 2000; telegram, Andy Matson to Hayden, n.d., and Weaver to McFarland, February 3, 1942, FCCR; *Coconino Sun,* July 24, 1942.

24. See Weaver correspondence with McFarland, Thomas, and Hayden, and various documents in Navajo Ordnance Depot 1942 files, FCCR; Hayden to O. C. Williams, February 16, 1942, Ordnance Depot, Bellemont, 1942, Osborn Collection.

25. *Coconino Sun,* October 31, 1941; January 30, February 13, 1942.

26. "Navajo Ordnance Depot, vol. I," Exhibit Construction Information, RG 156, National Archives; Cline, *Mountain Town,* 310; Navajo Army Depot Information Brochure (1964), box 5, 1942–1968, MS 44, SCA, CL.

27. Demmie H. Cox, "Completion Report, Navajo Ordnance Depot, Bellemont, Arizona, January 30, 1943," JOB M(1), 19, XXII–XXIII, JOB P(1), 1, II–III, Construction Completion Reports, 1917–43, Fort Myer to Nebraska, Records of the Office of the Chief of Engineers, RG 77, National Archives, Washington, D.C.; "Navajo Ordnance Depot, vol. I," 6.

28. *Coconino Sun,* January 30, February 13, March 13, 1942; interview with Henry Giclas, November 9, 1999.

29. *Coconino Sun,* March 6, 20, 1942.

30. *Kane County Standard* (Kanab, Utah), June 12, 1942; *Coconino Sun,* April 17, 1942; Cox, "Completion Report," JOB M(1), VIII, XXII–XXIII, RG 77; "Navajo Ordnance Depot, vol. I," 7, RG 156. For a history of the Atkinson Company, see "Guy F. Atkinson Company," *America's Builders* 5, no. 11 (September 1959): 1–12.

31. Cox, "Completion Report," JOB M(1), 19–22, XXII–XXIII and JOB P(1), 19–24, VIII, RG 77.

32. Telegram, Hayden to Weaver, July 20, 1942, FCCR.

33. Interview with Howard C. Wren, July 9, 2001.

34. Interview with Joe D. Richards, November 18, 1999; Wren interview.

35. Dowell interview.

36. Wren interview.

37. Wren interview; Duane Atkinson to Tom Jennett, July 10, 1981, author's files.

38. Cox, "Completion Report," JOB M(1), 31, 37, RG 77.

39. Interview with Elgymae Connelley, November 18, 2001, Stanfield, Arizona.

40. Giclas interviews; interview with Richard K. Mangum, November 10, 1999; Weaver to Hayden, June 26, 1942, in Open Shop, 1942 file, FCCR.

41. *Coconino Sun,* March 13, October 9, 16, December 4, 1942; Giclas interviews; Wren interview; interview with Eleuto Roybal, January 9, 2000; Weaver to Thomas, December 31, 1942 and Major E. B. Myrick to Chief of Ordnance, August 29, 1942, both in Navajo Ordnance Depot, 1942, FCCR.

42. *Coconino Sun,* May 29, 1942; interview with Lazaro A. Diaz, June 4, 2000; interview with Platt Cline, May 13, 1998; Roybal interview; Michelbach interview; Cox, "Completion Report," JOB M(1), 31, RG 77; "History of Navajo Ordnance Depot, Third Quarter, 1943," 75–76, RG 156, National Archives.

43. Michelbach interview; "Historical Summary, Third Quarter, 1943," 76–77, RG 156.

44. Michelbach interview; Wren interview; conversation with Richard Mangum, February 6, 2002.

45. "Historical Summary, Third Quarter, 1943," 76–79; Michelbach interview; *Arizona Daily Sun,* May 19, 1967.

46. Richards interview; "Historical Summary, Third Quarter, 1943."

47. Wren interview.

48. *Coconino Sun,* March 27, May 1, 22, September 4, 1942.

49. *Coconino Sun,* December 11, 1942. For accidents see the *Coconino Sun,* June 5, 12, July 3, 24, September 8, October 2, and December 18, 1942.

50. Interview with Lucile Michael, January 26, 2000; *Coconino Sun*, January 15, 1943; *Arizona Daily Sun*, August 20, 1984; *Twenty-Fifth Anniversary Navajo Army Depot* brochure, MS 44, SCA, CL; "Navajo Ordnance Depot, vol. I," 10, RG 156; Navajo Army Depot Information Brochure (1964), 1.

51. *Arizona Daily Sun*, May 19, 1967.

52. Michael interview; Weaver to Thomas, December 31, 1942; Navajo Army Depot Information Brochure (1964), 1; "Navajo Ordnance Depot, vol. I," 10, 11, RG 156.

53. "Navajo Ordnance Depot, vol. I," 11, RG 156.

54. *Arizona Daily Sun*, May 19, 1967; Cox, "Completion Reports."

55. Mangum interview; Cox, "Completion Report," RG 77.

56. Cox, "Completion Report," RG 77; "Navajo Ordnance Depot, vol. I," 7–9, RG 156; "Navajo Army Depot, 1942–1968," 17, Commanders' Scrapbooks, 1942–89, MS 44, SCA, CL.

57. *Coconino Sun*, October 30, 1942; "Navajo Ordnance Depot, vol. I," exhibit 9, RG 156.

58. "Navajo Ordnance Depot, vol. I," 14; *Coconino Sun*, November 13, 1942.

59. "Navajo Ordnance Depot, vol. I," 15–18, RG 156; *Coconino Sun*, December 4, 11, 1942; Weaver to Thomas, December 31, 1942.

60. Interview with Paul A. Sweitzer, November 11, 1999; Mangum interviews; "Historical Summary, Third Quarter, 1943," 9, RG 156; Cox, "Completion Report," JOB M(1), 31, 35–36, 38, 41, RG 77; *Coconino Sun*, July 16, 1943.

Chapter 3. Boxcars Coming

1. *Coconino Sun*, January 22, 1943; "Historical Summary, First Quarter, 1943," 17.

2. "Navajo Ordnance Depot, vol. I," 22, RG 156, National Archives.

3. "Historical Summary, First Quarter 1943," 41; NOD Organizational Chart, December 15, 1943, located in the "Navajo Ordnance Depot, vols. 2–5"; *ibid.*, Organizational Diagram, vol. 7, RG 156.

4. "Navajo Ordnance Depot, vol. I," 11, 19, 20; U.S. Army–DARCOM, *History of Fort Wingate Depot*, n.d., 44.

5. "Navajo Ordnance Depot, vol. I," 11, 19, 20.

6. "Historical Summaries, First Quarter, 1943," 15; "Third Quarter, 1943," 8; *Arizona Daily Sun* (Flagstaff), March 19, 1956.

7. *Arizona Daily Sun*, March 19, 1956; interviews with Guillermo "Gus" Florez and Earl C. Hedges, March 29, 2000.

8. "Historical Summaries, First Quarter, 1943," 17; "Fourth Quarter, 1943," 82, 85, 87, 117.

9. "Historical Summaries, Third Quarter 1943," 9, 89; "Fourth Quarter, 1943 and 1944."

10. "Historical Summaries, Second Quarter, 1943," 76; "Third Quarter, 1943," 8–12; "First Quarter, 1944," 46–47, 167; interview with Sally Coddington, January 26, 2000.

11. "Historical Summary, Second Quarter, 1943," 4, 10, 42–43.

12. *Arizona Daily Sun,* May 19, 1967.

13. "Historical Summaries, 1943–1945," passim; "Third Quarter, 1943," 6; and "Second Quarter, 1945," 7; *Arizona Daily Sun,* March 19, 1956.

14. "Historical Summaries, First Quarter, 1943," 1–14; "Second Quarter, 1945," 71; and other wartime summaries.

15. "Historical Summaries, 1942–45," passim; and "Third Quarter, 1943," 2; Green, Thomson, and Roots, *The Ordnance Department,* 9.

16. "Historical Summary, Third Quarter, 1943," 2; Lucile Michael interview. *Coconino Sun,* January 15, 1943; November 2, 16, 1945.

17. Cline interview.

18. Michelbach, Giclas, and Michael interviews; interview with Eleanor Lois F. Price, December 22, 1998; and Coddington interviews May 12 and November 17, 1999, January 26, 2000, all in author's files.

19. "Historical Summaries, Fourth Quarter 1943," 81–88, 118–19; "First Quarter, 1944," I, 272; "Second Quarter, 1945," 96–97.

20. "Historical Summary, First Quarter, 1944," 281–83; Bullis and Mielke, *Strategic and Critical Materials,* 37; Campbell, *The History of Basic Metals,* 35.

21. "Historical Summaries, Second Quarter, 1944," 26–29, 154; "Fourth Quarter, 1944," 80; "First Quarter, 1945," 10, 85–86; "Second Quarter, 1945," 20; "POW Population Lists, 1942–45, Reports on Camps by Location and Types of Work," 185, microfilm, Records of the Army Adjutant General, RG 407, National Archives, College Park, Maryland; Hoza, *PW,* 43.

22. *Coconino Sun,* August 18, November 10, 1944; "Historical Summaries, Third Quarter, 1943," 23; "Fourth Quarter, 1943," 22; "First Quarter, 1944," 21, 52, 55, 84, 102; "Second Quarter, 1944," 19; "Third Quarter, 1944," 62, 78.

23. *Coconino Sun,* June 11, 1943; May 25, July 27, 1945; "Historical Summaries, First Quarter, 1944," 112, 115, 194–99; "Second Quarter, 1944," 159–62; "Third Quarter, 1944," 54; telegram, Carl Hayden to Leo Weaver, September 17, 1943, in Navajo Ordnance Depot, 1942 file, FCCR, MS 193, SCA, CL.; "Background Information on Ordnance Field Service" (Washington, D.C.: The Pentagon, [c1955]), 12.

24. *Coconino Sun,* December 3, 1943; "Historical Summary, Fourth Quarter, 1943," 9–15; Isabel Simmons interview by Susan L. Rogers, January 13, 1976, 4, Flagstaff Oral History Project (hereafter FOHP), SCA, CL.

25. Interview with Sally O'Connell Veazey, March 29, 2002.

26. Veazey interview; "Historical Summaries, First Quarter, 1944," IV, 45, 97–98, 101, 220; "Second Quarter, 1944," 74, 97, 186; "Third Quarter, 1944," 141–42; "Fourth Quarter, 1944," 40, 52; "First Quarter, 1945," 15, 18; "Second Quarter, 1945," 60; Coddington interview, January 26, 2000; *Coconino Sun*, September 3, October 1, 1943; December 22, 1944.

27. *Coconino Sun*, May 12, 1944; "Historical Summary, Second Quarter, 1944," 6.

28. "Historical Summaries, Fourth Quarter, 1943," 75; "First Quarter, 1944," I, 192, 202, 205, 263; "Second Quarter, 1944," 133, 148, 167, 169; *Coconino Sun*, May 12, 1944.

29. "Historical Summary, First Quarter, 1944," 169; *Coconino Sun*, May 12, 1944.

30. *Coconino Sun*, September 29, 1944; "Historical Summaries, Third Quarter, 1944," 65A, 96; "First–Third Quarter, 1944," passim.

31. "Historical Summaries, Second Quarter 1943," 63–65, 100; "Second Quarter, 1944," 4, 130: "Third Quarter, 1944," 10; "Fourth Quarter, 1944," 71, 73, Exhibit A, Special Orders 157, October 12, 1944; *Coconino Sun*, October 6, 13, November 24, 1944; *Coconino Sun*, March 23, 1945.

32. "Historical Summary, First Quarter, 1945," 18, 68; *Coconino Sun*, December 22, 29, 1944.

33. Gilbert, *Auschwitz*, 31, 100; Marrus, *The Holocaust*, 158.

34. "Historical Summary, First Quarter, 1945," 13, 60–64, 77, 87, 101–3; "Second Quarter, 1945," 102; "Arizona," A-43, in Navajo Army Depot, 1942–present, folder 8166, Arizona Museum of Military History, Phoenix; Brophy et al., *Chemical Warfare Service*, 51–62.

35. "Historical Summaries, First Quarter, 1945," 77–82; "Second Quarter, 1945," 85, 86, 89, 90, 94.

36. Ibid., "Second Quarter, 1945," 93, 99–100.

37. *Coconino Sun*, March 30, 1945.

38. "Historical Summary, Second Quarter, 1945," 17–19; *Coconino Sun*, May 11, 18, 1945.

39. "Historical Summary, Second Quarter, 1945," 17; *Coconino Sun*, May 11, 1945.

40. *Coconino Sun*, May 11, 1945.

41. Ibid., March 23, 1945.

42. Ibid., May 18, June 8, 1945; "Navajo Ordnance Depot, vol. I," passim; "Historical Summaries, 1943–45," passim.

43. *Coconino Sun*, June 8, 1945.

44. *Coconino Sun,* April 6, June 8, 22, 1945; "Historical Summary, Second Quarter, 1945," 95, 101.

45. *Coconino Sun,* June 22, 1945; "Historical Summary, Second Quarter, 1945," 86–100.

Chapter 4. Warriors All

1. "Historical Summaries, First Quarter, 1944," 213–14; "Second Quarter, 1944," 13; *Arizona Daily Sun,* May 19, 1967.

2. Sheridan, *Arizona,* 294–98; Iverson, *Navajo Nation,* 24–45; Parman, *Navajos,* 43–44, 56–57, 97; Philp, *John Collier's Crusade,* 187–93; White, *Roots of Dependency,* 259–62.

3. Philp, *Termination Revisited,* 4–6; White, *Roots of Dependency,* 270; Iverson, *Navajo Nation,* 30–34, 49; Franco, "Navajos in World War II," 1–5. Also see Franco, "Loyal and Heroic Service," 391–406.

4. McCoy, "Navajo Code Talkers," 68; Stewart, "Navajo Indian at War," 21. Also see Franco, "Navajos in World War II," 1, 6; idem, "Patriotism on Trial," 90, 100–101, and Thomas, "First Families," 96.

5. Thomas, "First Families," 99; Leo Weaver to E. R. Fryer, Navajo Service, Window Rock, Arizona, February 10 [1942], in Indian Affairs, 1942 file, FCCR, MS 193, SCA, CL.

6. Parman, *Indians and the American West,* 63; Townsend, *World War II and the American Indian,* 61–62; "Navajo Ordnance Depot, vol. I," 10, 11, 20; Stewart, "Navajo Indian at War," 43; "Historical Summary, Third Quarter, 1943," 7; *Coconino Sun,* May 7, 1943; Doyle, Byrkit, and Swaim, *Historic Building Survey,* 2.

7. Brew, "Hopi Prehistory," 514–15; Pritzker, *Native Americans: An Encyclopedia,* 42–47; Malinowski and Sheets, ed., *Gale Encyclopedia,* 121–22.

8. Rushforth and Upham, *Hopi Social History,* 155, 160; *Navajo Times* (Window Rock, Arizona), May 18, 1967; Franco, *Crossing the Pond,* 53–55.

9. Interview with Scott B. Franklin, May 17, 2000; interview with Lazaro A. Diaz, June 4, 2000.

10. Boyce, *Too Many Sheep,* 120.

11. Ibid., 120; Stewart, "Navajo Indian at War," 43; Grenda, *Archaeological Survey,* 59.

12. "Navajo Ordnance Depot, vol. I," 10; LaRouche, "War Comes First," 19; interview with Amy Franklin, May 18, 2000.

13. "Historical Summary, First Quarter, 1944," 61; interview with Imo Wardlow, March 22, 2000; LaRouche, "War Comes First," 19.

14. Interview with Scott B. Franklin, July 31, 2000; "Navajo Ordnance Depot, vol. I," 10; Negri, "Bombs and Hogans," 43; Wardlow interview; *Arizona Daily Sun,* May 11, 1962.

15. "Navajo Ordnance Depot, vol. I," 11, 19–20; "Indian Labor at Navajo Ordnance Depot," folder 6, box 5, Navajo Army Depot Collection, MS 44, SCA, CL.

16. "Navajo Ordnance Depot, vol. I," 10; "Historical Summary, First Quarter, 1943," 23; Boyce, *Too Many Sheep,* 119–20.

17. Guy Multine to Myrick, June 1, 1943, "Navajo Army Depot," folder 3, box 5, MS 44, SCA, CL.; "Historical Summary, Third Quarter, 1943," 51.

18. Negri, "Town the War Built"; Multine to Myrick; "Historical Summary, First Quarter, 1944," 70–72.

19. Boyce, *Too Many Sheep,* 120.

20. Richardson, *Navajo Trader,* xi, 29–31; Negri, "Town the War Built"; photo 3432, Richardson's Trading Post, MS 44, SCA, CL.

21. Negri, "Town the War Built"; "Sanitary Sewer," engineer drawing, and Richardson's Trading Post photos, 3429–35, both in MS 44, SCA, CL.; Isabel Simmons interview by Susan L. Rogers, FOHP, January 13, 1976, 9; Wardlow interview; interview with John R. Young, Camp Verde, May 7, 2000.

22. Scott B. Franklin interviews; Young interview; Richardson's Trading Post photos, 3429–35, MS 44, SCA, CL.; interview with Kee and Mary Ester Tsinnie, January 8, 2002.

23. Multine to Myrick.

24. Negri, "Town the War Built"; Tsinnie interview.

25. Ibid.

26. *Coconino Sun,* May 26, 1944; *Arizona Daily Sun,* September 11, 1986; Wardlow interview; Richards interviews; "Historical Summary, Fourth Quarter, 1944," 34, 36.

27. John R. Young interview.

28. Simmons interview, 10; "Historical Summary, Third Quarter, 1943," 10.

29. "Historical Summaries, 1942–44," passim; "Indian Labor at Navajo Ordnance Depot."

30. Kambouris to author, August 11, 1999.

31. *Arizona Daily Sun,* March 19, 1956; Veazey interview.

32. "Historical Summaries, Third Quarter, 1943," 52; "Fourth Quarter, 1943," 87; "Second Quarter, 1944," 211; "Fourth Quarter, 1944," 35–36; "First Quarter, 1945," 12; *Coconino Sun,* May 12, December 1, 1944; Hansen, "Some Realities," 9; "Indian Labor at Navajo Ordnance Depot"; Underhill, *Here Come the Navajo!,* 259.

33. Amy Franklin interview.

34. Begay, "Munitions Plant Work," 48–50; Scott Franklin interviews.

35. *Coconino Sun,* May 11, 1945; "Historical Summaries, 1943–1945," passim.

36. "Historical Summary, First Quarter, 1943," 34; "Navajo Ordnance Depot, vol. I," 3, app. 2.

37. "Historical Summaries, Third Quarter, 1943," 50–51; "Fourth Quarter, 1943," 23; "First Quarter, 1944," 42; "Second Quarter, 1944," 15; "Fourth Quarter, 1944," 35; Hansen, "Some Realities," 7–8; *Coconino Sun,* September 18, 1942; May 7, 1943; LaRouche, "War Comes First," 19; *Navajo Times,* May 18, 1967.

38. "Indian Employment" in Indian Affairs, 1942 file and Weaver to Myrick, August 6, 1942, Navajo Ordnance Depot, 1942 file, both in FCCR, MS 193, SCA, CL.

39. *Coconino Sun,* September 18, 1942; October 12, 1945; Scott B. Franklin interviews.

40. "Historical Summary, First Quarter, 1944," 70–72; "Third Quarter, 1943," 137; "First Quarter, 1944," 70–72; "Third Quarter, 1944," 52, Exhibit D, n.p.; interview with George S. Barreras, May 3, 2000; Lautzenheiser et al., "Flagstaff and Bell[e]mont, Arizona," 36.

41. *Coconino Sun,* May 7, September 3, 1943; photos 2191–2215, Navajo Army Depot Collection, MS 44, SCA, CL; *Arizona Daily Sun,* May 11, 1962; *Arizona Republic,* June 19, 1985; Wardlow interview; "Historical Summary, First Quarter, 1944," 213–14; Boyce, *Too Many Sheep,* 120; Grenda, *Archaeological Survey,* 31.

42. "Sanitary Sewer," engineer drawing; Wardlow interview; *Coconino Sun,* May 7, 1943; December 1, 1944; February 23, 1945; *Arizona Republic,* November 30, 1944; June 19, 1985; "Historical Summary, 2 September 1945–30 June 1951"; Also see photos 2191–215, MS 44, SCA, CL.

43. Rushforth and Upham, *Hopi Social History,* 160; *Arizona Republic,* February 6, 1955; Tsinnie interview; Peplow, *History of Arizona,* vol. 2, 522.

44. "Navajo Ordnance Depot, vol. I," 11, 19–20; "Historical Summaries, Third Quarter, 1943," 7; "Fourth Quarter, 1943," 1; "First Quarter, 1944," 45; "Second Quarter, 1944," 4; "Third Quarter, 1944," 10; "Fourth Quarter, 1944," 31; "First Quarter, 1945," 11; "Second Quarter, 1945," 39.

45. Interview with Al Henderson, January 31, 2000; Hansen, "Some Realities," 16.

46. Scott B. Franklin interviews.

47. Coddington interview, 26 January 2000; Wardlow interview; Young interview; Hansen, "Some Realities," 13–16; *Arizona Daily Sun,* September 11, 1986; "Historical Summary, First Quarter, 1945," 13.

48. R. C. Gorman to author, March 12, 1997; interview with Josef Papp, October 13–16, 1998.

49. Boyce, *Too Many Sheep,* 119–21.

50. *Arizona Daily Sun,* March 29, 1956; "Historical Summary, Third Quarter," 1943, 10–11; "First Quarter, 1944," 61.

51. *Arizona Daily Sun,* March 29, 1956.

52. *Arizona Daily Sun,* March 29, 1956; "Historical Summary, First Quarter, 1944," 61.

53. *Arizona Daily Sun,* March 29, 1956.

54. "Historical Summaries, Third Quarter, 1943," 83; "First Quarter, 1944," 61.

55. *Coconino Sun,* March 19, 1943; Hoffman, *Navajo Biographies,* vol. 1, 204.

56. *Coconino Sun,* July 30, 1943; *Winslow Mail* (Winslow, Arizona), November 26, 1943.

57. *Coconino Sun,* May 26, 1944; "Historical Summary, Second Quarter, 1944," 38.

58. "Indian Labor at Navajo Ordnance Depot."

59. Ibid.; "Historical Summaries, Third Quarter, 1943," 11; "First Quarter, 1944," 114; LaRouche, "War Comes First," 19.

60. *Arizona Republic,* October 9, 1986; *Winslow Mail,* October 1, November 12, 1943; *Coconino Sun,* December 3, 1943.

61. Begay, "Munitions Plant Work," 48–49; *Coconino Sun,* February 23, 1945; "Historical Summaries, Third Quarter, 1943," 57; "Second Quarter, 1945," 13–14; "Indian Labor at Navajo Ordnance Depot."

62. "Historical Summary, Third Quarter, 1943," 57–58; *Coconino Sun,* February 23, 1945.

63. LaRouche, "War Comes First," 19.

64. Simmons interview, 12; Wardlow interview.

65. Richards interview; Connelley interview.

66. Amy Franklin interview; Gus Kambouris to author, 11 August 1999.

67. Interview with Ward C. Olson, November 15–19, 1999.

68. Kee Tsinnie interview.

69. Olson interview; interview with Robert Crozier Jr., February 21, 2001; Kambouris to author.

70. Simmons interview, 22; Olson interview.

71. Simmons interview, 22.

72. Ibid., 13.

Chapter 5. "Don't Do Anything Stupid!"

1. Lewis and Mewha, *Prisoner of War Utilization*, fn 41 p. 57, 68, 74, 90; Pluth, "German Prisoner of War Camps," 15–16.

2. Lewis and Mewha, *Prisoner of War Utilization*, 90; Krammer, *Nazi Prisoners of War*, 2.

3. Krammer, *Nazi Prisoners of War*, 27–28; Lewis and Mewha, *Prisoner of War Utilization*, 84–86.

4. Hoza, *PW*, 67–68; Lewis and Mewha, *Prisoner of War Utilization*, 82, fn 22 p. 82, 84–85; *Los Angeles Times*, September 27, 1943.

5. Interviews with Josef Papp, Hinterbrühl, Austria, October 5, 2000; Flagstaff, October 13–16, 1998; interview by David Kitterman, November 20, 1997.

6. Papp interview, October 5, 2000; interview with Walter Gastgeb, Vienna, Austria, October 6, 2000; interview with Friedrich Gröbner, translated by Alexander Grimme, Vienna, October 6, 2000; Walter Gastgeb to author, December 22, 1998 and Friedrich Gröbner to author, March 20, 1999, both translated by André Rupp.

7. Papp interview, October 5, 2000; *Los Angeles Times*, September 23, 1943.

8. *Los Angeles Times*, September 23, 1943; Gröbner interview; Gastgeb interview.

9. Krammer, *Nazi Prisoners of War*, 182; R. W. Flournoy to Mr. Hackworth, April 17, 1945, decimal file 711.63/4-1745, Records of the Department of State, RG 59, National Archives, College Park, Maryland. Lothar Burchardt to author, e-mail, August 28, 1998, includes segments of Adolf Berle's diary located at the Franklin D. Roosevelt Library at Hyde Park, New York.

10. Krammer, *Nazi Prisoners of War*, 192; Burchardt to author; Costelle, *Les Prisonniers*, 69–70; Kramer to author, e-mail, August 29, 1998; Department of State memorandum of conversation, W. M. Franklin, June 29, 1945, decimal file 711.62114/6-2045, and Memorandum for the Liaison Officer, State Department, from Edward H. Miller, July 29, 1945, decimal file 711.62114/7-2045, both in RG 59, National Archives; *Freiheit für Oesterreich* (New York) 1, no. 3 (August 1942): 1.

11. Gastgeb interview; POW signed statement, Otto Grünberger, October 24, 1944, author's files.

12. Field Service Report, Camp Florence, Arizona, January 10–12, 1945, Provost Marshal General Office Inspection Reports, Florence file, Enemy POW Information Bureau Reporting Branch, 1942–46, RG 389, National Archives; Hoza, *PW*, 69; Powell, *German Prisoners of War in Utah*, 65.

13. Papp interviews, October 13–16, 1998, October 5, 2000; Lewis and

Mewha, *Prisoner of War Utilization*, 91; Gerhard Lux, Camp Spokesman, to the International Committee of the Red Cross (ICRC), Geneva, Switzerland, October 7, 1944, Camp Florence, POW Special Projects Division, Administrative Branch, decimal file, 1943–46, RG 389, National Archives.

14. Lewis and Mewha, *Prisoner of War Utilization*, 91, fn 44 p. 91, 92; Krammer, *Nazi Prisoners of War*, 28, 35.

15. Hoza, *PW,* 86.

16. Powell, *German Prisoners of War in Utah*, 63–65, 73, 143, 214, 223–224, 233–234.

17. "Historical Summaries, Second Quarter, 1944," 26–29; "Second Quarter, 1945," 20; *Coconino Sun*, March 30, 1945.

18. *Coconino Sun*, March 30, 1945; Hoza, *PW,* 126–27.

19. *Coconino Sun*, March 30, 1945.

20. *Coconino Sun*, April 6, 1945.

21. Ibid.

22. Krammer, *Nazi Prisoners of War*, 35–36; Lewis and Mewha, *Prisoner of War Utilization*, 79.

23. Tomas Jaehn to author, e-mail, August 26, 1998.

24. *Coconino Sun*, April 6, 1945.

25. Ibid., April 13, 1945.

26. Ibid., April 20, 1945.

27. Ibid.

28. "Historical Summary, Second Quarter, 1945," 21–23.

29. Ibid., 24–25.

30. *Coconino Sun*, May 18, 1945; ICRC POW camp inspection report, Navajo Ordnance Depot, June 21, 1945, from the ICRC archives, Geneva, Switzerland, translated from French by author, author's files.

31. ICRC camp inspection report, June 21, 1945; Report of POW camp inspection, July 12, 1945, in Navajo Ordnance Depot file, Enemy POW Information Bureau, Reporting Branch, 1942–46, RG 389, National Archives.

32. Papp interviews; *Arizona Daily Sun*, October 12, 2001; time capsule items and letter signed by Reverend Isfried Friedrich Schmid, Hospital Order of Saint John, translated by Dorothea Rebhahn.

33. ICRC camp inspection report, June 21, 1945; Monthly Sanitary Reports, Navajo Ordnance Depot, February 3, 1945–August 2, 1946, Navajo Ordnance Depot file, Geographic Series, 1945–46, Records of the Surgeon General's Office, RG 2, National Archives, College Park, Maryland.

34. *Coconino Sun*, July 27, 1945; Papp interview by Kitterman.

35. ICRC camp inspection report, June 21, 1945.

36. Robin, *Barbed-Wire College,* 59–60; Krammer, *Nazi Prisoners of War,* 189, 194, 200–202.

37. *Arizona Sonne,* January 27, 1946.

38. Gröbner interview, to author, June 8, 1999, and copies of drawings, author's files; *Coconino Sun,* July 27, 1945.

39. ICRC camp inspection report, June 21, 1945; Gröbner interview; Gorman to author, March 12, 1997; Gastgeb interview; Scott Franklin interview.

40. "Historical Summaries, 1945," passim; Papp, Gastgeb, Gröbner, and Grünberger interviews.

41. Doerry, "Karl May," 243, 246–48; Kitchen, *Nazi Germany at War,* 276.

42. Young interview; Gastgeb to author, December 22, 1998.

43. Gorman to author.

44. Interview with Sally O'Connell Veazey, March 29, 2002.

45. *Coconino Sun,* May 18, 25, 1945; Papp interview, October 5, 2000; Gastgeb interview.

46. Josef Papp, interview by Richard Helt, December 5, 1997; Papp interviews, October 13–16, 1998, October 5, 2000.

47. Gastgeb interview; Price interview; Papp interviews; Peggy Davern to author, September 9, 2000.

48. Papp interview by Kitterman.

49. Ibid.; interview with Platt Cline, May 13, 1998; Papp interview, October 5, 2000.

50. Michelbach interview.

51. Ford McElroy, interview by Kristine Prennace, Flagstaff Oral History Project, August 24–26, 1976; Prisoner of War Strength Reports.

52. Krammer, *Nazi Prisoners of War,* 256–59.

53. Gastgeb interview; Papp interview, October 5, 2000.

54. Sweitzer interview.

55. Papp interview, October 5, 2000; ICRC camp inspection report, June 21, 1945.

56. Grünberger, Gastgeb correspondence, translated by André Rupp, author's files.

57. Papp interview by Kitterman; Papp interview, October 5, 2000; Gröbner interview; Report of POW camp inspection, July 12, 1945; *Arizona Daily Sun,* October 15, 1998; Report of Visit to Prisoner of War Camp, Navajo Ordnance Depot, Arizona, December 8, 1945, Navajo Ordnance Depot file, POW Special Projects Division, RG 389, National Archives; ICRC camp inspection reports, June 21, 1945 and January 24, 1946, author's files. The 1946 ICRC report, written in German, translated by Thomas Fuller, is also from the ICRC archives in Geneva, Switzerland.

58. Sweitzer interview; interview with Platt Cline, October 20, 1997; *Coconino Sun*, August 3, 1945.

59. Papp interviews, October 13–16, 1998, October 5, 2000; ICRC camp inspection report, June 21, 1945; Prisoner of War Strength Reports, March 31, 1945–March 13, 1946, Enemy POW Information Bureau, Camp Labor Report, Ninth Service Command, Navajo Ordnance file, RG 389, National Archives.

60. Prisoner of War Strength Reports.

61. "Historical Summary, September 2, 1945–June 30, 1951"; Prisoner of War Strength Reports; Report of POW camp inspection, July 12, 1945; ICRC camp inspection report, January 24, 1946; Papp, Gröbner, Gastgeb, and Grünberger correspondence and interviews.

Chapter 6. The Fleet's In!

1. Cline, *Mountain Campus Centennial*, 199, 276, 292; interview with Betty Jean Oliver Gatlin, April 15, 2002.

2. See the Thomas J. Tormey Collection, RG 1.8, Special Collections and Archives, Cline Library, Northern Arizona University; Hutchinson, *Northern Arizona University*, 146.

3. Laina Siniaho Van Campen, Donald R. Kirk, William H. Cummings, and Estella Marie Melton Ferrell, NAU Alumni Centennial Questionnaire, 1996, SCA, CL.

4. *Coconino Sun*, January 9, 1942; Cline, *Mountain Campus Centennial*, 185.

5. *Coconino Sun*, August 21, September 25, 1942, July 30, 1943; Cline, *Mountain Campus Centennial*, 173, 185; Hutchinson, *Northern Arizona University*, 141; *History of the Civil Aeronautics Administration*, 7.

6. Gatlin interview; Cline, *Mountain Campus Centennial*, 182; *The Pine* (ASTC, Flagstaff), February 16, 1943.

7. Cline, *Mountain Campus Centennial*, 182–83, 509; *La Cuesta* (ASTC yearbook), 1943–44; interview with Beverly Bellwood Burns, September 10, 2000; interview with Dorothy Schick Perry, September 21, 2000; *The Pine*, February 16, 1943.

8. *Coconino Sun*, May 14, 1943; Cline, *Mountain Campus Centennial*, 182–83.

9. Cardozier, *Colleges and Universities*, 7–8, 12–13.

10. Cline, *Mountain Campus Centennial*, 183–85; Schneider, *Navy V-12 Program*, 15; *Coconino Sun*, March 5, 1943.

11. *Coconino Sun*, March 5, 12, 26, 1943.

12. Hutchinson, *Northern Arizona University*, 141, 144.

13. *Coconino Sun*, March 19, 26, 1943.

14. Ibid., March 26, 1943; interview with Howard Wren, July 9, 2001; conversation with Howard Wren, April 30, 2002.

15. *Coconino Sun*, March 21, May 14, 1943. Schneider, *Navy V-12 Program*, 10.

16. Martin, *Lamp in the Desert*, 192, 196; *Arizona Republic*, December 3, 1978.

17. Schneider, *Navy V-12 Program*, 12, 460, 522–23, 529, 538, 540.

18. *Coconino Sun*, May 14, 21, 1943.

19. Ibid., June 4, 25, September 7, 1943; *The Pine*, July 13, 1943. Notes in Navy V-12 Unit file, folder 53, box 2; Gerard Swope Jr. to Tom O. Bellwood, May 10, 1945; State Auditor's Report, Budget Information, 1943–44 file, box 1; and ration checks in Navy Contract vertical file, all in Bellwood Collection, RG 1.9, SCA, CL.; Cline, *Mountain Campus Centennial*, 184; Winkler, *Home Front U.S.A.*, 39; Hutchinson, *Northern Arizona University*, 142, 145; Oliver interview.

20. *Coconino Sun*, October 16, 1945; Earl M. Bay to author, February 26, 2002; *The Pine*, October 16, 1945; Don H. Horner, NAU Alumni Centennial Questionnaire, 1996, SCA, CL.

21. *Coconino Sun*, June 18, 25, 1943; Schneider, *Navy V-12 Program*, 15.

22. Schneider, *Navy V-12 Program*, 76, 522; Cline, *Mountain Campus Centennial*, 184–85.

23. Betty Jean Oliver Gatlin, NAU Alumni Centennial Questionnaire, 1996, SCA, CL.

24. Jerry Garlock to Howard Wren, December 13, 2001, author's files; Wren interview; *The Pine*, March 7, 1944; Victor Myers to Howard Wren, December 13, 2001, author's files; conversation with Art Mehagian, February 13, 2002; Bay to author.

25. Lorraine O. Inman to author, December, 2001; Schneider; "Arizona State Teachers College"; notes in Navy V-12 Unit file, folder 53, box 2; Schneider, *Navy V-12 Unit*, in the Navy Contract vertical file, all in Bellwood Collection; interview with Harold L. and Marion Elliott, August 25, 2000; Kathryn M. Custis McGinis to author, September 28, 2000.

26. *Manual for the Operation of a V-12 Unit* ([Washington, D.C.]: Department of the Navy, June 18, 1943), iv, copy in Navy V-12 Unit file, folder 52, box 2, Bellwood Collection.

27. Cardozier, *Colleges and Universities*, 52–53; *Coconino Sun*, April 9, June 18, 1943; Elliott interview.

28. Interview with Ruth Corbett Kunkle, September 11, 2000; Marycarol Pryor Bazacos to author, September 16, 2000; *The Pine*, November 9, 1943, October 17, 1944; *Coconino Sun*, July 2, 1943.

29. Elliott interview.

30. Wren interview; *The Pine*, January 25, 1944; Garlock to Wren; conversation with Earl M. Bay, April 29, 2002.

31. *The Pine*, November 9, 1943; Myers to Wren.

32. Conversation with Earl M. Bay, April 29, 2002.

33. *The Pine*, July 13, 1943, January 11, February 1, 8, September 5, 1944, passim.

34. Boots on Parade brochure, Navy V-12 Unit file, box 2, Bellwood Collection; Hutchinson, *Northern Arizona University*, 144.

35. Boots on Parade brochure, Bellwood Collection; *The Pine*, July 27, September 21, 1943; *Coconino Sun*, August 20, 1943.

36. *The Pine*, February 8, 1944; Garlock to Wren.

37. *Coconino Sun*, June 25, 1943; Bay to author; *The Pine*, July 27, 1943, January 25, 1944.

38. *The Pine*, August 17, 1943, August 4, 1944.

39. Ibid., August 4, 1944; Bay to author and conversations with Earl M. Bay, March 3, April 29, 2002.

40. Sherman R. Payne to author, September 2000.

41. Ibid.

42. Ibid; conversation with Arthur S. Mehagian, April 29, 2002.

43. *NAU Football Guide, 2001,* 90; *Coconino Sun*, July 16, 30, 1943; conversation with Robert E. Brickey, April 25, 2002; minutes, spring meeting, Border Intercollegiate Athletic Conference, May 22, 1943, El Paso, Texas, NAU Athletic Department archives.

44. *Coconino Sun*, July 16, 30, 1943; *The Pine*, July 27, 1943; Brickey conversation.

45. *The Pine*, August 31, 1943; Bay to author; Brickey conversation.

46. *The Pine*, August 31, October 12, 26, 1943, February 20, 1945; *NAU Football Guide, 2001,* 90.

47. Elliott interview; Lorraine O. Inman to author, October 3, 2000.

48. *Coconino Sun*, September 1, 1944; Hutchinson, *Northern Arizona University*, 149.

49. Bay to author; *The Pine*, passim; Iola Aston Sanders and Marycarol Pryor Bazacos, NAU Alumni Centennial Questionnaire, 1996, SCA, CL.

50. Elliott interview; Burns interview; Betty Jean Oliver Gatlin to author, September 18, 2000, and Gatlin interview; Perry interview; Inman to author; Marycarol Pryor Bazacos to author, October 8, 2001.

51. Burns interview; Peggy Davern to author, September 9, 2000; interview with Betty Lou Decker Cummings, September 15, 2000; Bazacos to author; McGinis to author; Patricia Herold, NAU Alumni Centennial Questionnaire, 1996, SCA, CL.

52. *The Pine*, March 21, 1944, passim; Myers to Wren.

53. Interview with Rose Titus Davis, October 2, 2000.

54. *The Pine*, January 18, 25, April 11, May 23, 1944; Perry interview.

55. *The Pine*, November 9, 1943.

56. *Coconino Sun*, October 8, 1943, June 16, 1944; *The Pine*, February 15, 1944.

57. Oliver Briggs Jr. to author February 9, 2002; *The Pine*, passim; memorial service brochure, Navy V-12 Unit file, box 2, Bellwood Collection.

58. Lola M. Dunaway, NAU Alumni Centennial Questionnaire, SCA, CL.

59. Bay and Briggs to author; Davis interview.

60. Bay to author; *Coconino Sun*, July 16, 1943.

61. *The Pine*, October 19, 1943; Davis interview.

62. *The Pine*, July 13, 1943, January 11, February 1, March 14, April 25, 1944, February 13, 1945; *Coconino Sun*, June 11, 1943.

63. Schneider, *Navy V-12 Program*, 522; Garlock to Wren; *Coconino Sun*, August 20, 1943; *The Pine*, August 8, 1944.

64. Oliver interview.

65. Revenues, Budget Information, 1942–43 file, box 6, Tormey Collection; revenues, Budget Information, 1943–44 file, box 1, and Tom O. Bellwood to instructors, February 19, 1945, Navy V-12 Unit file, box 2, both in Bellwood Collection; Minutes of a Meeting of the Board of Regents of the University and State Colleges of Arizona, May 20, 1946. All in SCA, CL.

66. *The Pine*, March 7, 1944, October 9, 23, 1945.

Chapter 7. Arman Peterson

1. Peterson, *Colonel "Pete"*, 35–37; *Coconino Sun*, July 9, 30, August 13, 1943; Fry, *Eagles of Duxford*, 33.

2. Baillie, *Two Battlefronts*, 39.

3. McManus, *Deadly Sky*, 144, 153.

4. Freeman, *Mighty Eighth War Diary*, 74.

5. Ibid., 74; Frazer, "Gallery of Fighters," 59; Peterson, *Colonel "Pete"*, 33–37; Fry, *Eagles of Duxford*, 33.

6. Duxford Aviation Society, *Duxford Diary*, 1–3; Peterson, *Colonel "Pete"*, 35–37; *Coconino Sun*, July 9, August 13, 1943; Baillie, *Two Battlefronts*, 40–41; Fry, *Eagles of Duxford*, 33.

7. *Coconino Sun*, July 23, 1943; news clippings (without newspaper names or dates), Peterson family records.

8. Peterson, *Colonel "Pete"*, 35–36.

9. Ibid., 6; *Coconino Sun*, July 9, 1943; news clippings, Peterson family records.

10. *Coconino Sun*, August 13, 1943; Peterson, *Colonel "Pete"*, 9, 12, 18–20; news clippings, Peterson family records; Dale Peterson to author, May 16, 2002.

11. Peterson, *Colonel "Pete"*, 20–24; *Coconino Sun*, August 13, 1943; Fry, *Eagles of Duxford*, 1.

12. Peterson, *Colonel "Pete"*, 27–29.

13. Ibid., 18, 30; Peterson to author, May 16, 2002.

14. Peterson, *Colonel "Pete"*, 31; *Oakland Tribune*, May 11, 1942; Fry, *Eagles of Duxford*, 1–7, 9, 23, 31; Bowyer, "Duxford Reflections," 1, website; Duxford Aviation Society, *Duxford Diary*, 1.

15. Freeman, *Mighty Eighth War Diary*, 53–55; news clippings, Peterson family records; *Coconino Sun*, July 9, August 13, 1943; Duxford Aviation Society, *Duxford Diary*, 2–3; Fry, *Eagles of Duxford*, 10, 15–16, 18, 21.

16. Duxford Aviation Society, *Duxford Diary*, 3; Baillie, *Two Battlefronts*, 14, 38, 41; Arman Peterson to Peterson family, June 18, 1943, and news clippings, Peterson family records; Freeman, *Mighty Eighth War Diary*, 3; Peterson, *Colonel "Pete"*, 54; *Coconino Sun*, July 9, August 13, 1943; Fry, *Eagles of Duxford*, 32.

17. Fry, *Eagles of Duxford*, 28, 33; Peterson, *Colonel "Pete"*, 35–36; *Coconino Sun*, August 13, 1943; Cline, *Mountain Town*, 346; Anthony Eden to General Ira C. Eaker, July 9, 1943, Peterson family records; House Concurrent Resolution, State of Arizona, Sixteenth Legislature, Second Special Session, February 28, 1944; C. Wind, curator, Gemeentebestuur van West-voorne, Rockanje, the Netherlands, to author, September 9, 2002.

18. Cline, *Mountain Town*, 348.

Chapter 8. A Town on the Move

1. Cline, *Mountain Town*, 339; Gallup Survey, in Navajo Ordnance Depot, 1942 file, FCCR, MS 193, SCA, CL.

2. Jesus Gil, interviewed by Susan L. Rogers, January 8, 1976, 17–18, FOHP; *Flagstaff Telephone Directory*, 1942, 18–19; Flagstaff Rental Complaints, Rentals, 1942 file, FCCR, SCA, CL; interview with Shelton G. Dowell Jr., March 27, 2002.

3. Flagstaff Rental Complaints, FCCR.

4. *Coconino Sun*, March 13, May 1, June 12, 19, July 31, October 2, 1942 and correspondence in Rentals, 1942, FCCR.

5. *Coconino Sun*, October 2, 9, 16, 30, November 6, 1942; Fred and Lois Metz, interviewed by Kristine Prennace, Flagstaff, July 14, 1976, 70–71, FOHP.

6. *Coconino Sun*, November 13, 1942.

7. Winkler, *Home Front U.S.A.*, 45.

8. *Coconino Sun*, December 4, 1942, January 29, 1943.

9. Finnerty, *Del Webb*, 12, 23, 30, 33–34.

10. *Coconino Sun*, January 22, 29, May 21, 28, 1943, August 17, 1945; Cline, *Mountain Town*, 337; Wren interview; Richard Mangum to author, June 17, 2002.

11. Green et al., *Ordnance Department*, 154; Winkler, *Home Front U.S.A.*, 50; Amy Franklin interview; interview with Jessie Jimenez Alonzo, June 3, 2002.

12. Green et al., *Ordnance Department*, 154–55; *Coconino Sun*, October 16, 1942, July 9, 1943; Winkler, *Home Front U.S.A.*, 50; Evans, *Born For Liberty*, 221.

13. *Coconino Sun*, July 9, 1943.

14. Winkler, *Home Front U.S.A.*, 50; Chafe, *American Women*, 141.

15. Evans, *Born For Liberty*, 223; Amy Franklin, Coddington, and Price interviews; interview with Pete L. Hernandez, June 4, 2002; "Navajo Ordnance Depot Historical Summaries, 1942–45," passim.

16. Interview with Eleanor Lois Ferguson Price, December 22, 1998.

17. Mangum to author.

18. Alonzo interview; Fred and Lois Metz interview, 73, FOHP.

19. *Coconino Sun*, January 7, 1944.

20. Ibid., March 3, 1943, January 7, February 5, 18, June 30, 1944.

21. Cline, *Mountain Town*, 339; *Coconino Sun*, January 25, March 5, 1943, December 1, 1944.

22. Ynfante, "*Coconino Sun* Index," 52–53; Evans, *Born For Liberty*, 219–20.

23. *Coconino Sun*, March 13, April 3, 1942, January 29, March 3, 12, July 23, 1943.

24. Ibid., August 31, 1945.

25. Ibid., April 3, July 31, 1942, January 22, July 23, 1943; Evans, *Born For Liberty*, 221.

26. *Coconino Sun*, July 31, 1942, July 16, 1943; Evans, *Born for Liberty*, 220, 224.

27. *Coconino Sun*, July 23, November 12, 1943.

28. Ibid., January 29, 1943, January 19, February 16, May 18, 1945.

29. *Coconino Sun*, March 13, April 10, 1942, January 28, February 4, 11, 18, March 10, April 14, 28, 1944, May 18, 1945.

30. Ibid., January 16, March 20, December 11, 1942, March 19, 1943; *USA Today*, March 7, 2002; Kennedy, *Freedom From Fear*, 645.

31. Conversation with Richard Mangum, February 6, 2002.

32. Fred and Lois Metz interview, 71–72, FOHP.

33. Ibid., 72.

34. *Coconino Sun,* September 18, 1942.

35. *Coconino Sun,* February 5, 1943; "Historical Summary, First Quarter, 1944," 213–14; Cline, *Mountain Town,* 340.

36. 368th Infantry General Orders No. 6, January 2, 1942, in Dec. 1941–July 1943 file, World War II Operations Reports, 1940–48, Ninety-Third Infantry Division, RG 407, Records of the Adjutant General's Office, National Archives; Lee, *Employment of Negro Troops,* 5, 106, 127–28, 489; Nash, *American West Transformed,* 88–93.

37. *Coconino Sun,* April 10, July 17, September 18, 1942; Lee, *Employment of Negro Troops,* 500; conversation with Pat Stein, September 20, 2000; Mangum, "The CCC in Flagstaff": 47.

38. Wallace, "Across Arizona to the Big Colorado," 329–30; Stein, *Logging Railroads,* 12; Arizona State Teachers College, *Arizona: A State Guide* (reprint edition), 188; Vance, "Lumber and Sawmill Workers," 40–41.

39. Leo Weaver to Governor Sidney P. Osborn and Osborn's reply, March 17 and 19, 1943, both in Flagstaff, 1943 file, Osborn Collection, RG 1, Arizona State Archives, Phoenix.

40. Cline, *Mountain Town,* 340–41; Henry T. Lewis to author, December 15, 1999, author's files.

41. *Coconino Sun,* July 17, November 13, 1942; Michelbach interview; *Winslow Mail,* July 17, 1942.

42. *Coconino Sun,* July 17, November 13, 1942.

43. Ibid., July 17, September 18, October 9, 1942.

44. Ibid., July 16, 1943.

45. Ibid., July 12, 1894; Matheny, "Lumbering in Arizona," 261–68; Vance, "Lumber and Sawmill Workers," 16, 67, 73; various letters in Indian Affairs, 1942 file, FCCR.

46. Cline, *Mountain Town,* 337; Vatter, *U.S. Economy,* 119–20.

47. See various letters and [Leo Weaver] to Senator Elmer Thomas, n.d., in the Indian Affairs, 1942 file and telegram, Leo Weaver to Senator Carl Hayden, n.d., and Senator Carl Hayden to Lt. Col. C. D. Barker, May 14, 1942, both in the Open Shop, 1942 file, all in FCCR. Also see Wade, *Bitter Issue,* 17–19, 25–26; *Coconino Sun,* May 22, 1942.

48. Samuel A. Boorstin to Flagstaff Chamber of Commerce, August 10, 1942, and Leo Weaver to Samuel A. Boorstin, August 12, 1942, and telegram [Leo Weaver] to Senator Carl Hayden, May 12, 1942, all in Open Shop, 1942 file, FCCR; *Coconino Sun,* May 15, 1942.

49. Senator Hayden to Barker; Cline, *Mountain Town,* 337; *Coconino Sun,* June 5, 12, 1942; *Flagstaff Journal,* May 28, 1942.

50. Telegrams, Leo Weaver to Commissioner John Collier and Senator Carl

Hayden, n.d., Open Shop, 1942 file, FCCR.

51. The *Arizona Fax*, as quoted in the *Coconino Sun*, June 12, 1942.

52. Ibid.

53. See letters in the Open Shop, 1942 file, FCCR; *Honolulu Star Bulletin*, July 9, 1942.

54. *Honolulu Star Bulletin*, July 9, 1942; *Coconino Sun*, June 5, 12, 1942; letters, Open Shop, 1942 file, FCCR.

55. Weaver to Boorstin; *Coconino Sun*, July 24, 1942.

56. *Coconino Sun*, March 12, April 2, May 21, 1943, July 28, 1944; Cline, *Mountain Town*, 332–33, 342–43; *Arizona Republic*, December 3, 1978.

57. *Coconino Sun*, July 20, 1945; Stanton, *In Harm's Way*, 34–37; Mee, *Meeting at Potsdam*, 81–82.

58. *Coconino Sun*, August 10, 1945; Mee, *Meeting at Potsdam*, 80.

59. *Coconino Sun*, August 17, 1945, August 13, 1999; Cline, *Mountain Town*, 349–50; Lois Ferguson Price interview.

60. *Coconino Sun*, August 17, 24, 1945.

Chapter 9. Conclusion

1. *Coconino Sun*, March 9, 1945; Lotchin, *Martial Metropolis*, 223–32. For V-12 and CPT revenues see Navy V-12 files, Bellwood Collection, SCA, CL.

2. *Coconino Sun*, July 31, 1942, January 15, 1943.

3. Flagstaff City Records, Balance Sheet, April 1943, and Statement of Working Capital, April 1944, from Monthly Reports—Expenditures and Receipts, 1943–49, FPL.

4. Ibid.; Ynfante, *Coconino Sun Index*, Introduction.

5. E. D. Babbitt Motor Company, folder 413, box 19, series 6, and Babbitt and Roberts, 1919–60, folder 338, box 14, series 4, both in MS 83, Babbitt Brothers Trading Company Records, SCA, CL.

6. Schneider, "Arizona State Teachers College" and *Navy V-12 Program*, cover, xi; Martin, ed. *Navy V-12*, 62.

7. Burns and Perry interviews; Davern to author; Inman to author.

8. Perry and Burns interviews; BonnyLee Hughey Champion, NAU Alumni Centennial Questionnaire, 1996; *Arizona Daily Sun* on-line, October 31, 2001; *The Lumberjack*, February 1, 1973, October 29, 1987, October 28, 1992, October 28–November 3, 1998, and other articles in the Morton Hall Ghost file, vertical files, SCA, CL.

9. Schneider, *Navy V-12 Program*, cover, xi, and "Arizona State Teachers College"; Martin, ed. *Navy V-12*, 62.

10. Schneider, *Navy V-12 Program*, 341, 354.

11. Schneider, "Arizona State Teachers College" and notes in Navy V–12 Unit file, folder 53, box 2, RG 1.9, Bellwood Collection; Also see Schneider, *Navy V-12 Unit* and *Navy V-12 Program*, 343.

12. Schneider, *Navy V-12 Program*, 14; *Coconino Sun*, October 12, 1945; Myers to author.

13. Bazacos to author; Burns interview; Gatlin to author; Curtis McGinis to author.

14. Rose Titus Davis, Marycarol Pryor Bazacos, and Iola Aston Sanders, NAU Alumni Centennial Questionnaire, 1996, SCA, CL.

15. *Coconino Sun*, September 28, October 5, 12, 1945, February 1, 1946; Report of Visit to Prisoner of War Camp, December 8, 1945.

16. Gastgeb interview; Doyle, "German Prisoners of War," 41, 123; Papp interviews, October 13–16, 1998, October 5, 2000; Report of Visit to Prisoner of War Camp, December 8, 1945. Also see the *Arizona Daily Sun*, October 15, 1998.

17. Krammer, *Nazi Prisoners of War*, 238; Bischof and Ambrose, *Eisenhower and the German POWs*, 9.

18. ICRC camp inspection report, January 24, 1946.

19. "Historical Summary, 2 September 1945–30 June 1951," 21; *Coconino Sun*, February 1, 1946; Papp interview, October 5, 2000; Prisoner of War Strength Reports.

20. Heinrich Mueller to Ern[e]st Harris, November 13, 1946, copy provided to author by Gerald and Wilma Harris; Gastgeb to author and interview; Krammer, *Nazi Prisoners of War*, 247; Papp interview, October 5, 2000.

21. Hernandez interview; Coddington interview; interview with Tommie Coleman, February 16, 2000.

22. J. M. Stewart to Fred H. Daiker, July 5, 1943, Central Classified Files, 1943–1948, Navajo 916–922, file 23932—1943—Navajo—920, Records of the Bureau of Indian Affairs, RG 75, National Archives; Iverson, *Navajo Nation*, 49.

23. Interview with Mary Ester Tsinnie, January 8, 2002.

24. Adams, *Shonto*, 50.

25. *Arizona Republic*, October 9, 1986.

26. Ibid.; *Navajo Times*, May 18, 1967; *Arizona Daily Sun*, September 11, 1986; Scott Franklin interview.

27. Conte, "Changing Woman," 536; Lautzenheiser et al., "Flagstaff and Bellemont, Arizona," 37, 41, 48, 50.

28. Lois Metz interview, FOHP.

29. Frank L. Hoover to author, July 28, 1999.

30. Stewart, "Navajo Indian at War," 43.

31. Ibid.

32. Winkler, *Home Front U.S.A.*, 41; Wade, *Bitter Issue*, 36, 82.

33. Ynfante, *Coconino Sun Index*, Introduction, SCA, CL.

34. Ibid.

35. Mangum to author.

36. John G. Babbitt, interviewed by Susan L. Rogers, November 21, 1975, 8, and Olive McNerney, interviewed by Kristine Prennace, June 18, 1976, 16–17, and Agnes Allen interview, 26, all in FOHP.

Chapter 10. Epilogue

1. *Coconino Sun*, October 12, 1945.

2. Carr, *Game and Fish Stories*, 54–57; Mangum interview; Dwight F. Johns to A. B. Custis, August 13, 1948, and Custis to Governor D. E. Garvey, September 22, 1949, both in Navajo Ordnance Depot, 1943–49, box 45, RG 1, Governor's Office, Subgroup Garvey, Arizona State Archives, Phoenix; interview with Imo Wardlow, March 22, 2000.

3. Carr, *Game and Fish Stories*, 54–57.

4. *Arizona Republic*, June 17, 1966; Coddington interview, January 26, 2000; Gus Kambouris to author, August 11, 1999.

5. Wardlow interview; Armstrong, *Life Poured Out*, 87–90, 94; *Arizona Daily Sun*, August 20, 1952.

6. "Historical Summary, September 2, 1945–June 30, 1951," 8; *Arizona Daily Sun*, July 9, August 22, September 24, 1952, April 6, 1992; "Data on NAD Bellemont," file 10, MS 155, Roger Kelly Collection, SCA, CL; *Navajo Ordnance Depot News Bulletin* 1, no. 2 (November 1953): 1; Kambouris to author.

7. William R. Horbaly to author, September 15, 1998.

8. Kambouris to author; reports and letters found in decimal file 333.1, 1945–46, Navajo Ordnance Depot, RG 112, Records of the Surgeon General's Office, National Archives.

9. "Historical Summaries, January 1, 1954 to June 30, 1959," passim; Dildine, "Navajo Army Depot," 6–7; *Arizona Daily Sun*, May 16, 1959, October 31, 1969; *Arizona Republic*, August 10, 1958.

10. "Historical Summaries, January 1, 1955 to June 30, 1964," passim; *Arizona Daily Sun*, June 25, 1956, October 10, 1957, October 17, 1959, June 1, 1960, May 18, 1962; "Navajo," Historical Data—Post, Camp, Station, or Air Field; *Arizona Republic*, August 10, 1958.

11. "Historical Summaries, July 1, 1962–June 30, 1963," 12; "July 1, 1970–June 30, 1971," 27.

12. R. [O. A. Ramnes] to Harry Field, May 17, 1956, copy in author's pos-

session; interview with Ward Olson, November 15, 1999; *Navajo Ordnance Depot News Bulletin* 1, no. 2 (November 1953): 6.

13. "Historical Summaries, January 1, 1961–June 30, 1961," 34–39; "July 1, 1961–December 31, 1961," 36; "January 1, 1962–June 30, 1962," 63; *Arizona Daily Sun*, March 9, 28, 1961.

14. Various letters, folder 11, box 563, MSS 001, Hayden Collection, Carl Hayden Library, Arizona State University, Tempe; *Arizona Daily Sun*, April 5, 1951, June 16, 1952, September 18, 1952, April 25, June 20, July 1, 1955, January 13, 1970.

15. *Arizona Daily Sun*, May 8, 1953, May 19, 1967; *Arizona Republic*, February 6, 1955.

16. *Arizona Daily Sun*, June 24, 1966, November 2, 1967.

17. "Historical Summary, July 1, 1966–June 30, 1967," 2, and "Historical Summaries, July 1, 1967 to June 30, 1969," passim; *Arizona Republic*, June 13, 1965.

18. Interview with Isabel Simmons by Susan L. Rogers, January 13, 1976, FOHP, SCA, CL; *Arizona Daily Sun*, February 2, 1971, April 6, 1992; "Historical Summary, July 1, 1967–June 30, 1968," 2.

19. "Historical Summaries, July 1, 1969 to June 30, 1971," passim; *Williams News*, August 27, 1970; *Arizona Daily Sun*, January 8, 21, February 25, 1971.

20. "Historical Summaries, 1962–71," passim; *Arizona Daily Sun*, February 25, March 27, June 11, 1964, June 11, 1965, August 20, 1966, March 27, 1969, June 9, October 10, 1972, February 5, 9, 1973; Kambouris to author.

21. Mangum interview, March 21, 2001; Giclas interviews.

22. *Arizona Republic*, October 11, 1979, June 12, 1980; *Arizona Daily Sun*, September 27, October 1, 11, 30, 1979.

23. *Arizona Daily Sun*, September 28, 30, 1979.

24. Ibid., October 1, 2, 4, 5, 7, 1979, August 1, 1980.

25. *Arizona Republic*, April 19, 1981; Mangum interview; *Arizona Daily Sun*, March 30, 1984, February 4, July 14, 1991.

26. Johnson, "Navajo Army Depot Activity," 1–4.

27. Ibid., July 30, 1990.

28. U.S. Senator Dennis DeConcini et al., to the Honorable Edward R. Madigan, Secretary, Department of Agriculture, March 20, 1992, Camp Navajo Congressional Hearing files; *Arizona Daily Sun*, March 27, 1992.

29. Lall and Marlin, *Building a Peace Economy*, 102, 110–11.

30. *Arizona Daily Sun*, October 23, November 21, 1991; *Arizona Republic*, July 30, 1990, March 8, 1992.

31. *Arizona Daily Sun*, March 2, 1993, July 13, 1995; John Morrow, fact

sheet, "Camp Navajo Environmental Accomplishments, 1987–Present" [March 2001].

32. Interview with Tim Cowan, March 28, 2001.

33. *Arizona Daily Sun,* March 8, 1995; *Arizona Republic,* March 8, 1995.

34. *Coconino Sun,* March 12, 1943, November 16, 1945; *Arizona Daily Sun,* May 11, 1962.

35. *Coconino Sun,* April 14, 1951.

36. *Arizona Daily Sun,* December 28, 1970, May 24, 1990.

37. "Historical Summary, January 1, 1962–June 30, 1962," 18–21; *Arizona Daily Sun,* May 19, 1967.

38. Peterson, *Colonel "Pete",* 36, 38.

39. Interview with Mary Lynch, March 28, 2001.

BIBLIOGRAPHY

Manuscript Collections

Babbitt Brothers Trading Company Records. MS 83, Special Collections and Archives, Cline Library, Northern Arizona University, Flagstaff.

Bellwood, Tom O. Collection, RG 1.9, Cline Library.

Flagstaff All-Indian Pow-Wow Collection. MS 51, Northern Arizona Pioneers Historical Society, Cline Library.

Flagstaff Chamber of Commerce Records. MS 193, Cline Library.

Flagstaff City Records. Flagstaff Public Library.

Flagstaff Oral History Project. Flagstaff Public Library and Cline Library.

Garvey, Dan E. RG 1, Governor's Office, Arizona State Archives, Phoenix.

Hayden, Carl. Collection, Carl Hayden Library, Arizona State University, Tempe, Arizona.

Hill, Walter J. Prisoner Information Collection, prisoner files no. 18975 and 23962, San Quentin Prison, California State Archives, Sacramento, California.

Kelly, Roger. Collection, MS 155, Cline Library.

Navajo Army Depot Collection. MS 44, Cline Library.

Northern Arizona Pioneers Historical Society. Manuscript Collection, Cline Library.

Northern Arizona University Alumni Centennial Questionnaire. Cline Library.

Osborn, Sidney P. Collection, RG 1, Governor's Office, Arizona State Archives, Phoenix.

Peterson, Arman. Family records provided by Jon Hales, Flagstaff, and Mary Ann Johanson, Salt Lake City, Utah.

Reilly, P. T. Collection, MS 275, Cline Library.

Santa Fe Railway Archives. Kansas State Historical Society, Topeka, Kansas.

Tormey, Thomas J. Collection, RG 1.8, Cline Library.

U.S. Army. Records of the Army Adjutant General. RG 407, National Archives, College Park, Maryland.

—————. Records of the Office of the Chief of Engineers. RG 77, National

Archives—Pacific Southwest Region, Laguna Niguel, California, and National Archives Building, Washington, D.C.

————. Records of the Office of the Chief of Ordnance. RG 156, National Archives, College Park, Maryland. Navajo Ordnance Depot, Official Histories, Post World War I Divisions, Services, and Other Units, Executive Division, Histories of Ordnance Installations and Activities, vol. I, Basic History thru December 31, 1942; summaries, January 1943 through June 1971. Most copies also found in the Navajo Army Depot Collection, MS 44, Special Collections and Archives, Cline Library. "Navajo Ordnance Depot Basic History, vol. I, thru December 31, 1942," [Exum B. Myrick]; "1943," [Exum B. Myrick]; "First Quarter, 1944," Ruth C. Leslie; "Second Quarter, 1944," Mary Cecilia Marks; "Third Quarter, 1944," Mary Cecilia Marks; "Fourth Quarter, 1944," Beryl W. Webb; "First Quarter, 1945," Beryl W. Webb; "Second Quarter, 1945," Beryl W. Webb; "September 2, 1945 to June 30, 1951," Louise E. Wensel; "July 1, 1951 to December 31, 1951," Ida S. Mathews; all 1952–1961 summaries are by Louise E. Wensel; "January 1, 1962 to June 30, 1962," Isabel Simmons; all 1965–1970 summaries are by Isabel Simmons.

————. Records of the Provost Marshal General. RG 389, National Archives, College Park, Maryland.

————. Records of the Surgeon General's Office. RG 112, National Archives, College Park, Maryland.

U.S. Department of the Interior. Records of the Bureau of Indian Affairs. RG 75, National Archives, Washington, D.C.

U.S. Department of State. Records of the Department of State. RG 59, National Archives, College Park, Maryland.

Walkup, Lawrence J., Collection. RG 1.11, Cline Library.

Unpublished Documents

"Arizona." A-43 in "Navajo Army Depot, 1942–Present," folder 8166, Arizona Museum of Military History, Phoenix.

"Background Information on Ordnance Field Service," Washington, D.C.: Information Officer for the Chief of Ordnance, the Pentagon, n.d.

Dildine, James. "The Navajo Army Depot: A bomb, a boom, or a bust?" Unpublished manuscript, 1993. Copy in the author's possession.

"Forest Service Map of the San Francisco Mountain Forest Reserve in Arizona," 1906. U.S. Department of Agriculture. Special Collections and Archives, Cline Library, Northern Arizona University.

Franco, Jeré. "Navajos in World War II." Unpublished manuscript, n.d. Arizona Historical Foundation, Phoenix.

Hansen, Carol. "Some Realities of the Navajo Ordnance Depot/Bellemont Experience." Unpublished manuscript, July 1, 1999. Copy in the author's possession.

"History of Navajo Army Depot Activity," [c1991], from Camp Navajo files. Copy in the author's possession.

"NAD Fact Sheet," April 4, 1979. Camp Navajo files.

"Navajo Depot Activity General Water Map." Colorado Springs: Higginbotham and Associates, 1987. Camp Navajo.

"Navajo," Historical Data—Post, Camp, Station, or Air Field. U.S. Army Center of Military History, Washington, D.C.

"Navajo Ordnance Depot General Information and Operational Data." [1955] From the collection of Harry L. Field Jr. Copy in the author's possession.

Prisoner of War Camp Inspection Reports, Navajo Ordnance Depot, International Committee of the Red Cross, June 21, 1945; January 24, 1946, Geneva, Switzerland. Copies in the author's possession.

Schneider, James G. "Arizona State Teachers College, Flagstaff, Arizona." Navy Contract vertical file, RG 1.9, Bellwood Collection, Cline Library, Northern Arizona University.

————. *Navy V-12 Unit, Arizona State College, 1 July 1943 to 30 November 1945.* Navy Contract vertical file, RG 1.9, Bellwood Collection, Cline Library, Northern Arizona University.

Interviews

Interviews were conducted by the author in Flagstaff or Bellemont unless otherwise noted. Transcripts or tapes are in the author's possession.

Alonzo, Jessie Jimenez, June 3, 2002.

Barreras, George S., May 3, 2000.

Burns, Beverly Bellwood, September 10, 2000.

Cline, Platt, October 20, 1997; May 13, 1998.

Coddington, Sally, May 12, November 17, 1999; January 26, 2000; February 26, 2001.

Coleman, Tommie, February 16, 2000.

Connelley, Elgymae, Stanfield, Arizona, November 18, 2001.

Cowan, Timothy J., November 4, 1998; March 26, 28, 2001.

Crozier, Robert, Jr., February 21, 2001.

Cummings, Betty Lou Decker, September 15, 2000.

Davis, Rose Titus, October 2, 2000.

Diaz, Lazaro A., June 4, 2000.

Dowell, Shelton G. Jr., March 27, 2002.

Elliott, Harold L. and Marion, August 25, 2000.

Florez, Guillermo, "Gus," March 29, 2000.

Franklin, Amy, May 18, 2000.

Franklin, Scott B., May 17 and July 31, 2000.

Gastgeb, Walter, Vienna, Austria, October 6, 2000.

Gatlin, Betty Jean Oliver, April 15, 2002.

Giclas, Henry, November 9, 1999; January 7, 2000.

Gröbner, Friedrich, translated by Alexander Grimme, Vienna, Austria, October 6, 2000.

Hedges, Earl C., March 29, 2000.

Henderson, Al, January 31, 2000.

Hernandez, Pete L., June 4, 2002.

Kunkle, Ruth Corbett, September 11, 2000.

Lynch, Mary, March 28, 2001.

Mangum, Richard K., November 10, 1999; March 20, 21, 2001.

Martinez, Gregorio "Curly," November 1, 1998.

Michael, Lucile, January 26, 2000.

Michelbach, A. P. "Pete," Sedona, May 17, 1998.

Mulnix, Martha, January 19, 2001.

Olson, Ward C., November 15, 1999.

Papp, Josef. Interview by David Kitterman, Flagstaff, November 20, 1997.

————. Interview by Richard Helt, Flagstaff, December 5, 1997.

————. Interview by author, Hinterbrühl, Austria, October 13–16, 1998; October 5, 2000.

Perry, Dorothy Schick, September 21, 2000.

Price, Eleanor Lois Ferguson, December 22, 1998.

Richards, Joe D., November 18, 1999; February 27, 2001.

Roybal, Eleuto, January 9, 2000.

Sweitzer, Paul A., November 11, 1999.

Thorstenson, Don, December 1, 1998.

Tsinnie, Kee and Mary Ester, January 8, 2002.

Veazey, Sally O'Connell, March 29, 2002.

Young, John R., Camp Verde, May 7, 2000; February 27, 2001.

Wardlow, Imo, March 22, 2000.

Wren, Howard, July 9, 2001.

Newspapers and Periodicals

Arizona Champion, Flagstaff, 1883, 1887.

Arizona Daily Star, Tucson, 1951.

Arizona Daily Sun, Flagstaff, 1949–98.

Arizona Miner (Weekly Arizona Journal–Miner), Prescott, 1882.

Arizona Republic, Phoenix, 1938–2000.

Arizona Sonne, Camp Florence, 1946. "German Prisoner of War Camp Papers Published in the United States," microfilm, vol. 21, reel 6, Library of Congress, Washington, D.C.

Army Times, 1982.

Atlanta Journal, 1995.

Coconino Sun, Flagstaff, 1912, 1931–46, 1951.

Flagstaff Journal, 1942.

Flagstaff Sun-Democrat, 1897.

Freiheit für Oesterreich, New York, 1942, 1943. Hoover Institution, Stanford University.

Honolulu Star Bulletin, 1942.

Kane County Standard, Kanab, Utah, 1942.

Los Angeles Times, 1943.

Lumberjack, Northern Arizona University, Flagstaff, 1973, 1987, 1992, 1998.

Navajo Times, Window Rock, Arizona, 1967.

Oakland Tribune, 1942.

Phoenix Gazette, 1979.

Pine, Arizona State Teachers College, Flagstaff, 1943–45.

USA Today, 2002.

Williams News, Williams, Arizona, 1970.

Winslow Mail, Winslow, Arizona, 1942–43.

Essential Secondary Sources

Aaseng, Nathan. *Navajo Code Talkers.* New York: Walker, 1992.

Adams, William Y. *Shonto: A Study of the Role of the Trader in a Modern Navajo Community.* Bureau of Ethnology Bulletin 188. Washington, D.C.: Smithsonian Institution, 1963.

All-Indian Pow-Wow, July 4-5–6, 1947. Flagstaff: Pow-Wow, Inc., 1947.

Arizona State Teachers College at Flagstaff. The Arizona WPA Writers' Project. *Arizona: A State Guide.* New York: Hastings House, 1940; reprinted as *The WPA Guide to 1930s Arizona.* Tucson: University of Arizona Press, 1989.

Armstrong, Hart. *A Life Poured Out: The Life and Ministry of Katherine Ruth Beard*. Wichita: Christian Communications, 1988.

Arrington, Leonard J., and Thomas G. Alexander. "They Kept 'em Rolling: The Tooele Army Depot, 1942–1962." *Utah Historical Quarterly* 31, no. 1 (winter 1963): 3–25.

Ashworth, Donna. *Biography of a Small Mountain*. Flagstaff: Small Mountain Books, 1991.

Baillie, Hugh. *Two Battlefronts*. New York: United Press Associations, 1943.

Barnes, Will C. *Arizona Place Names*. University of Arizona Bulletin, vol. 6, no. 1, 1935. Reprint, Tucson: University of Arizona Press, 1988.

Begay, Agnes R. "Munitions Plant Work during World War II." In Keats Begay, *Navajos and World War II*, ed. Broderick H. Johnson. Tsaile, Navajo Nation, Ariz.: Navajo Community College Press, 1977.

Bernstein, Alison R. *American Indians and World War II*. Norman: University of Oklahoma Press, 1991.

Bischof, Günter, and Stephen E. Ambrose, eds. *Eisenhower and the German POWs: Facts against Falsehood*. Baton Rouge: Louisiana State University Press, 1992.

Bixler, Margaret T. *Winds of Freedom: The Story of the Navajo Code Talkers of World War II*. Darien, Conn.: Two Bytes, 1992.

Bowyer, Michael J. F. Seventy-Eighth Fighter Group Unit History, "Duxford Reflections," 1975, website, http://www.78thfightergroup.com/history/index.html, accessed June 3, 2003.

Boyce, George A. *When Navajos Had Too Many Sheep: The 1940s*. San Francisco: Indian Historian Press, 1974.

Brew, J. O. "Hopi Prehistory and History to 1850." In *Handbook of North American Indians*, ed. William C. Sturtevant, vol. 9, 514–23. Washington, D.C.: Smithsonian Institution, 1979.

Brophy, Leo P., Wyndham D. Miles, and Rexmond C. Cochrane. *The Chemical Warfare Service: From Laboratory to Field*. United States Army in World War II series. Washington, D.C.: Center of Military History, 1959.

Bullis, Harold L., and James E. Mielke. *Strategic and Critical Materials*. Boulder: Westview Press, 1985.

Byrkit, James W., and Gerald A. Doyle & Associates, P.C., in association with Swaim Associates, Ltd. *Camp Navajo, Arizona, Ethnographic Survey: A Determination of Native American Presence near Volunteer Spring at Bellemont, Arizona*. [Phoenix]: November 22, 1994.

Campbell, Robert F. *The History of Basic Metals: Price Control in World War II*. New York: Columbia University Press, 1948.

Cardozier, V. R. *Colleges and Universities in World War II*. Westport, Conn.: Praeger, 1993.

Carr, John N. *It Was a Rough Road! . . . and Other Arizona Game & Fish Stories.* Phoenix: Heart Track Publications, 1994.

Chafe, William H. *The American Woman: Her Changing Social, Economic, and Political Roles, 1920–1970.* New York: Oxford University Press, 1972.

Civil Aeronautics Administration. *Wartime History of the Civil Aeronautics Administration.* Washington, D.C.: Civil Aeronautics Administration, 1946.

Cline, Platt. *They Came to the Mountain: The Story of Flagstaff's Beginnings.* Flagstaff: Northland Publishing, with Northern Arizona University, 1976.

————. *Mountain Campus: The Story of Northern Arizona University.* Flagstaff: Northland Press, 1983.

————. *Mountain Town: Flagstaff's First Century.* Flagstaff: Northland Publishing, 1994.

————. *Mountain Campus Centennial.* Flagstaff: Northern Arizona University, 1999.

Conte, Christine. "Changing Woman Meets Madonna: Navajo Women's Networks and Sex-Gender Values in Transition." In *Writing the Range: Race, Class, and Culture in the Women's West,* ed. Elizabeth Jameson and Susan Armitage. Norman: University of Oklahoma Press, 1997.

Costelle, Daniel. *Les Prisonniers.* Paris: Flammarion, 1975.

Doerry, Karl W. "Karl May." In *Nineteenth-Century German Writers, 1841–1900, Dictionary of Literary Biography,* vol. 29, ed. James Hardin and Siegfried Mews, 241–51. Detroit: Gale Research, 1993.

Doyle, Frederick Joseph. "German Prisoners of War in the Southwest United States during World War II: An Oral History." Ph.D. diss., University of Denver, 1978.

Doyle, Gerald A., James W. Byrkit, and Swaim Associates. *Camp Navajo, Arizona, Historic Building Survey.* Phoenix: Arizona Army National Guard, November 22, 1994.

Duxford Aviation Society. *Duxford Diary.* 3d ed. [London]: Black Bear Press, 1989.

Evans, Sara M. *Born for Liberty: A History of Women in America.* New York: Simon & Schuster, 1997.

Finnerty, Margaret. *Del Webb: A Man, A Company.* Flagstaff: Heritage Publishers, 1991.

Franco, Jeré. "Loyal and Heroic Service: The Navajos and World War II." *Journal of Arizona History* 27, no. 4 (winter 1986): 391–406.

————. "Patriotism on Trial: Native Americans in World War II." Ph.D. diss., University of Arizona, 1990.

————. *Crossing the Pond: The Native American Effort in World War II.* Denton: University of North Texas Press, 1999.

Frazer, Charles D. "Gallery of Fighters." *Air Force* (New York), February 1944, 57–59.

Freeman, Roger A. *Mighty Eighth War Diary.* London: Jane's Publishing, 1981.

Fry, Garry L. *Eagles of Duxford: The 78th Fighter Group in World War II.* St. Paul, Minn.: Phalanx Publishing, 1991.

Fuchs, James R. *A History of Williams, Arizona, 1876–1951.* Social Science Bulletin no. 23. Tucson: University of Arizona, 1955.

Gilbert, Martin. *Auschwitz and the Allies.* New York: Henry Holt, 1981.

Green, Constance McLaughlin, Harry C. Thomson, and Peter C. Roots. *The Technical Services—The Ordnance Department: Planning Munitions for War.* United States Army in World War II series. Washington, D.C.: Chief of Military History, Department of the Army, 1955.

Grenda, Donn R. *Land Use in North-Central Arizona: An Archaeological Survey of Navajo Army Depot, Coconino County, Arizona.* Tucson: Statistical Research Inc., 1993.

Griffith, Janice P. "In Love with Northern Arizona." *Arizona Republic,* April 23, 2000, p. F6.

Haskett, Bert. "History of the Sheep Industry in Arizona." *Arizona Historical Review* 7, no. 3 (July 1936): 3–49.

Hoffman, Virginia. *Navajo Biographies.* Vol. 1. Phoenix: Navajo Curriculum Center Press, 1974.

Housley, Harold Ray. "A History of United States Highway 66 in Arizona." Masters thesis, Arizona State University, 1996.

Hoza, Steve. *PW: First-Person Accounts of German Prisoners of War in Arizona.* Phoenix: Steve Hoza, 1995.

Hutchinson, Melvin T. *The Making of Northern Arizona University: A Chronicle.* Flagstaff: Northern Arizona University, 1972.

Igloo Area History Committee, with Suzanne Julin. *IGLOO: A History of the Black Hills Ordnance Depot.* South Dakota: Fall River County Historical Society, 1984.

Iverson, Peter. *The Navajo Nation.* Albuquerque: University of New Mexico Press, 1981.

Johnson, Broderick H., and Virginia Hoffman. *Navajo Biographies.* Vol. 2. Rough Rock, Ariz.: Navajo Curriculum Center, 1978.

Kennedy, David M. *Freedom from Fear: The American People in Depression and War, 1929–1945.* New York: Oxford University Press, 1999.

Kitchen, Martin *Nazi Germany at War.* New York: Longman, 1995.

Krammer, Arnold. *Nazi Prisoners of War in America.* New York: Stein and Day, 1979. Reprint, Lanham, Md.: Scarborough House, 1996.

La Cuesta. Arizona State Teachers College yearbook, 1943–44. Special Collections and Archives, Cline Library, Northern Arizona University.

Lagerquist, Syble. *Philip Johnston and the Navajo Code Talkers.* Billings, Mont.: Council for Indian Educators, 1996.

Lall, Betty G., John Tepper Marlin, et al. *Building a Peace Economy: Opportunities and Problems of Post–Cold War Defense Cuts.* Boulder, Colo.: Westview Press, 1992.

LaRouche, F. W. "War Comes First in Navajo Life." *Indians at Work* 10, nos. 2–6 (winter 1942–43): 17–24.

Lautzenheiser, E. L., S. H. Kerr, and E. J. Lincoln. "Flagstaff and Bell[e]mont, Arizona." In *Indian and Non-Indian Communities.* Window Rock, Ariz.: Navajo Agency, Bureau of Indian Affairs, 1952.

Lee, Ulysses. *The Employment of Negro Troops* United States Army in World War II Series. Washington, D.C.: Chief of Military History, Department of the Army, 1966.

Lewis, George, and John Mewha. *History of Prisoner of War Utilization by the United States Army, 1776–1945.* Department of the Army Pamphlet 20-213, June 1955. Reprint, Washington, D.C.: Chief of Military History, Department of the Army, 1988.

Locke, Raymond Friday. *The Book of the Navajo.* 4th ed. Los Angeles: Mankind, 1989.

Lotchin, Roger W., ed. *The Martial Metropolis: U.S. Cities in War and Peace.* New York: Praeger, 1984.

Malinowski, Sharon, and Anna Sheets, eds. *The Gale Encyclopedia of Native American Tribes* Vol 2. New York: Gale, 1998.

Mangum, Richard K. "The CCC in Flagstaff: The Schultz Pass Camp." *Mountain Living Magazine* (Flagstaff, September 1996): 47.

————. "The Underpass." *Mountain Living Magazine* (January 2001): 67.

————. "Flu." *Mountain Living Magazine* (December 2001): 76.

————. "Pioneer Doctor Remembers the Early Days." *Mountain Living Magazine* (August 2002): 76.

Marrus, Michael R. *The Holocaust in History.* New York: Penguin, 1987.

Martin, Douglas D. *The Lamp in the Desert: The Story of the University of Arizona.* Tucson: University of Arizona Press, 1960.

Martin, Robert J., ed. *Navy V-12.* Paducah, Ky.: Turner Publishing Co., 1996.

Matheny, Robert Lavesco. "The History of Lumbering in Arizona before World War II." Ph.D. diss., University of Arizona, 1975.

McCoy, Ron. "Navajo Code Talkers of World War II." *American West* 18, no. 6 (November/December 1981): 67–75.

McManus, John C. *Deadly Sky: The American Combat Airman in World War II.* Novato, Calif.: Presidio Press, 2000.

McNitt, Frank. *Navajo Wars: Military Campaigns, Slave Raids, and Reprisals.* Albuquerque: University of New Mexico Press, 1972.

Mee, Charles L., Jr. *Meeting at Potsdam.* London: André Deutsch, 1975.

Midgley, G. T. "I, Highway 66." *Arizona Highways* 12, no. 9 (September 1937): 17–18.

Mountain States Telephone and Telegraph, *Flagstaff Telephone Directory.* Phoenix: 1942.

Myrick, David F. *The Santa Fe Route: Railroads of Arizona.* Vol. 4. Wilton, Calif.: Signature Press, 1998.

Nash, Gerald D. *The American West in the Twentieth Century: A Short History of an Urban Oasis.* Englewood Cliffs, N.J.: Prentice-Hall, 1973. Reprint, Albuquerque: University of New Mexico Press, 1985.

——. *The American West Transformed: The Impact of the Second World War.* Bloomington: Indiana University Press, 1985. Reprint, Lincoln: University of Nebraska Press, 1990.

——. *World War II and the West: Reshaping the Economy.* Lincoln: University of Nebraska Press, 1990.

——. *The Federal Landscape: An Economic History of the Twentieth Century West.* Tucson: University of Arizona Press, 1999.

Navajo Ordnance Depot News Bulletin, 1, nos. 1 and 2 (May and November 1953).

Negri, Sam. "The Town the War Built." *Arizona Republic,* June 19, 1985.

——. "Bombs and Hogans at Bellemont." *Arizona Highways* 64, no. 7 (July 1988): 43.

Parman, Donald L. *The Navajos and the New Deal.* New Haven: Yale University Press, 1976.

——. *Indians and the American West in the Twentieth Century.* Bloomington: Indiana University Press, 1994.

Paul, Doris A. *The Navajo Code Talkers.* Pittsburgh: Dorrance Publishing Co., 1998.

Peplow, Edward H., Jr. *History of Arizona.* Vol. 2. New York: Lewis Historical Publishing, 1958.

Peterson, Dale. *Colonel "Pete": The Story of Colonel Arman Peterson.* Salt Lake City: Dalila Family Trust, 1996.

Peterson, Thomas H., Jr. "Cash Up or No Go: The Stagecoach Era in Arizona." *Journal of Arizona History* 14, no. 3 (fall 1971): 205–22.

Philp, Kenneth R. *John Collier's Crusade for Indian Reform, 1920–1954.* Tucson: University of Arizona Press, 1977.

————. *Termination Revisited: American Indians on the Trail to Self-Determination, 1933–1953.* Lincoln: University of Nebraska Press, 1999.

Plopper, Zach. "Requiem for Old Bellemont." *Northern Arizona Outdoors,* February 1994, pp. 14–15.

Pluth, Edward J. "The Administration and Operation of German Prisoner of War Camps in the United States during World War II." Ph.D. diss., Ball State University, 1970.

Powell, Allen Kent. *Splinters of a Nation: German Prisoners of War in Utah.* Salt Lake City: University of Utah Press, 1989.

Pritzker, Barry M. *Native Americans: An Encyclopedia of History, Culture, and Peoples.* Santa Barbara: ABC-CLIO, 1998.

Putt, Patrick John. *South Kaibab National Forest: A Historical Overview.* Kaibab National Forest and the Center for Colorado Plateau Studies at Northern Arizona University, June 30, 1991.

Reilly, P. T. *Lee's Ferry: From Mormon Crossing to National Park.* Ed. Robert H. Webb. Logan: Utah State University Press, 1999.

Richardson, Gladwell. *Navajo Trader.* Ed. Philip Reed Rulon. Tucson: University of Arizona Press, 1986.

Richmond, Al. "Apex: A Vanished Arizona Logging Community." *Journal of Arizona History* 29, no. 1 (spring 1988): 75–88.

Robbins, William G. *American Forestry: A History of National, State, and Private Cooperation.* Lincoln: University of Nebraska Press, 1985.

Robin, Ron. *The Barbed-Wire College: Reeducating German POWs in the United States during World War II.* Princeton: Princeton University Press, 1995.

Rothman, Hal. *On Rims & Ridges: The Los Alamos Area since 1880.* Lincoln: University of Nebraska Press, 1992.

Rushforth, Scott, and Steadman Upham. *A Hopi Social History: Anthropological Perspectives on Sociocultural Persistence and Change.* Austin: University of Texas Press, 1992.

Schneider, James G. *The Navy V-12 Program: Leadership for a Lifetime.* Boston: Houghton Mifflin Company, 1987.

Scott, Quinta, and Susan Croce Kelly. *Route 66: The Highway and Its People.* Norman: University of Oklahoma Press, 1991.

Sheridan, Thomas E. *Arizona: A History.* Tucson: University of Arizona Press, 1995.

Stanton, Doug. *In Harm's Way: The Sinking of the USS* Indianapolis *and the Extraordinary Story of Its Survivors.* New York: Henry Holt, 2001.

Stein, Pat. *Logging Railroads of the Coconino and Kaibab National Forest: Supplemental Report to a National Register of Historic Places Multiple Property Documentation Form.* Flagstaff: SWCA, Inc., 1993.

Steinbeck, John. *The Grapes of Wrath.* New York: Viking Press, 1939.

Stewart, James M. "The Navajo Indian at War." *Arizona Highways* 19, no. 6 (June 1943): 20–43.

Szasz, Margaret Connell. *Between Indian and White Worlds: The Cultural Broker.* Norman: University of Oklahoma Press, 1994.

Thomas, Estelle Webb. "America's First Families on the Warpath." *Common Ground* 2, no. 4 (1942): 95–99.

Thomson, Harry C., and Lida Mayo. *The Technical Services: The Ordnance Department; Procurement and Supply.* United States Army in World War II series. Washington, D.C.: Chief of Military History, Department of the Army, 1960.

Thorstenson, Don, and L. Sue Beard, "Geology and Fracture Analysis of Camp Navajo, Arizona Army National Guard, Arizona." Department of the Interior, U.S. Geological Survey, February 17, 1997.

Tinker, George H. *Northern Arizona and Flagstaff in 1887: The People and Resources.* Glendale, Calif.: Arthur H. Clark, 1969.

Townsend, Kenneth William. *World War II and the American Indian.* Albuquerque: University of New Mexico Press, 2000.

Underhill, Ruth. *Here Come the Navajo!* Lawrence, Kans.: United States Indian Service, Indian Life and Customs, no. 8, 1953.

U.S. Army–DARCOM. *History of Fort Wingate.* N.d.

U.S. Bureau of the Census. *Thirteenth Census of the United States: 1910; Arizona.* Washington, D.C.: Government Printing Office, 1913.

————. *Fifteenth Census of the United States: 1930; Arizona.* Washington, D.C.: Government Printing Office, 1931.

Vance, Robert. "Lumber and Sawmill Workers in the Flagstaff Timber Industry, 1917–1947: Migration, Adaptation, and Organization." Master's thesis, Northern Arizona University, 1992.

Vatter, Harold G. *The U.S. Economy in World War II.* New York: Columbia University Press, 1985.

Wade, Michael S. *The Bitter Issue: The Right to Work Law in Arizona.* Tucson: Arizona Historical Society, 1976.

Wallace, Andrew. "Across Arizona to the Big Colorado: The Sitgreaves Expedition of 1851." *Arizona and the West* 26, no. 4 (winter 1984): 325–64.

Westerlund, John S. "Rommel's Afrika Korps in Northern Arizona: Austrian Prisoners of War at Navajo Ordnance Depot." *Journal of Arizona History* 39, no. 4 (winter 1998): 405–20.

————. "Boom to Bust in Bellemont: The Tragic Story of Northern Arizona Pioneer Walter J. Hill." *Journal of Arizona History* 41, no. 2 (summer 2000): 181–96.

————. " 'U.S. Project Men Here': Building Navajo Ordnance Depot at Flagstaff." *Journal of Arizona History* 42, no. 2 (summer 2001): 201–26.

————. "Bombs From Bellemont: Navajo Ordnance Depot During World War II." *Journal of Arizona History* 42, no. 3 (fall 2001): 321–50.

————. "Anchors Aweigh: The U.S. Navy's WWII Port of Call at Flagstaff." *Journal of Arizona History*, 43, no. 1 (spring 2002): 69–86.

White, Richard. *The Roots of Dependency: Subsistence, Environment, and Social Change among the Choctaws, Pawnees, and Navajos.* Lincoln: University of Nebraska Press, 1983.

Winkler, Allan M. *Home Front U.S.A.: America during World War II.* Arlington Heights, Ill.: Harlan Davidson, 1986.

Ynfante, Charles. *The Coconino Sun: An Index for the Period December 12, 1941 through February 1946.* Flagstaff: Northern Arizona University, 1993.

————. "Arizona during the Second World War, 1941–1945: A Survey of Selected Topics." Ph.D. diss., Northern Arizona University, 1997.

ILLUSTRATION CREDITS

Camp Navajo

Demmie H. Cox's headquarters, 1942
Igloo construction frame
Aboveground magazine construction
"Southwest Mounted Police"
Earth-covered igloos
Col. John Huling Jr.
Victory Village dormitory
Ammunition handlers at a bond rally
Storing chemical bombs
Ammunition handlers
Indian Village hogans
Indian Village tents
Richardson's Trading Post
Women at assembly line work
Navajo Depot hospital
Moving bombs into igloos
Indian Village apartments
Indian Field Day
Jim Boone, gang boss and foreman
Trini Lopez at the depot hospital
Ballistic missile motor

Elliott, Harold

Seaman Harold Elliott and friends

Gröbner, Friedrich

Sketch from Friedrich Gröbner's window

Special Collections and Archives, Cline Library, Northern Arizona University

Indian Wagon. NAU.PH.85.3.000.239

Flagstaff's All-Indian Fourth of July Parade. Fronske Collection. NAU.PH.85.03.ON.13

All-Indian Rodeo. Fronske Collection. NAU.PH.85.3.000.205

Enjoying the Carnival. Fronske Collection. NAU.PH.85.3.12.254

Leo Weaver. P. T. Reilly Collection. NAU.PH.97.46.112-71

Maj. Exum B. Myrick. Navajo Army Depot Collection. NAD 3509

Bellemont day school. Navajo Army Depot Collection. NAD 4039

Navajo Tribal Chairman Chee Dodge. Leo Crane Collection. NAU.PH.658.995

Prisoner of war camp. Navajo Army Depot Collection.

Civil Aeronautics Administration flight training. Fronske Collection. NAU.PH.85.3.26.31

Navy V-12 marching. Fronske Collection. NAU.PH.85.3.14.63

Students on the ASTC campus. NAU Archives. NAU.ARC 1945-4-1d

Picnic lunch at ASTC. NAU Archives. NAU.ARC 1944-6-4

Gamma Chi dance. NAU Archives. NAU.ARC 1945-6-23

Arman Peterson. Fronske Collection. NAU.PH.85.3.17.184

Arman Peterson and his plane at Flagstaff. Fronske Collection. NAU.PH.85.3.000.195

Jessie Jimenez (Alonzo). Los Recuerdos del Barrio en Flagstaff Collection. NAU.PH.22.1.10

African American soldiers in Flagstaff. Fronske Collection. NAU.PH.85.3.24.185

MAP CREDITS

Navajo Ordnance Depot, 1942. Navajo Ordnance Depot Collection, National
    Archives II, College Park, Md.
Prisoner of war camps in Arizona. Map by Don Larson Mapping Specialists.
    Based on a map in Steve Hoza, *PW: First Person Accounts of German*
    Prisoners of War In Arizona (Phoenix: Steve Hoza, 1995).
Map of the Prisoner of War Camp at Bellemont. Map by Don Larson Mapping
    Specialists. Based on Hospital & Prisoner of War Area Map, MS 44,
    Navajo Army Depot Collection. Special Collections and Archives, Cline
    Library, Northern Arizona University.

INDEX

Page numbers in italics refer to illustrations.